Browning's Hatreds

BROWNING'S HATREDS

DANIEL KARLIN

CLARENDON PRESS · OXFORD
1993

Oxford University Press, Walton Street, Oxford OX2 6DP

Oxford New York Toronto
Delhi Bombay Calcutta Madras Karachi
Kuala Lumpur Singapore Hong Kong Tokyo
Nairobi Dar es Salaam Cape Town
Melbourne Auckland Madrid

and associated companies in
Berlin Ibadan

Oxford is a trade mark of Oxford University Press

Published in the United States
by Oxford University Press Inc., New York

British Library Cataloguing in Publication Data
Data available

Library of Congress Cataloging in Publication Data

Karlin, Daniel, 1953–
Browning's hatreds/Daniel Carlin.
Includes bibliographical references
1. Browning, Robert, 1812–1889—Criticism and interpretation.
2. Hate in literature. I. Title.
PR4242.H34K37   1993
821'.8—dc20   93-2907
ISBN 0-19-811229-7

Typeset by Datix International Limited, Bungay, Suffolk

Printed in Great Britain
on acid-free paper by
Biddles Ltd
Guildford and King's Lynn

FOR PAT

'What an illustration of the law by which opposite ideas suggest opposite, and contrary images come together!'

Acknowledgements

THE extracts from the lyrics of Bob Dylan's 'Masters of War' and 'It's Alright, Ma (I'm Only Bleeding)' on p. 115 are copyright © 1963 and © 1965 by Warner Bros. Inc. All rights reserved. Some of the material in Chapter 7 first appeared in *Browning Society Notes*; I am grateful to the editor, Michael Meredith, for permission to reprint it. Parts of Chapters 2, 3, and 10 were given as seminar papers; I would like to thank the staff and students of the English Departments of University College and King's College, London, and also the members of the Victorian Studies seminar held at Birkbeck College. Sarah Squire's careful research helped my task at the outset; I have benefited throughout, as always, from the stimulus and encouragement of John Woolford's ideas and conversation.

Contents

I

The Idea of Hatred

Nature seems (the more we look into it) made up of antipathies: without something to hate, we should lose the very spring of thought and action. Life would turn to a stagnant pool . . . Love turns, with a little indulgence, to indifference or disgust: hatred alone is immortal.

(Hazlitt)[1]

THE idea for this book grew from its opposite. I had written a study of Browning's courtship, and was planning a book on his marriage. I was used to thinking of Browning as a lover, and as a writer about love. (So are many other readers and critics; I was helping to deepen a familiar track.) I was reading one of Browning's most famous love-poems, 'One Word More'—famous because, coming at the end of *Men and Women*, it declares itself *not* to be a dramatic monologue: 'Let me speak this once in my true person, | Not as Lippo, Roland or Andrea' (ll. 137–8). For Browning, an advocate of poetic 'impersonality' long before T. S. Eliot, this statement has more than ordinary force. He had long disclaimed any autobiographical or confessional intention in his poetry—'so many utterances of so many imaginary persons, not mine'[2]—so the act of addressing himself directly to his beloved gives the poem an exceptional interest. And in this rare, if not unique, utterance, I came across (as though for the first time) the following lines on another famous poet-lover:

> Dante once prepared to paint an angel:
> Whom to please? You whisper 'Beatrice.'
> While he mused and traced it and retraced it,
> (Peradventure with a pen corroded
> Still by drops of that hot ink he dipped for,

[1] 'On the Pleasure of Hating', *The Plain Speaker: Opinions on Books, Men and Things* (1826) in Hazlitt: xii. 128.
[2] Advertisement to *Dramatic Lyrics* (1842).

When, his left hand i' the hair o' the wicked,
Back he held the brow and pricked its stigma,
Bit into the live man's flesh for parchment,
Loosed him, laughed to see the writing rankle,
Let the wretch go festering through Florence)—
Dante, who loved well because he hated,
Hated wickedness that hinders loving,
Dante standing, studying his angel,—
In there broke the folk of his Inferno.
Says he—'Certain people of importance'
(Such he gave his daily, dreadful line to)
Entered and would seize, forsooth, the poet.
Says the poet—'Then I stopped my painting.'

(ll. 32–49)

Here, at the heart of Browning's tenderest and most personally expressive lyric, is a figure of astonishing violence and cruelty, a figure of hatred, blistering, savage, demonic. Indeed, the source of Dante's gesture is his own behaviour at the climax of the *Inferno* (xxxii. 97–104) when he seizes the traitor Bocca degli Abati 'per la cuticagna' (by the afterscalp) and tears at his hair to make him reveal his name; and his next encounter is with the most haunting and bestial image of hatred in the whole of the *Inferno*, that of Count Ugolino gnawing eternally at the skull of Archbishop Ruggieri. Browning's image of Dante here is made sharper when you realize that it is the product of a deliberate and double anachronism, since the episode of Dante's drawing of the angel, which he relates in the *Vita Nuova*, is not contemporary with the writing of the *Inferno*, but pre-dates it by as much as a decade, and was not done to 'please' the living Beatrice but to commemorate her. What, then, is the figure of hatred doing here? And what larger questions does it raise about Browning's creativity?

In trying to answer these questions I was led to reflect on other instances of hatred and hating in Browning's work. 'One Word More' itself throws a bridge between Browning's own feelings of, and ideas about, hatred, and those expressed by characters in 'dramatic' works. I could think of several such at random; but in order to be thorough I went to the Browning Concordance and looked up all the occurrences of hatred and its cognates, as well as associated words such as *loathe, detest, resent, abhor, abominate, spite, aversion, malice, malign, grudge*. The results surprised me. I found 681 occurrences: *hate* alone (as both verb and noun) had 234, with *hated, hateful, hatefullest, hater, haters, hate's, hates, hatest, hating, hatred,* and *hatred's* accounting for a further 149. These occurrences ranged from Browning's first publication, *Pauline*, in 1833 ('But I begin to know what thing hate is— | To sicken and to quiver and grow white—', ll. 650–1) to his last, *Asolando*, in 1889 ('by hate taught love', 'Rephan', l. 88). Looking beyond individual lines and passages, it became clear that there were a large number of poems entirely preoccupied with hatred, or in which hatred played a significant part. Among such works I would cite (in order of publication) *Paracelsus, Strafford, Sordello, Pippa Passes*, 'My Last Duchess', 'Soliloquy of the Spanish Cloister', *The Return of the Druses, Luria, A Soul's Tragedy*, 'The Laboratory', 'Instans Tyrannus', 'Childe Roland to the Dark Tower Came', 'The Patriot', 'Caliban upon Setebos', *The Ring and the Book, The Inn Album, Aristophanes' Apology*, 'Of Pacchiarotto, and How He Worked in Distemper', 'A Forgiveness', 'Filippo Baldinucci on the Privilege of Burial', 'Halbert and Hob', and 'Ixion'. This is a selective list, and a conservative one; I have not, for example, cited 'Italy in England',[3] though to the speaker of that poem, an Italian nationalist at the time of the *risorgimento*, hatred of the Austrians is almost the guiding principle of his life, to the extent that two of his three wishes at the end are violent and vengeful, one of them being to 'grasp Metternich until | I felt his red wet throat distil | In blood thro' these two hands' (ll. 121–3), and the other that a 'perjured traitor' to the cause 'Should die slow of a broken heart | Under his new employers' (ll. 125–7).

I am less concerned to pile up these instances, however, than to try to suggest some of the reasons for their number. I hope to show that Browning's bizarre and disturbing outburst in 'One Word More' takes its place in a complex and fascinating pattern of ideas and associations in his thinking about poetry and in his poetry itself, a pattern which makes the dualism between love and hate look very different. Like Keats's 'Chamber of Maiden Thought', Browning's poetry of love 'becomes gradually darkened and at the same time on all sides of it many doors are set open — but all dark—all leading to dark passages'.[4] It seems to me that Browning's 'genius', as Keats said of Wordsworth's, is 'explorative of these dark passages', and it

---

[3] Published in *Dramatic Lyrics* (1842); when it was reprinted in *Poems* (1849) it was retitled 'The Italian in England'.
[4] Letter of 3 May 1818 to J. H. Reynolds.

is these journeys of exploration that I have attempted to follow.

What did Browning understand by hatred? Where does his concept of it derive, and how does this concept shape his representation of it as a physical, psychological, and linguistic phenomenon?

As with many other terms in our vocabulary of the emotions, 'hatred' is deceptively simple. Dr Johnson (whose *Dictionary* Browning is said to have read through as part of his preparation for becoming a poet[5]) is typically direct: for the verb 'hate' he gives 'To detest; to abhor; to abominate; to regard with the passion contrary to love', and for 'hatred' 'Hate; ill-will; malignity; malevolence; dislike; abhorrence; detestation; abomination; the passion contrary to love'. These are all (with one exception) what I would call 'strong' senses, and fit the description of hatred as a 'passion' or, as Johnson again defines it, 'violent commotion of the mind'. The quotations back this up: for example, under 'hate', from *The Merchant of Venice*:

BASSANIO. Do all men kill the things they do not love?
SHYLOCK. Hates any man the thing he would not kill?
BASSANIO. Every offence is not a hate at first.

(IV. i. 66–8)

Both Bassanio and Shylock agree that hatred is an extreme emotion; Shylock's point is that he really does *hate* Bassanio, that his feeling cannot be diminished into 'do not love' (which is, in itself, a long way from what Johnson means by 'the passion contrary to love'). But the weak link in Johnson's list of synonyms for 'hatred' is 'dislike'; the weakness leads to a split in the *Oxford English Dictionary* into two definitions of the verb 'hate' which broadly govern two great branches of its application. The first is still the 'strong' definition: 'to hold in very strong dislike: to detest; to bear malice to'. The second, 'weak' definition is 'to dislike greatly, be extremely averse (to do something)': here 'hate' is merely an intensified or rhetorically heightened way of expressing a taste or preference. The statements 'I hate beetroot' and 'I hate you' have the same form but refer (apparently) to different kinds of feeling: in the former case 'hate' is a hyperbolic way of expressing a trivial dislike, whereas in the latter it is, potentially at any rate, the expression of a serious personal

---

[5] Orr: 53. All quotations from Johnson are from the facsimile of the first edition of the *Dictionary* (1755) published by Longman.

feeling.[6] Of course, there is a problem in trying to distinguish in this way between rhetorical and 'literal' senses of a word. 'He hates to be call'd *parson*, like the *devil!*' writes Swift ('Mrs Harris' Petition', l. 54): this seems designed precisely to occupy a borderline between strong and weak senses, but is assigned to the former by *OED*. Definition means choice, and choice may define meaning in a way that obscures meaning itself.

Uncertainty about the dividing-line between 'strong' and 'weak' uses of hate is only the beginning of the difficulties which start to crowd in on you as soon as you start thinking not of the definition of a word but of its uses. Another difficulty concerns the different objects of hatred, and whether these differences correspond to different kinds of hatred itself. Group hatred, for example—national, racial, tribal, social—seems the most intractable of all human social phenomena, in our century as much as in others. But is group hatred an extension of personal hatred, or separate from it? If your neighbours are Jewish, and you hate them, can there be a distinction between hating them as neighbours and hating them as Jews? It may be that there are species of hatred, like plants, peculiar to the soil in which they flourish; or that old man hatred is protean, a shape-changer, but always at bottom himself. 'An intellectual hatred is the worst', declares Yeats in 'A Prayer for My Daughter'; but does this mean that hating an idea is like hating a person, only worse, or that, on the contrary, hating an idea is worse precisely because it is *un*like hating a person, that is, has an inhuman and soul-less quality which degrades rather than animates?

Most 'basic' words are like this, as philosophers and psychologists (and, indeed, poets) have long recognized: their strong, simple, and unified appearance conceals a tangled and intractable hinterland of interpretation. But we need to recognize the importance of this deceptive appearance as well as seeing through it. Names are active constituents of meaning, not passive carriers of it. It may well be that 'I hate beetroot' *means*, in effect, 'I strongly dislike the taste of beetroot'; but it is not the *same* as saying that; the word 'hate' has an active property of its own. 'I hate all Boets and Bainters', King George I is said to have declared; his royal philistinism might be taken more seriously were it not modulated into comedy by his

---

[6] Since the context of any utterance determines its meaning, with a small amount of ingenuity we could devise circumstances in which 'I hate beetroot' became a tragically serious remark and 'I hate you' a frivolous one; but this would not affect the semantic issue itself.

funny accent. No such humour affects Wellington's snort of disdain: 'I hate the whole race ... There is no believing a word they say—your professional poets I mean—there never existed a more worthless set than Byron and his friends.' For a parson to hate being called one *like the devil* implies both that the parson is, really, devilish in his aversion to his own profession, and that he has trivialized the devil in the comparison, reduced him to a term of colloquial dislike. When Iago says of Othello, 'I do hate him as I do hell-pains' (I. i. 155), we give the comparison its full value even if, like Verdi's librettist Boito, we think of Iago as an atheist; Nelson's adjuration to his sailors, 'you must hate a Frenchman as you hate the devil', has a faint trace of professional jocularity about it. (Though even here a residual idea of the devil's *inhuman* malice, however colloquially and untheologically conjured up, helps to justify the inhuman malice without which wars could not be fought.) Hatred, you might say, covers a multitude of sins, but there is a unifying force in the term itself; the house of hatred has many mansions, but it remains one house in part because of the sign over the door.

The gloss in my edition of Cruden's concordance to the Bible says of 'hate' (agreeing with the *OED*'s distinction) that it 'is used in the Bible frequently, as it is now, not for literal hatred, but a dislike, or even a lesser degree of love for one than for another'. There are numerous examples in Browning's poetry of just this secondary or weakened form: in 'Pictor Ignotus', for example, where the speaker disdains the 'daily pettiness' of conversation about art: "This I love or this I hate, | This likes me more and this affects me less!"' (ll. 55–6); or in 'Rabbi Ben Ezra', where the speaker refers to the relativity of judgement: 'Now, who shall arbitrate? | Ten men love what I hate, | Shun what I follow, slight what I receive' (ll. 127–9); or in *Sordello*, where Sordello finds it wearisome to keep up with the preoccupations of the common herd:

> And as for Men in turn . . . contrive
> Who could to take eternal interest
> In them, so hate the worst, so love the best!
> Though in pursuance of his passive plan
> He hailed, decried the proper way.
>
> (ii. 758–62)

But this last example may again alert us to the danger of severing the link between 'weak' and 'strong' senses of hatred. Sordello's 'passive plan' of conformity to conventional opinion is a symptom of the breakdown he is suffering as man and artist; in his spiritual lethargy the phrases 'hate the worst . . . love the best' lose their meaning for him and become the token counters of social exchange. Later on in the poem it is precisely an 'eternal interest' that Sordello discovers in mankind: value floods back into his judgements about them, and into the dry sponges of 'love' and 'hate'.

The use of 'hate' as a conventional or hyperbolic way of saying 'dislike' is not, therefore, adequately accounted for by simply equating the strong word with the weak meaning. The example which Cruden's concordance gives for 'hate' as 'a lesser degree of love' is Deuteronomy 21: 15, which turns out to beg the question:

If a man have two wives, one beloved, and another hated, and they have born him children, both the beloved and the hated; and if the firstborn son be hers that was hated: then it shall be, when he maketh his sons to inherit that which he hath, that he may not make the son of the beloved firstborn before the son of the hated, which is indeed the firstborn: but he shall acknowledge the son of the hated for the firstborn, by giving him a double portion of all that he hath: for he is the beginning of his strength; the right of the firstborn is his.

It is hard to see how the injunction to read 'hated' here as meaning 'loved less' could be sensibly followed, whatever the philological arguments; as Browning's Pippa remarks, 'Lovers grow cold, men learn to hate their wives',[7] and the impulse to accord 'hated' its full value (especially in contrast with 'beloved') will at the very least modify, if not absolutely determine, the way we respond to the situation which is evoked and the moral code which is applied to it.[8] This impulse is triggered *by the word itself*: after all, if 'hated' does mean no more than 'loved less', why not use the latter phrase? But it seems the translators of the Authorized Version were subtler psychologists than the editors of Cruden's.

If Browning found in the Bible (especially the Old Testament) what most people would endorse, even today, as the 'natural' categories of emotion (such as love, hatred, fear, anger, jealousy, and

---

[7] This line was added after l. 129 of the introductory section in the heavily revised version of *Pippa Passes* included in *Poems* (1849): see Woolford and Karlin: ii. 25.

[8] The abstract situation given here in legalistic formulas is fleshed out in Genesis in the relationship between Jacob, Leah, and Rachel: 'and he [Jacob] loved also Rachel more than Leah . . . and when the Lord saw that Leah was hated, he opened her womb: but Rachel was barren' (29: 30–1).

pride), he would also have found these categories to be multiple, and
their names to conceal a suggestive instability. 'Hatred' can refer to a
relatively simple emotion, with an understandable source: 'And Esau
hated Jacob because of the blessing wherewith his father blessed
him: and Esau said in his heart, The days of mourning for my father
are at hand; then will I slay my brother Jacob' (Genesis 27: 41); but
when God refers to the same story in one of the prophetic books, his
words, offered as proof of his love for Israel, rest on a more troubled
base: 'I have loved you, saith the Lord. Yet ye say, Wherein hast
thou loved us? Was not Esau Jacob's brother? saith the Lord: yet I
loved Jacob, and I hated Esau, and laid his mountains and his
heritage waste for the dragons of the wilderness' (Malachi 1: 2–3). In
human terms, 'hatred' can describe a more complex psychological
condition than Esau's, such as Amnon's reaction after he rapes his
sister Tamar: 'Then Amnon hated her exceedingly; so that the hatred
wherewith he hated her was greater than the love wherewith he had
loved her' (2 Samuel 13: 15). But the same term which represents
Esau's jealous rage and Amnon's sickness (both the sickness of his
original desire and the sickness of his revulsion from it) also serves to
describe the psalmist's feelings of righteous indignation against the
wicked: 'Do not I hate them, O Lord, that hate thee? and am I not
grieved with those that rise up against thee? I hate them with perfect
hatred: I count them mine enemies' (Psalms 139: 21–2). A theologian
might well argue that these different hatreds are, indeed, linked; that the
Bible takes for granted both the flexible application of a single term,
'hatred', to a variety of psychological states, and the essential unity
of those states, which the very use of a single term helps to maintain.

Browning's concept of hatred (and other emotions) is similarly
governed by a tension between the single, unitary term and the
multiplicity of its applications. And it is also the case, I think, that
for Browning the singleness of the term is an emblem of the unity of
the concept: all 'hatreds' flow from 'hatred', all are organically
related, descendants of the same ancestral root. This attitude stems
from the narrow and primitive analytical framework which underlies
the enormous profusion of Browning's work. He was a writer of
extraordinary intelligence and subtlety, but the conceptual premisses
of his art were narrow and remained constant throughout his career.
I do not mean that Browning never developed or changed his mind.
He did, of course: in politics, for example, he began with a heady
fusion of Shelley's utopian radicalism and Carlyle's sardonic pessi-

mism, and ended up as a liberal individualist sceptical of both authority and dissent; in religion the Incarnation (the 'proof' of God's humanity and love) fought with and eventually displaced the Resurrection (the manifestation of God's transcendent power) as his central spiritual symbol, with incalculable consequences for his attitude to poetry and poetic language. But such changes involved a re-evaluation or reordering, not a fundamental redefinition, of Browning's conceptual vocabulary.

This vocabulary derives essentially from two sources: from religion (principally, as I have suggested, the Bible itself, but also the tradition of Puritan polemical writing in all its richness, incorporating the tracts of forgotten Puritan divines as well as the works of Jeremy Taylor, Milton, and Bunyan); and from the intellectual discourse of the eighteenth and early nineteenth century, both from the period we call the 'Enlightenment' and from that which followed it, the period of 'Romanticism'. For Browning, as for many of his contemporaries, these two periods were not separated, as we tend to see them today, by a sort of intellectual ha-ha. They were continuous with one another, and influential figures belonged to both camps (Goethe, for example, and Rousseau). Browning was as much an admirer of Diderot and the whole tradition of Enlightenment rationalism and scepticism as he was of Keats and Shelley.[9]

Browning seems to have been especially influenced by the preoccupation of his immediate intellectual precursors with analysis, taxonomy, and accurate definition. The eighteenth century is the heroic age of dictionaries, encyclopaedias, maps, and catalogues: instruments of knowledge which did not merely accumulate observations, but attempted to order their material according to rational principles, and, above all, to fix the stable 'laws' by which the phenomena of life were governed. The operation of the human mind was at the forefront of this intellectual enterprise, from Locke to the writers of the *Encyclopédie*. And one of its results was the representation of identity in terms of primary and essential constituents of feeling, motive, and conduct. Enlightenment philosophers drew heavily on Descartes, whose philosophic method relied on the twin processes of analysis (of the complex into the simple) and re-combination, and whose *Traité des passions de l'âme* (1649) proposed six fundamental human passions: love, hate,

---

[9] He wrote to Elizabeth Barrett of refuting a believer in mesmerism with 'a mere cupful of Diderot's rinsings' (1 July 1845, Kintner: 110).

admiration, desire, joy, and sadness.[10] These essential human feelings can be studied in various orders, categories, and combinations, but remain what they are in themselves. The physical sciences, as so often, provided an analogy here: there were a number of elemental emotions, and though human chemistry might produce an infinite variety of states of feeling it was powerless to add to the basic elements or change their nature. Browning himself (if, as seems probable, he wrote the words which follow in the *Life of Strafford* on which he collaborated with the named author, John Forster, and which was published in 1836) fully displays this Cartesian and scientific bent in a passage reflecting on 'those who carry their researches into the moral nature of mankind': 'Infinitely and distinctly various as appear the shifting hues of our common nature when subjected to the prism of CIRCUMSTANCE, each ray into which it is broken is no less in itself a primitive colour, susceptible, indeed, of vast modification, but incapable of further division' (Firth and Furnivall: 61).[11]

The physical sciences did more than provide Browning with an analogy for the moral world, however; he would have found suggestions of a closer link in passages such as the following, from Shelley's *Queen Mab*:

> Every grain
> Is sentient both in unity and part,
> And the minutest atom comprehends
> A world of loves and hatreds; these beget
> Evil and good: hence truth and falsehood spring;
> Hence will and thought and action, all the germs
> Of pain or pleasure, sympathy or hate
> That variegate the eternal universe.
>
> (iv. 143–50)

Shelley's description of the universe as a feeling organism may seem quintessentially 'Romantic' to us, but it, too, is rooted in Enlightenment speculations as to the sentience of matter, which Shelley would have found even in so uncompromising a materialist as Holbach. A passage from Holbach's *Système de la nature* (1770) argues that what

---

[10] Part 2, Article LXIX.

[11] The prism-image, one of Browning's favourites, strongly suggests his authorship here, even to those who remain sceptical of (in particular) Furnivall's claims as to the extent of Browning's involvement in the book. Michael Mason cites this passage (in Armstrong: 253–4) as evidence of Browning's idea of 'consistency' of character, a line of thought very close to the one I am following in this chapter.

moralists call 'love' and 'hate' are properties which derive from the
physical states of 'attraction' and 'repulsion' inherent in all matter.[12]

The influence of this physical and analytical model of human
identity on Browning's poetry shows itself early. In *Pauline*, the
narrator's Romantic and confessional impulses are matched by a
pseudo-scientific bent in self-analysis:

> I strip my mind bare—whose first elements
> I shall unveil . . .
>
> .   .   .   .   .   .
>
> And then I shall show how these elements
> Produced my present state, and what it is.
>
> (ll. 260–7)

'First' here means not just first in time, but 'primary', as in the
phrase 'first principles'. This interest in identifying the 'first elements'
of a mind is accompanied by the notion that such elements, like
those in the physical world, are intrinsic and unvarying. In a passage
from another early work, *Paracelsus*, the poet Aprile expounds his
ideal of universal artistic achievement, first as a sculptor and painter:

> Every passion sprung from man, conceived by man,
> Would I express and clothe in its fit form,
> Or show repress'd by an ungainly form,
> Or blend with others struggling in one form.
>
> (ii. 381–4)

—then as a poet:

> When those who look'd on pined to hear the hopes,
> And fears, and hates, and loves which moved the crowd,
> I would throw down the pencil as the chisel,
> And I would speak: no thought which ever stirr'd
> A human breast should be untold; all passions,
> All soft emotions, from the turbulent stir
> Within a heart fed with desires like mine—
> To the last comfort, shutting the tired lids
> Of him who sleeps the sultry noon away
> Beneath the tent-tree by the way-side well:
> And this in language as the need should be,
> Now pour'd at once forth in a burning flow,
> Now piled up in a grand array of words.
>
> (ii. 410–22)

---

[12] Quoted in Matthews and Everest: 305.

—and last, as a composer:

> This done, to perfect and consummate all,
> Even as a luminous haze links star to star,
> I would supply all chasms with music, breathing
> Mysterious motions of the soul, no way
> To be defined save in strange melodies.
>
> (ii. 423–7)

This last passage is interesting as negative evidence for the case I am making, because the Romantic notion of music which it outlines (a repository for that which escapes intellectual definition) rapidly disappears from Browning's work, to be replaced (in 'Saul', 'A Toccata of Galuppi's', 'Abt Vogler', and *Fifine at the Fair*) by an account which grants music as concrete and specific a power to represent the 'elements' of identity as any of the other arts.[13] As for the plastic and graphic arts, their mode of representation is strictly subservient to the unalterable essences they depict: the act of painting or writing does not create the subject, whose reality is attested by the response of the audience to the artist's fidelity in handling his materials. The aesthetics here are certainly pre-Romantic: the sculptor who uses his talent to 'express and clothe' passion belongs more to Pope than to Shelley (let alone Blake). Whether the poet's utterance is lyrical and volcanically 'natural' ('pour'd at once forth in a burning flow'), or measured, architectural, and ordered ('piled up in a grand array of words') matters less, again, than its truthfulness to the 'passions' which it mimes.

The painter in 'Pictor Ignotus', a poem published twelve years after *Paracelsus*, shows the persistence in Browning's thinking of this concept of art as a means of representing fixed, elementary states of feeling. The anonymous painter of the title sees his unfulfilled mission as his having been

---

[13] The idea that music expresses the otherwise inexpressible (for whose possible source in German Romantic aesthetics see Woolford and Karlin: i. 48) comes dangerously close to the idea that music is purely abstract and has no correspondence at all with recognizable human feelings, something which Browning's aesthetics could not long have tolerated. It is possible that Aprile's words are intended to show him up, but support for the fact that in his youth Browning himself thought about music in this way comes from another early poem, *Pauline*, whose protagonist describes music as 'earnest of a heaven, | Seeing we know emotions strange by it, | Not else to be revealed' (ll. 365–7).

Sent calmly and inquisitive to scan
  The license and the limit, space and bound,
    Allowed to Truth made visible in Man.
And, like that youth ye praise so, all I saw,
  Over the canvass could my hand have flung,
Each face obedient to its passion's law,
  Each passion clear proclaimed without a tongue;
Whether Hope rose at once in all the blood,
  A-tiptoe for the blessing of embrace,
Or Rapture drooped the eyes as when her brood
  Pull down the nesting dove's heart to its place,
Or Confidence lit swift the forehead up,
  And locked the mouth fast, like a castle braved,—

(ll. 10–22)

Physiognomy and gesture provide the artist with an iconographic repertoire, a dictionary of 'Truth made visible in Man': to each feeling, in its 'pure' state, will correspond some physical attitude or expression, 'obedient to its passion's law'. Once again the influence of eighteenth-century rationalism is evident, with its emphasis on definable and measurable characteristics (here, specifically physical: the movement of blood, of the eyes, of the muscles of the face) and on the operation of immutable 'laws' governing human nature. Not surprisingly, we find in Browning's physical and physiognomical descriptions of hatred a set of recurring facial expressions and gestures, along with a set of recurring images. *Whiteness*, for example: from *Pauline*:

But I begin to know what thing hate is—
To sicken, and to quiver, and grow white . . .

(ll. 650–1)

from *Paracelsus*:

The wroth sea's waves are edged
With foam, white as the bitten lip of Hate . . .

(v. 644–5)

and from *Sordello*, where the 'livid' colour of wrath combines with the image of hatred itself as a physical substance:

gathering in its ancient market-place,
Talked group with restless group, and not a face
But wrath made livid, for among them were

> Death's staunch purveyors, such as have in care
> To feast him. Fear had long since taken root
> In every breast, and now these crushed its fruit,
> The ripe hate, like a wine . . .
>
> (i. 88–93)

This image, with its biblical source in the winepress of God's wrath (Revelation 14) is given a characteristically vulgar twist by 'Half-Rome' in *The Ring and the Book*, describing Pietro and Violante Comparini's supposed ingratitude towards their son-in-law Guido Franceschini and his family:

> when the drunkenness of hate
> Hiccupped return for hospitality,
> Befouled the table they had feasted on . . .
>
> (ii. 677–9)

The image of the winepress returns in Other Half-Rome's florid account of Guido going murderously over the top:

> Then did the winch o' the winepress of all hate,
> Vanity, disappointment, grudge and greed,
> Take the last turn that screws out pure revenge
> With a bright bubble at the brim beside . . .
>
> (iii. 1542–5)[14]

Another physical characteristic of hatred is bound up with *looking*: in 'Soliloquy of the Spanish Cloister' the speaker's obsessive watching of Brother Lawrence, in 'Count Gismond' the cousins 'glancing sideways with still head' at the woman they intend to destroy (l. 24), and in 'The Laboratory' the speaker's eerie and unhinged amazement at the small amount of poison she will require to kill her rival:

> For only last night, as they whispered, I brought
> My own eyes to bear on her so, that I thought,
> Could I keep them one half minute fixed, she'd fall
> Shrivelled: she fell not; yet this does it all!
>
> (ll. 33–6)

The artist who represents the passion of hatred employs a symbolic, but at the same time quasi-scientific, naturalism: the effect is the

---

[14] Browning is recalling Keats's 'beaker full of the warm South . . . with beaded bubbles winking at the brim | And purple-stainèd mouth' ('Ode to a Nightingale', ll. 15–18): Guido, a product of the 'warm South', drinks blood for wine.

reverse of the 'arresting strangeness, the special beauty' which Swann, in *A la recherche du temps perdu*, teaches the Narrator to admire in Giotto's Paduan frescoes of the Virtues and Vices:

By a fine stroke of the painter's invention she [Charity] is trampling all the treasures of the earth beneath her feet, but exactly as if she were treading grapes in a wine-press to extract their juice, or rather as if she had climbed on to a heap of sacks to raise herself higher; and she is holding out her flaming heart to God, or shall we say 'handing' it to him, exactly as a cook might hand up a corkscrew through the skylight of her basement kitchen to someone who has called down for it from the ground-floor window. The 'Invidia,' again, should have had some look of envy on her face. But in this fresco, too, the symbol occupies so large a place and is represented with such realism, the serpent hissing between the lips of Envy is so huge, and so completely fills her wide-opened mouth, that the muscles of her face are strained and contorted, like those of a child blowing up a balloon, and her attention—and ours too for that matter—is so utterly concentrated on the activity of her lips as to leave little time to spare for envious thoughts.   (Proust: i. 87–8)

Despite this difference in the mode of representation Proust's account of the Giotto frescoes reminds us that the nature of these passions, and their essential fixity, is more or less taken for granted in either case. Where Giotto's symbolism is *de*familiarizing, that of Browning's Aprile and Pictor is *re*familiarizing: they celebrate the power of art to depict with seductive intensity that which we already know. In 'Fra Lippo Lippi' (published ten years after 'Pictor Ignotus') the painter is still harping on the same theme:

> Take the prettiest face,
> The Prior's niece . . . patron-saint—is it so pretty
> You can't discover if it means hope, fear,
> Sorrow or joy?
>
> (ll. 208–11)[15]

What a face 'means' is given its most elaborate treatment in *Fifine at the Fair* (published in 1872) in which the speaker of the poem, Don Juan, tells of a protracted day-dream which comes to him when he falls asleep after playing Schumann's 'Carnaval'. He finds himself in Venice, in the middle of a 'prodigious Fair, | Concourse immense of

---

[15] See also ll. 280–311 of this poem for an important elaboration of Lippo Lippi's aesthetic.

men and women' (ll. 1696–7), all masked, but whose masks in fact denote their identity:

> On each hand,
> I soon became aware, flocked the infinitude
> Of passions, loves and hates, man pampers till his mood
> Becomes himself, the whole sole face we name him by,
> Nor want denotement else, if age or youth supply
> The rest of him: old, young,—classed creature: in the main
> A love, a hate, a hope, a fear, each soul a-strain
> Some one way through the flesh—the face, the evidence
> O' the soul at work inside . . .
>
> (ll. 1718–26)

Age and youth are the only permitted variables here; otherwise the 'soul' is defined in terms of a ruling passion, expressed in such a way as to seem absolute and self-sufficient: we are not told what the love and hate and hope and fear are love and hate and hope and fear *of*, simply that they are 'at work inside'.

In the course of his day-dream, Juan comes to complicate and subtilize his initial vision of humanity as a masque of ruling passions, but the principle of identity which underlies it remains unaltered. The observer of human nature, he says, is like

> the chemist when he winds
> Thread up and up, till clue be fairly clutched,—unbinds
> The composite, ties fast the simple to its mate,
> And, tracing each effect back to its cause, elate,
> Constructs in fancy, from the fewest primitives,
> The complex and complete, all diverse life, that lives
> Not only in beast, bird, fish, reptile, insect, but
> The very plants and earths and ores.
>
> (ll. 1793–1800)[16]

The psychologist works in the same Cartesian fashion as the chemist; so for that matter does the metaphysician, whose faith, in the resounding last lines of the 'Epilogue' to *Dramatis Personae* (1864), 'decomposes but to recompose, | Becomes my universe that feels and knows'. Another such analyst appears in 'A Forgiveness' (published in *Pacchiarotto . . . with Other Poems*, 1876), whose speaker, confronted with his wife's infidelity, tells her that he

---

[16] Contrast Paracelsus's description of his chemical researches (iv. 375–90).

went
Back to the house, that day, and brought my mind
To bear upon your action, uncombined
Motive from motive, till the dross, deprived
Of every purer particle, survived
At last in native simple hideousness,
Utter contemptibility, nor less
Nor more.

(ll. 320–7)[17]

As it happens, the speaker's deductions here are based on a false premiss (that his wife hates him), but that is nothing to do with the rigour of his method. An analysis of Browning's poetry like that undertaken by the 'chemist' in Juan's image would break down its 'complex and complete' world into its 'fewest primitives', that is the 'passions', of which Juan's summary list—love, hate, hope, and fear—are the ones to which Browning most constantly alludes.[18] In *Sordello* they occur in a description of the way dramatic poetry presents its characters in action:

behold
How such, with fit assistance to unfold,
Or obstacles to crush them, disengage
Their forms, love, hate, hope, fear, peace make, war wage,
In presence of you all!

(v. 586–91)

Again the terms (verbs here instead of indefinite nouns, but the effect is the same) have no defined object: they are more significant as elemental 'forms' of behaviour than as components of an Aristotelian 'action'. In *La Saisiaz*, a philosophical elegy for his friend Anne Egerton Smith, published in 1878, the same quartet reappears: Browning speculates that the earth might be 'Only a machine for teaching love and hate and hope and fear | To myself' (ll. 320–1).

The passions are therefore, for Browning, the elements of identity; they are also, as a necessary consequence, the elements of motive. 'Tracing each effect back to its cause', in Juan's words, is a key both

[17] I discuss 'A Forgiveness' in detail in Ch. 9.
[18] Obviously the dualism of these terms, the way they come in opposed pairs (love/hate, hope/fear) is important, and I shall discuss it in a later chapter. The conventional nature of the list is indicated by Johnson's lines in *The Vanity of Human Wishes*: 'Then say how hope and fear, desire and hate | O'erspread with snares the cloudy maze of fate'.

to the psychologist and to the storyteller: just as the psychologist analyses identity according to elementary principles, so the storyteller concentrates not on the outward form of an action but on its inward springs. In *Sordello*, the actions of the two main characters who affect Sordello's fate, Palma and Taurello Salinguerra, are each governed by a ruling passion, in Palma's case her love of Sordello, in Taurello's case his hatred of the Este family. Without this key their actions are enigmatic: Palma's behaviour only becomes clear to Sordello (and to us) when she reveals, first of all that love itself, in an absolute sense, is the quality that expresses her inmost self, secondly that she had spent her youth waiting for the embodiment of her desire, an 'out-soul' to direct her own, and thirdly that she had found this embodiment in Sordello.[19] Similarly, Taurello's energetic effort on behalf of Ecelin Romano, even after Ecelin has turned his back on their lifelong struggle against the rival Este clan, puzzles onlookers until they remember 'somewhat late | A laughing old outrageous stifled hate | He bore that Este' (iv. 649–51; the clashing epithets perfectly convey both the depth and intensity of Taurello's hatred and his desire to keep it hidden or cover it with affected nonchalance).

Sordello realizes at the climax of the poem that in their submission to a ruling 'love' or 'hate' Taurello and Palma are typical of the mass of mankind, who likewise 'had some core | Within . . . Some love, hate even' (vi. 59–60, 82).[20] It is this 'core' which fires Browning's interest in character: as he explained in the preface to the first edition of *Paracelsus* (1835): 'instead of having recourse to an external machinery of incidents to create and evolve the crisis I desire to produce, I have ventured to display somewhat minutely the mood itself in its rise and progress'. Browning followed this method in his development of the dramatic monologue, where the speaker's 'mood' is the predominant object of interest and the story's 'incidents' serve mainly

---

[19] Browning was influenced by Dante's placing of Cunizza (Palma's original) in the heaven of Venus in the *Paradiso* (ix. 13 ff.), 'perche mi vinse il lume d'esta stella' (because the light of this star overcame me); Dante refers to Cunizza's many scandalous love-affairs, but Browning takes the dominance of Venus on an altogether higher metaphysical plane: Palma's 'love' means the impulse to entire self-devotion, not as self-sacrifice but as the means of liberating and putting into play the resources of her nature (see *Sordello* iii. 304 ff.).

[20] Sordello's problem turns out to be an inability to share in this common human lot: 'not that a Palma's Love, | A Salinguerra's Hate would equal prove | To swaying all Sordello', he reflects (vi. 89–91).

to 'display' it. 'My Last Duchess' is not in this sense a thriller (even an enigmatic one) about what happened to the Duke's first wife; it is a 'display' of the Duke's ruling passion, that of self-love (and, contained within his monologue, a counter-display of his wife's opposing passion, that of love for others). To take a less obvious example: it seems clear that Browning made the historical background of 'How They Brought the Good News from Ghent to Aix' deliberately vague and impressionistic in order to focus attention on the ride itself (and its 'mood' of physical exhilaration); he was annoyed by repeated enquiries about the historical authenticity of the story and the nature of the 'good news' itself.[21] Readers who wonder, as the poem progresses, whether the 'good news' will get through or not have not properly grasped the title, which is in the past tense and resolves any suspense before the action begins.

Though Browning's analysis of motive searches out the 'fewest primitives' that form the basis of all human action, he is not interested (as Coleridge was, or Freud) in the origin of these primitive elements themselves. He takes them as given. Coleridge speculated that the archetype of hatred is oral rejection, and linked this idea to the aspirate sound of the word: *h* is an expulsion of breath; *h* + *ate* = I reject what I have ingested, I hate (Coleridge: 3). (He could have cited Milton's devils, chewing 'bitter ashes, which the offended taste | With spattering noise rejected', and who 'With hatefullest disrelish writhed their jaws' (*Paradise Lost* x. 566–9).) There is nothing equivalent to this in Browning, though there is much else that links his curious, ingenious, and fanciful intelligence to that of Coleridge. Nor is there anything equivalent to Freud's account of the development of hatred in, for example, his 1915 paper 'Instincts and their Vicissitudes', as deriving from 'the narcissistic ego's primordial repudiation of the external world with its outpouring of stimuli' (Freud 1984: 137). This is not to say that Browning's writing about hatred cannot be read in terms of psychological theory, only that such theory is not, in itself, the subject of his writing. An illustration of this difference relates to what Freud, both in 'Instincts and their Vicissitudes' and in *The Ego and the Id* (1923), calls the 'ambivalence' of love and hate. Browning, too, recognizes and is fascinated by this ambivalence: he was as disturbed as Freud to find 'not only that love is with unexpected regularity accompanied by hate . . . but also that

---

[21] See Woolford and Karlin: ii. 239–40.

in a number of circumstances hate changes into love and love into hate' (Freud 1984: 383). Freud seeks to *account* for this ambivalence—that is, to demonstrate that it is not an ambivalence at all, or that it is not the kind of ambivalence it appears. He is compelled to do so because if such an ambivalence were admitted without qualification, 'then clearly the ground is cut away from under a distinction so fundamental as that between erotic instincts and death instincts, one which presupposes physiological processes running in opposite directions' (ibid.). Freud's dualism must therefore find some way of accommodating the shifts and dissolves to which emotion is subject, but Browning's dualism, though it is quite as strong as Freud's, is under no such obligation. On the contrary: Keats's principle of 'negative capability' works to the poet's advantage here, and Browning shows himself 'capable of being in uncertainties, mysteries, doubts, without any irritable reaching after fact and reason'.[22] It is the phenomenon itself that absorbs him, and not its place in a larger system of ideas.

Why *should* Browning have been so absorbed by hatred, so interested in (as he wrote to Julia Wedgwood) 'morbid cases of the soul', so drawn to landscapes 'overrun with weed | —Docks, quitchgrass, loathly mallows no man plants' (*Sordello*, iv. 22–3)?[23] The answer lies, I think, in the association of hatred with conflict and aggression, and therefore with one of Browning's deepest beliefs about human nature. In his writing there are dozens of occurrences of the rhyme 'strife/life': conflict is a universal law, struggle is the condition of existence, all progress is dependent on a perpetual warfare between opposed forces (whether characterized politically, morally, or aesthetically, as revolution versus reaction, good versus evil, romantic versus classical).[24] This belief in dialectical struggle is predominant both in nineteenth-century intellectual culture (Carlyle, Hegel, Marx, Darwin, and Freud all subscribe to it in one form or another) and in

[22] Letter of 22 Dec. 1817 to George and Thomas Keats.

[23] For the Julia Wedgwood letter, see pp. 219–20.

[24] Of the 85 occurrences of 'strife' in Browning's poetry, 41 rhyme with 'life' (including 3 examples of internal rhyme). Two examples: the first from *Sordello*: 'And, lo, Sordello vanished utterly, | Sundered in twain; each spectral part at strife | With each; one jarred against another life' (ii. 656–8), and the second from *Fifine at the Fair*: 'we must learn to live, | Case-hardened at all points, not bare and sensitive, | But plated for defence, nay, furnished for attack, | With spikes at the due place, that neither front nor back | May suffer in that squeeze with nature, we find—life. | Are we not here to learn the good of peace through strife, | Of love through hate, and reach knowledge by ignorance?' (ll. 1763–9).

literature: among English writers alone can be counted Tennyson, Charlotte Brontë, Eliot, Dickens, Trollope, Meredith, Clough, and Hardy; perhaps the one dissenter is Thackeray, that great and lovable humanist whom the idea of success at others' expense revolted, and who immortalized its exponent, Becky Sharp, in *Vanity Fair*.

The belief in struggle manifests itself in Browning's language by a proliferation of metaphors drawn from physical aggression, a figurative violence which attaches itself to any and every activity, and forms one of the principal image-clusters in his rhetorical universe. In *Luria*, Luria's friend Husain claims to have seen through the false opposition between the rational and intellectual Florentines and the wild and warlike Moors:

> They called our thirst of war a transient thing;
> The battle element must pass away
> From life, they said, and leave a tranquil world:
> —Master, I took their light and turned it full
> On that dull turgid vein they said would burst
> And pass away; and as I looked on Life,
> Still everywhere I tracked this, though it hid
> And shifted, lay so silent as it thought,
> Changed oft the hue yet ever was the same:
> Why 'twas all fighting, all their nobler life!
> All work was fighting, every harm— defeat,
> And every joy obtained—a victory!
>
> (iv. 172–83)

The 'dull turgid vein' of violence has a medical connotation (when it bursts the patient will be tranquil, as after a blood-letting); it is also like a vein of mineral ore, which can be traced across different formations and contours; lastly it is animated like a snake, subtle and deceptive. Elizabeth Barrett approved of Husain's 'true doctrine',[25] but it is doubtful whether she had thought through some of the implications of these images; for the unexceptionably worthy idea that all work is fighting leads in the end to Guido in his death-cell, calling his 'civilized' auditors to account. To the Cardinal who condones his sentence he asks:

---

[25] In her note on the line when she read the play in manuscript: see Woolford and Karlin: ii. 432.

Was this strict inquisition made for blood
When first you showed us scarlet on your back,
Called to the College? That straightforward way
To that legitimate end, — I think it passed
Over a scantling of heads brained, hearts broke,
Lives trodden into dust, — how otherwise?
Such is the way o' the world, and so you walk:
Does memory haunt your pillow? Not a whit.

(*The Ring and the Book*, xi. 2233–40)

The Cardinal's scarlet robe, the sign of his success, is also a mark of
Cain; his 'straightforward' and 'legitimate' progress to high office
has been as murderous as Guido's crooked path to the scaffold.
Browning's endorsement of Husain's 'true doctrine' runs all the way
from the noble to the bestial, and his own compulsive self-image as a
'fighter' (in 'Prospice' and, above all, the 'Epilogue' to *Asolando*) is
riven with ambivalence. For what Guido accuses the Cardinal of is
not immorality but hypocrisy, and in this he is at one with Browning.
It is not violence that is bad, but the pretence that violence is
something else, something 'legitimate'. Nor can Browning resist the
lure of this violence, the seductive shifts and changes of hue with
which it finds its way into the heart of the 'nobler life'. 'Prospice' is
based on the image of the 'strong man' confronting death like a
warrior, and specifically like Bunyan's spiritual warrior, Mr Great-
heart, in the second part of *Pilgrim's Progress*:

For the journey is done and the summit attained,
    And the barriers fall,
Though a battle's to fight ere the guerdon be gained,
    The reward of it all.
I was ever a fighter, — so — one fight more,
    The best and the last!

(ll. 9–12)

The word 'best' here has two meanings, one official and one illicit.
The official meaning is that the last fight is the best because it *is* the
last (the 'reward of it all' is not having to fight any more); the illicit
meaning is that it is the best because Death is the ultimate antagonist,
the 'Arch Fear in a visible form' (l. 7). As though uneasily conscious
that he has said something double-edged, the speaker of the poem

goes on to characterize the fight against death as the 'worst' possible experience, which is redeemed only by its outcome, salvation:

> For sudden the worst turns the best to the brave,
>   The black minute's at end,
> And the elements' rage, the fiend-voices that rave,
>   Shall dwindle, shall blend,
> Shall change, shall become first a peace out of pain,
>   Then a light, then thy breast,
> O thou soul of my soul!
>
> (ll. 21–7)

The 'best' fight is somehow also the 'worst' to endure; the 'black minute' whose end is welcomed belongs nevertheless to the many *minutes* and *moments* in Browning whose extreme intensity, whether of joy or suffering, is always a sign of their privileged value (the 'moment, one and infinite' of the lovers' blissful union in 'By the Fire-Side', the 'one moment' which 'knelled the woe of years' in 'Childe Roland to the Dark Tower Came'). In fact the very 'rage' and 'fiend-voices' which the speaker imagines do not disappear, but 'dwindle', 'blend', and 'change', so that the bliss which the speaker enters is made up of the same 'elements' and 'voices' as before. The 'battle-element' (to return to Husain's image) has not 'passed away from life' but has only 'shifted' and 'changed its hue'.

As with violence, so with hatred, its emotional correlate: Browning recognizes not just the animating quality of hatred but (more disturbingly, more scandalously even) what Hazlitt called 'the pleasure of hating', 'a secret affinity, a *hankering* after evil in the human mind' (Hazlitt: xii. 128). Browning records this pleasure in poem after poem: from the mob at Verona getting drunk on 'the ripe hate, like a wine' (*Sordello*, i. 93) to the refined discriminations of the Spanish grandee in 'A Forgiveness', from the gross enjoyment of the crowd at the execution of Jacques du Bourg-Molay in 'The Heretic's Tragedy' to Tertium Quid's cultivated, vicarious, and voyeuristic thrill at Guido's murder of Pompilia (*The Ring and the Book*, iv. 1382–9).[26] To read Browning is to encounter such emotions, and not necessarily in the spirit of moral condemnation. 'On the stage,' Hazlitt argues, 'every one takes part with Othello

---

[26] The passage from *Sordello* is cited above, pp. 13–14; for 'A Forgiveness', see Ch. 9; for 'The Heretic's Tragedy' see Ch. 6; Tertium Quid's lines are cited in Ch. 9.

against Iago.'[27] But what of the poet who, according to Keats, took 'as much delight in conceiving an Iago as an Imogen'?[28] Can we really separate ourselves, as readers, from Shakespeare's—or Browning's—'relish of the dark side of things', and is this relish not one of the qualities which, whether we admit it or not, most draws us to them?

[27] This is the one exception he allows, in 'On the Pleasure of Hating', to our 'hankering after evil': 'in reading we always take the right side, and make the case properly our own. Our imaginations are sufficiently excited, we have nothing to do with the matter but as a pure creation of the mind, and we therefore yield to the natural, unwarped impression of good and evil'. This exception comes in a footnote at the end of the essay.

[28] Letter to Richard Woodhouse, 27 Oct. 1818. The following phrase also comes from this letter.

2

Personal Hatred

We can scarcely hate anyone that we know.

(Hazlitt)[1]

ON 7 July 1889, Browning was leafing through a new book in a friend's garden. The book was *Letters and Literary Remains of Edward FitzGerald*, edited by W. Aldis Wright. FitzGerald would have been known to Browning for his friendship with Tennyson if for nothing else; he had also conducted an oblique argument with FitzGerald many years before through 'Rabbi Ben Ezra', a poem which 'answers' the one work for which FitzGerald is now remembered, the *Rubáiyát* of *Omar Khayyám*. In this volume of FitzGerald's letters Browning came across the following passage:

> Mrs Browning's Death is rather a relief to me, I must say: no more Aurora Leighs, thank God! A woman of real Genius, I know: but what is the upshot of it all? She and her Sex had better mind the Kitchen and their Children; and perhaps the Poor: except in such things as little Novels, they only devote themselves to what Men do much better, leaving that which Men do worse or not at all.

'I felt as if she had died yesterday', Browning told a friend.[2] He also described the effect of the event as having 'the directness of a sharp physical blow. He spoke of it, and for hours, even days, was known to feel it, as such' (Orr: 422). To his son Pen he wrote that he had 'really been the worse, physically, for this outrage', and his sister Sarianna confirmed that he was 'quite ill with the pain it gave him' (Hood: 312, 315). This may partly account for the physical imagery

---

[1] 'Why Distant Objects Please', *Table-Talk* (1822), in Hazlitt: viii. 262.

[2] This remark is not in a letter; it originates with Mrs Orr, and may have been made to her (Orr: 423). She adds that it was made 'in half deprecation, half denial of the too great fierceness of his reaction', but whether this represents his feelings or her gloss on them is impossible to say. I comment below on the criticism implied by 'too great fierceness'.

which dominates the poem he wrote the following day and sent to the *Athenaeum*, where it was published on 13 July (No. 3220, p. 64):

TO EDWARD FITZGERALD

I chanced upon a new book yesterday:
I opened it, and, where my finger lay
   'Twixt page and uncut page, these words I read
—Some six or seven at most—and learned thereby
That you, FitzGerald, whom by ear and eye
   She never knew, 'thanked God my wife was dead.'

Ay, dead! and were yourself alive, good Fitz,
How to return you thanks would task my wits:
   Kicking you seems the common lot of curs—
While more appropriate greeting lends you grace:
Surely to spit there glorifies your face—
   Spitting—from lips once sanctified by Hers.[3]

In his letter to Norman MacColl, the editor of the *Athenaeum*, Browning wrote: 'If you consider that the feeling I gave some faint expression to in the accompanying stanzas is discordant with the general tone of the poetry in your columns—pray let me have them again for publication elsewhere' (Hood: 311). After sending the poem, however, Browning had second thoughts and tried to retract it. He sent a telegram to MacColl which arrived as the issue was going to press; but MacColl, guessing the contents, 'so managed by talking to a friend before opening the telegram as to be able to inform Browning that it was too late to keep the stanzas from appearing' (Hood: 378).

Though Aldis Wright sent a formal apology to the *Athenaeum* for having allowed the passage to be published while Browning was still alive, he wrote privately to a friend of his calling it 'the unlucky paragraph', asserting that it had been 'twisted from its true meaning', and complaining: 'who could have imagined that it would produce the disgraceful insults which Browning has been guilty of?' (ibid.). The phrase 'unlucky paragraph' picks up Browning's 'chanced upon', as though the offensiveness of FitzGerald's words were a mere accident of circumstance: FitzGerald has been *unlucky* but Browning has been *disgraceful*. It might be thought to be the other way round: that Browning was unlucky enough, eight days after the thirty-eighth anniversary of Elizabeth Barrett Browning's death, and almost exactly

---

[3] The poem is dated 'July 8, 1889' in the *Athenaeum* text.

five months before his own, to 'chance upon' FitzGerald's disgraceful
paragraph.

In letters to his family written after the poem appeared we can see
Browning's anger cooling, so to speak, into hatred. To Pen, he
wrote: 'I was not going to let the people who are reading the book
suppose for a moment that I am inclined to let such a ruffian insult
the dead with impunity'; he referred to FitzGerald as a 'wretched
Irish fribble and "feather-head"' and as Tennyson's 'adulatory lick-
spittle', and concluded, passion getting the better of grammar and
fusing his and his wife's identity into 'one': 'all I know is that the
fellow insulted one unable to defend herself—who yet is able to
express his loathing for such a scamp' (Hood: 312). The reference to
Tennyson shows Browning attempting to characterize the relationship as one-sided and discreditable to FitzGerald; but the title of the
poem, and the phrase 'good Fitz' in l. 7, echo Tennyson's own
affectionate tribute 'To E. FitzGerald', published in 1885, which
opens with the words 'Old Fitz' and has 'My Fitz' at l. 51. Moreover,
this poem had been written in June 1883 as the dedication to
'Tiresias', while FitzGerald was still alive; he died before he saw it,
and Tennyson added an elegiac passage at the end of 'Tiresias',
'laying flowers . . . above his honoured head' (ll. 83–4).[4] FitzGerald is
not alive to respond to Tennyson, just as he is not alive to respond to
Browning; it is difficult to believe that Browning did not have
Tennyson's poem in mind when he wrote his own.

Despite affirming to Pen that he would not look at the book again,
it evidently fascinated him: he told his brother-in-law George Barrett
(in a letter, written three months after the incident, in which his
'horror and disgust' are freshly expressed): 'I ran my eye afterwards
through the proper names occurring therein—to see if any more
wanted notice' (Landis: 330). In the same letter Browning adds racial
abuse to his litany: 'I observe that having to find fault with Wordsworth's sonnets he needs must "wish old W. had his sonnets fastened
round his neck and was pitched into the Duddon," or a similar
bestiality—in the true Celtic strain: cruelty and fun together'.

At this point we reach the question of whether there was something
excessive or indecently violent in Browning's response—though
perhaps we should reserve these epithets for Julian Hawthorne's
outburst: 'No English gentleman would so have expressed himself;

---

[4] See Ricks: iii. 105 ff.

no mere man would have stooped to such words: it was a feminine screech of hate and spite, such as one might expect to hear from a raving street-walker in Spitalfields' (Hawthorne: 142). Yet the imagery is not in itself unusual in Browning. Kicking (especially associated with dogs) and spitting are familiar actions of hatred and contempt in his work (both poems and letters).[5] In the poem the implication is that kicking is too good for FitzGerald, who is hateful above the ordinary; what would be required would be the poetic reverse of what Caponsacchi imagines in *The Ring and the Book* when he says that killing Guido would have been 'A spittle wiped off from the face of God!' (vi. 1479). Christ is spat on (Matthew 26: 67); but should we, in turn, spit in the devil's face? In 'Childe Roland to the Dark Tower Came', Roland recalls the fate of 'Giles . . . the soul of honour':

> What honest men should dare (he said) he durst.
> Good—but the scene shifts—faugh! what hangman's hands
> Pin to his breast a parchment? his own bands
> Read it. Poor traitor, spit upon and curst!
>
> (ll. 83–6)

Giles's treason is shadowed by *Macbeth*, i. vii. 46–7 ('I dare do all that may become a man; | Who dares do more is none'), but it is the whole man who is remembered in his fall, and his fate elicits Roland's pity, not his condemnation. That there might be something dubious about the judgement itself is suggested by the barbaric rejoicing of the executioners in 'The Heretic's Tragedy':

> Then up they hoist me John in a chafe,
>   Sling him fast like a hog to scorch,
> Spit in his face, then leap back safe,
>   Sing 'Laudes' and bid clap-to the torch.
>
> (ll. 32–5)

The poem is based on the burning of Jacques du Bourg-Molay, Master of the Order of the Knights-Templar, who, as Browning would have been well aware, was innocent of the charges brought

---

[5] Two examples from letters will illustrate the point. Of the medium D. D. Home (see next chapter) Browning wrote: 'If I ever cross the fellow's path I shall probably be silly enough to soil my shoe by kicking him' (DeVane and Knickerbocker: 199). Of a former acquaintance who did not repay a debt he wrote to Isa Blagden: 'I spit at him and have done with it' (McAleer 1951: 322).

against him; the gross 'Christian' zeal of his executioners, their hatred and mockery of the victim, ironically align him with Christ himself. If there is an argument to be made against Browning's language in 'To Edward FitzGerald' it might be on this ground: that it does, indeed, 'lend [FitzGerald] grace', that people will feel about him as Roland feels about Giles, and that Browning will appear to them to be singing Laudes and clapping-to the torch.

Browning's family and friends were certainly embarrassed by the outburst—notably Pen, who irritated his father by saying that such expressions as FitzGerald's 'recoil sufficiently on those who use them' (Hood: 313), a thoroughly conventional sentiment which might equally apply to the poem itself. It stung Browning into an accusation of cowardice: 'One may decline any painful duty on very specious grounds—letting the thing recoil &c—but I said a little of my mind and there it will remain—I expect as long as FitzGerald's recorded "relief"—the blackguard' (p. 314). Pen's squeamishness has communicated itself to almost every biographer, starting with Browning's close friend Mrs Orr, who shrank from giving a full account of an 'incident . . . which deserved only to be forgotten', and wondered that 'he could be thus affected at an age usually destructive of the more violent emotions' (Orr: 422–3). Nor is the poem mentioned in the revised and updated editions of her *Handbook to the Works of Robert Browning* (first published in 1885) which appeared after Browning's death, though it would fit nicely in the section entitled 'Poems expressive of the Fiercer Emotions'. Griffin and Minchin, too, refrain from citing the poem itself and think it 'superfluous to dilate upon this unhappy affair' (p. 293). The standard modern biography wags its sage head at Browning's 'savagery': 'He had shown to the public a raw, brutal reaction, he had humiliated himself, and probably he knew that in doing so he had humiliated Elizabeth in a way FitzGerald never could' (Irvine and Honan: 514). So now the injury to his wife is *Browning's* fault! I think we need to look at this matter in a less reasonable light. Surely Chesterton is closer to the mark in linking the poem to the 'something very queer and dangerous that underlay all the good humour of Browning', and in commenting: 'if some of the prejudices that were really rooted in him were trodden on . . . his rage was something wholly transfiguring and alarming, something far removed from the shrill disapproval of Carlyle and Ruskin. It can only be said that he became a savage, and not always a very agreeable or presentable savage. The indecent fury which danced upon the bones of Edward FitzGerald was a thing which ought not to have astonished any one who had known much of Browning's character or even of his work' (Chesterton: 115–16). Chesterton further testified to his own 'dark and indescribable pleasure in this last burst of the old barbaric energy. The mountain had been tilled and forested, and laid out in gardens to the summit; but for one last night it had proved itself once more a volcano, and had lit up all the plains with its forgotten fire' (p. 131). In this sense the poem becomes a companion-piece of hate to the love-lyrics of Browning's last volume, *Asolando*, such as 'Now' or 'Summum Bonum', also habitually praised for their intense, late fire.

Here the question of context arises: specifically that of the biographical context. In comparing 'To Edward FitzGerald' either with love-lyrics in *Asolando*, or with expressions of hatred in other poems, am I really comparing like with like? Does the particular biographical occasion of 'To Edward FitzGerald' put it in a different category from these works, make it into a personal and non-dramatic utterance? If so, perhaps the hostility to the poem rests on an unspoken distinction between what is permissible in a work of fiction (Caponsacchi's loathing of Guido) and what is permissible in a 'real' utterance (Browning's loathing of FitzGerald). Leaving aside the fact that Caponsacchi and Guido were historical personages who did hate each other, the urgency of the question remains: should our reading of the poem be determined by its status as a literary text, or by its status as a historical document? And is the distinction between the two a useful, or indeed a tenable one?

The reluctance shown by every commentator on the poem that I have come across to treat it *as* a poem seems to indicate that its function as a record of Browning's actual feelings about Edward FitzGerald is thought to be more important than its form. Even Chesterton, who comes closest to suggesting its affinity with Browning's creativity, his poetic 'fire', doesn't say anything that could not equally have been said had 'To Edward FitzGerald' been a letter to the editor and not a poem at all. Supposing, however, we were to recast it in this form. It would then read something like this:

Dear Sir

I chanced upon a new book yesterday: I opened it, and, where my finger lay between one uncut page and the next, I read a few words by Edward FitzGerald saying that he 'thanked God for the death of my wife'—who, I should say, had never seen or heard of him. If Mr FitzGerald were still alive,

it would task my wits how to return his 'thanks': kicking him would be
treating him like a mere cur, but spitting in his face, though more appropriate,
would lend him a grace he did not deserve: for I would be spitting from lips
once sanctified by my wife's.

I am, Sir [etc.]

As a paraphrase this is doubly wrong: not only does it take away the
formal characteristics of the verse (rhythm, rhyme, alliteration, and
so on), but it alters the mode from direct to indirect address. Instead
of being *to* Edward FitzGerald the letter is *about* him. The person
addressed by a letter to a newspaper is the editor. But Browning's
real letter to MacColl, as we have seen, was purely functional; it was
intended to get the poem published. The newspaper itself was to be
no more than the medium of publication.[6] The poem rests on a
rhetorical contradiction: that FitzGerald can be spoken to as if he
were alive, though the content of what is said to him assumes that he
is not. (Browning's 'revision' of Tennyson's 'To E. FitzGerald' rests,
in part, on his acute grasp of the two-part structure of that poem, the
first written when Tennyson believed that FitzGerald would be alive
to read it, the second when he knew that he would not.) Browning
expresses his hatred to FitzGerald, not simply of him, even in the act
of saying that FitzGerald's death denies him the opportunity.

Poetry was always for Browning a creative, a resurrective power.
He insists on the fact that his wife 'by ear and eye . . . never knew'
FitzGerald because this condition is the mirror image of the one
FitzGerald now occupies towards himself. Blind and deaf to admoni-
tion, FitzGerald is nevertheless resurrected in poetry to be (or rather
not to be) kicked and spat on; but nothing will bring Elizabeth back;
the poem exists in a despairingly ironic relation to Milton's sonnet
about his dead wife, brought to him 'like Alcestis from the grave'
only to be lost again (and Browning was fascinated, indeed obsessed
by the Alcestis story in the years following Elizabeth's death).[7] On
the 'lips once sanctified by hers' Browning feels the kiss of his own
'late espoused Saint', cruelly delusive as Milton's had been: 'But O as

---

[6] A carefully chosen one, I would add: the privacy of Browning's feelings had been
violated by the publication of a private letter; hence the expedient of publishing his
response as widely as possible, rather than (say) writing privately to Aldis Wright.

[7] The major work here is of course *Balaustion's Adventure* (1871), which incorpo-
rates a translation of Euripides' *Alcestis*; see also 'Apollo and the Fates', the prologue
to *Parleyings with certain people of importance in their day* (1887). The Alcestis theme
appears in other guises, linked to the myths of Andromeda and Eurydice, for example
in *The Ring and the Book* and *Aristophanes' Apology*.

to embrace me she enclin'd | I wak'd, she fled, and day brought back my night'.[8] This 'night' has been brought back by FitzGerald: 'I felt as if she had died yesterday'. The kiss is replaced (or more properly *dis*placed) by spitting. As Darwin observed, 'Spitting seems an almost universal sign of contempt or disgust; and spitting obviously represents the rejection of anything offensive from the mouth' (Darwin: 272). The poem records the terrible substitution of a hating for a loving relationship. In the new creation generated by the 'new book', Browning and FitzGerald are 'I' and 'you', Elizabeth Barrett is 'she'. A love poem has become a hate poem. I said the substitution was terrible; but it is also (violently, erotically) pleasurable. Its last line enacts and withholds an ejaculation in which the memory of erotic intimacy winds itself luxuriantly around a desire to express scorn and repulsion.

My reading assumes that a poem cannot be an expression of opinion, or of feeling, and nothing more. 'To Edward FitzGerald' is the last in a series of poems by Browning in which an intellectual design subsumes a personal hostility. Among others: 'The Lost Leader' (Wordsworth), 'Mr. Sludge, "the Medium"' (D. D. Home), *Prince Hohenstiel-Schwangau, Saviour of Society* (Napoleon III), 'Of Pacchiarotto, and How He Worked in Distemper' (Alfred Austin), and *Parleying with George Bubb Dodington* (Disraeli). What distinguishes 'To Edward FitzGerald' from these works is the lack of disguise, the naming of its object; it is scandalously naked, but it is not different in kind. Chesterton's metaphor—that of Browning dancing on FitzGerald's bones—is inaccurate precisely in the measure that it takes the symbolic act as equivalent to the literal. 'To Edward FitzGerald' is fundamentally like 'The Lost Leader' because in it feeling is not simply vented, but compounded with the element of creative or aesthetic thought—that element so conspicuously missing from Browning's remarks in the aftermath of the poem's publication.

Why is 'The Lost Leader' not called 'To William Wordsworth'? In

---

[8] For another treatment of this ghostly kiss, also evidently influenced by Milton, see the last lines of 'Dubiety', published in *Asolando* (1889) and contemporary with 'To Edward FitzGerald': 'Perhaps but a memory after all! |—Of what came once when a woman leant | To feel for my brow where her kiss might fall. | Truth ever, truth only the excellent!' The exclamation at the end represents a 'waking' from fantasy and a refusal to be seduced by memory.

1875 the scholar Alexander Grosart asked Browning whether he had indeed been thinking of Wordsworth, and Browning replied:

I have been asked the question you now address me with, and as duly answered it, I can't remember how many times: there is no sort of objection to one more assurance, or rather confession, on my part that I *did* in my hasty youth presume to use the great and venerable personality of Wordsworth as a sort of painter's model; one from which this or the other particular feature may be selected and turned to account: had I intended more, above all, such a boldness as portraying the entire man, I should not have talked about 'handfuls of silver and bits of ribbon.' These never influenced the change of politics in the great poet; whose defection, nevertheless, accompanied as it was by a regular face-about of his special party, was to my juvenile apprehension, and even mature consideration, an event to deplore. But just as in the tapestry on my wall I can recognise figures which have *struck out* a fancy, on occasion, that though truly enough thus derived, yet would be preposterous as a copy, so, though I dare not deny the original of my little poem, I altogether refuse to have it considered as the 'very effigies' of such a moral and intellectual superiority.   (Hood: 166–7)[9]

It is hard not to accuse Browning of being disingenuous here, as though he were unaware of the biblical associations of the 'handful of silver', or even of the fact that the writers he idolized in the 1830s and 1840s (Byron, Shelley, Keats, Hazlitt) *did* believe that Wordsworth's 'change of politics' had been 'influenced' by material considerations. I don't doubt that Browning himself either thought so at one time, or was willing to think so because it fitted his prejudice against Wordsworth on other counts. In any case his denial that the poem was an attempt to portray 'the entire man' begs the question of whether the *truth* of a portrait depends on its literal likeness or completeness.

Here the image of the tapestry comes to Browning's mind, and it takes us back to two images of childhood in Browning's poetry. The first comes from Book I of *Sordello*, and describes Sordello's exploration of the castle at Goito:

> see him lurk
> ('Tis winter with its sullenest of storms)
> Beside that arras-length of broidered forms
> On tiptoe, lifting in both hands a light
> Which makes yon warrior's visage flutter bright

---

[9] Grosart published this letter in his edition of Wordsworth's prose (i, p. xxxvii). 'Very effigies' means 'exact likeness'.

> —Ecelo, dismal father of the brood,
> And Ecelin, close to the girl he wooed
> —Auria, and their Child, with all his wives
> From Agnes to the Tuscan that survives,
> Lady of the castle, Adelaide . . .

$$(\text{i. } 452\text{–}61)$$

Sordello is learning about the family to which he is attached as a page, but he is also learning about poetry and its transfiguring power. In Keats's *Eve of St Agnes* (it is a happy coincidence that an Agnes is mentioned in Browning's poem) the lovers flee from a castle during a storm while 'The arras, rich with horseman, hawk, and hound | Fluttered in the besieging wind's uproar' (ll. 358–9). These animated figures embody simultaneously the lovers' fears and the haste and boldness of their flight; in *Sordello*, however, they are 'fluttered' not by the wind but by the light that the boy holds in his hands, whose wavering makes 'bright' the 'dismal father of the brood'. The second tapestry comes near the beginning of Pompilia's monologue in *The Ring and the Book*; she tells how her mother

> brought a neighbour's child of my own age
> To play with me of rainy afternoons;
> And, since there hung a tapestry on the wall,
> We two agreed to find each other out
> Among the figures. 'Tisbe, that is you,
> With half-moon on your hair-knot, spear in hand,
> Flying, but no wings, only the great scarf
> Blown to a bluish rainbow at your back:
> Call off your hound and leave the stag alone!'
> '—And there are you, Pompilia, such green leaves
> Flourishing out of your five finger-ends,
> And all the rest of you so brown and rough:
> Why is it you are turned a sort of tree?'
> You know the figures never were ourselves
> Though we nicknamed them so.

$$(\text{vii. } 184\text{–}98)$$

Pompilia and Tisbe identify each other respectively with Diana and Daphne, huntress and victim, causer and sufferer of metamorphosis. Both are emblems of chastity, but of radically different kinds. One is a creature of the air, her magical flight symbolizing freedom, her weapons violence and fear; the other's flight (escape) ends in a

paradoxical stasis, earthbound yet 'flourishing'. The words *scar,
blow, blush,* and *bow* make ghostly appearances in Diana's 'scarf |
Blown to a bluish rainbow', an image of sexual shame translated
into pursuit and retribution; it is set against the green and brown of
the tree, the colours of organic life. That Pompilia speaks first and
identifies her friend with Diana implies either her self-identification
with Daphne, or her fear of being herself identified as Diana, or
both; at any rate she takes the initiative and pre-empts the interpretation. She was a child when the episode took place but is not one
when she recounts it in her monologue; her childish ignorance both
of the names of the mythical figures and their sexual associations is
deceptive, and in her adult telling the images are proleptic, like
Milton's imagery of the unfallen world in *Paradise Lost*.[10] Like
Daphne, Pompilia is a nymph who will flee from violation and
escape pursuit by a transcendent change. Like Diana, she is a
goddess who will hunt Guido to death: his last cry, 'Pompilia, will
you let them murder me', is a vain plea to her to call off her hounds.
These interpretations are 'metaphysical' but not perverse, so Pompilia
is quite 'wrong' (consciously so, however) to claim that 'the figures
never were ourselves'. Might she argue, as Browning does in his
letter to Grosart, that the 'figures . . . have struck out a fancy . . .
that though truly enough thus derived, yet would be preposterous
as a copy'? But the dividing line between 'fancy' and 'copy' depends on keeping apart two kinds of meaning which are always
threatening to collapse into each other. Browning's poem 'Waring'
opens with the famous question 'What's become of Waring?' and
imagines all kinds of exotic answers. Joseph Arnould called
'Waring' a 'fancy-portrait' of his and Browning's friend Alfred
Domett, who emigrated to New Zealand in 1842, so that the question in the opening line would be ridiculous if it were taken literally; both Browning and Arnould knew perfectly well what had
become of Domett. Yet it is arguable that the *meaning* (to Browning) of Alfred Domett's flight from England is more truly represented by such a portrait than by one more literally faithful, a
'very effigies'. Wordsworth in this sense is truly the *original* of the
Lost Leader, both as a point of departure and a point of return.

[10] Browning's handling of childhood impressions and their subsequent recuperation
in adult discourse anticipates Freud (see, for example, Freud's remarks on this subject
in 'From the History of an Infantile Neurosis' (the story of the 'Wolf Man'), Freud
1979: 277 n. 2).

The Lost Leader is the brightened image of his 'dismal father', not a 'copy' but 'truly enough derived' from him.

The speaker of Browning's great poem about portraits, 'A Likeness', owns an etching which he deprecatingly calls

> a study, a fancy, a fiction
> Yet a fact (take my conviction)
> Because it has more than a hint
>   Of a certain face, I never
> Saw elsewhere touch or trace of . . .
>
>   (ll. 35–9)

This ability of a work of art to be both false and true to its original, for 'likeness' to be governed by suggestion rather than literal fidelity, is linked to the idea that art is objective and self-sustaining, but depends on belief—*our* belief, as readers or viewers. The speaker's parenthetical exhortation to us to 'take [his] conviction' is not an idle phrase meant to shore up the rhyme; in fact the rhyme between *fiction* and *conviction* is vital to the poem. It echoes the opening lines of *Sordello*, where a similar act of faith is demanded:

> Who will, may hear Sordello's story told:
> His story? Who believes me shall behold
> The man, pursue his fortunes to the end
> Like me; for as the friendless people's friend
> Spied from his hill-top once, depite the din
> And dust of multitudes, Pentapolin
> Named o' the Naked Arm, I single out
> Sordello, compassed murkily about
> With ravage of six long sad hundred years:
> Only believe me. Ye believe?
>   Appears
> Verona . . .
>
>   (i. 1–11)

The allusion to Pentapolin is to an episode of *Don Quixote* in which the hero mistakes two flocks of sheep, enveloped in clouds of dust, for rival armies, commanded by legendary warriors. Browning is therefore asking his readers to 'believe' in 'a study, a fancy, a fiction' which will nevertheless enable them to 'behold | The man'.[11] The reader's act of will is not enough: that merely sets in motion a 'story', from which, it is implied, an essential truth is absent. The

---

[11] The enjambement disguises an echo of John 19: 5.

will to hear the story must be transformed into an assent to the
poet's claim that he can 'single out | Sordello', even though in doing
so he compares himself to the fictional Quixote who deludes himself
that he can single out Pentapolin. The poem's true object, Sordello,
is therefore doubly an *appearance*, conjured by the poet in a sleight
of imagination which answers to the degree of the reader's credulity.
Verona cannot 'appear' in writing, but can appear to the reader's
imagination; it can appear to appear, just as Pentapolin appears to
Don Quixote, illusory in one sense but (in Bob Dylan's phrase)
'really real' in another.[12]

I take it that Wordsworth 'appears' in 'The Lost Leader' in this
way, that we 'behold | The man' as Browning imagines him whether
or not this vision corresponds to 'the entire man', Wordsworth's
actual historical self. It is not an imaginary, but an imagined Wordsworth whom Browning hated.

Browning's direct personal knowledge of Wordsworth was slight.
He probably first met him at the dinner given to celebrate the success
of Talfourd's play *Ion* in 1836. *Paracelsus* had recently enjoyed a
considerable critical success, and Wordsworth publicly drank Browning's health. Later meetings took place at John Kenyon's house,
where Wordsworth usually stayed when he was in town. But there
was no warmth in the acquaintance on either side, and it never
ripened into friendship. Possibly Browning's citified manner grated
on Wordsworth. Carlyle remembered him at this period as 'a dainty
Leigh-Huntish kind of fellow, with much ingenuity, vivacity and
Cockney gracefulness' (quoted in Maynard: 7); another acquaintance
spoke of him as 'just a trifle of a dandy, addicted to lemon-coloured
kid-gloves and such things' (ibid.: 129), just the sort of person whom
Wordsworth would despise. Certainly Browning got to hear of
Wordsworth's sarcastic comment on his suburban home at New
Cross; 'there is a vast view from our greatest hill', he wrote to
Elizabeth Barrett, and then added:

did I ever tell you that Wordsworth was shown that hill or its neighbour;
—someone saying 'R. B. lives over *there* by that HILL'—'Hill'? interposed
Wordsworth—'we call that, such as that,—a rise'!   (Kintner: 627)[13]

[12] 'Spanish Harlem Incident' (*Another Side of Bob Dylan*, Columbia, 1964).
[13] This letter is dated 16 Apr. 1846; it would be interesting to know whether
Wordsworth's remark took place before or after the publication of 'The Lost Leader'
in *Dramatic Romances and Lyrics* (Nov. 1845), and, indeed, whether Wordsworth
read that poem and guessed its application.

Wordsworth condescends to Browning from the heights of Parnassus as well as the Lake District; Browning is a social and poetical upstart, and probably underbred; the similarity with Keats is striking.[14]

Browning, too, linked personal and poetic malice in his chortling over Wordsworth's ludicrous appearance at court in Samuel Rogers's ill-fitting costume and bag-wig, 'to the manifest advantage of the Laureate's pocket, but more problematic improvement in his person, when one thinks on the astounding difference of "build" in the two Poets' (Kintner: 83). Elizabeth Barrett, however, didn't see the joke:

> It is a large exaggeration I do not doubt—and then I never sympathized with the sighing kept up by people about that acceptance of the Laureateship which drew the bagwig as a corollary after it. Not that the Laureateship honored *him*, but that he honored it; & that, so honoring it, he preserves a symbol instructive to the masses, who are children & to be taught by symbols now as formerly. Isn't it true? or at least may it not be true? And wont the court-laurel (such as it is) be all the worthier of *you* for Wordsworth's having worn it first?   (Kintner: 84)

Elizabeth Barrett probably thought that the compliment at the end softened the sharp rebuff at the beginning, but her defence of the Laureateship may have struck Browning differently. It amounted to saying that poets should accept the privileges accorded by the establishment as tokens of their own kind of superiority over the childlike 'masses'. This equivalence of social and intellectual hierarchy was alien to Browning's republican aesthetic—an aesthetic which owed a great deal to the Wordsworth who wrote the Preface to *Lyrical Ballads* and the 'Essay, Supplementary to the Preface' to the *Poems* of 1815. But there never was much prospect of a middle-class dissenting poet like Browning, born and educated in London, becoming Poet Laureate, let alone Wordsworth's spiritual son and heir.[15] That role had been bagged by the genteel, Anglican, country-born, Cambridge-educated Tennyson. Aubrey de Vere recounts an incident which took place at a dinner given by Edward Moxon (who published all three poets) shortly after Wordsworth's presentation at Court—in

[14] See pp. 102–4. That Browning himself tells the anecdote implies, of course, that he thinks it says more about Wordsworth's arrogance than about his (Browning's) stature.

[15] Elizabeth Barrett would have had more chance than Browning, and indeed there was a small lobby on her behalf in 1850, whereas there was none for him.

other words at exactly the date of Browning's exchange with Elizabeth Barrett:

> There was another occasion on which the Poet whose great work was all but
> finished, and the youthful compeer whose chief labours were yet to come,
> met in my presence. It was at a dinner, given by Mr. Moxon. The ladies had
> withdrawn, and Wordsworth soon followed them. Several times Tennyson
> said to me in a low voice, 'I must go: I cannot wait any longer.' At last the
> cause of his disquiet revealed itself. It was painful to him to leave the house
> without expressing to the old Bard his sense of the obligation which all
> Englishmen owed to him, and yet he was averse to speak his thanks before a
> large company. Our host brought Wordsworth back to the dining-room; and
> Tennyson moved up to him. He spoke in a low voice, and with a perceptible
> emotion. I must not cite his words lest I should mar them; but they were
> few, simple and touching. The old man looked very much pleased, more so
> indeed than I ever saw him look on any other occasion; shook hands with
> him heartily, and thanked him affectionately. Wordsworth thus records the
> incident in a letter to his accomplished American friend Professor Reed: 'I
> saw Tennyson when I was in London several times. He is decidedly the first
> of our living poets, and I hope will live to give the world still better things.
> You will be pleased to hear that he expressed in the strongest terms his
> gratitude to my writings. To this I was far from indifferent.' (Tennyson:
> 174–5)

In his biography of Tennyson, Robert Bernard Martin comments
(with a Freudian *frisson*): 'It was an emblematic handing on of the
sceptre from the Romantic poet to the Victorian forty years his
junior, and it was totally appropriate that when Tennyson succeeded
as Poet Laureate he was presented to the Queen in the same court
suit, once more groaning at the seams, that Wordsworth had bor-
rowed from Rogers in 1845' (Martin: 290–1). The elaborate masculine
ritual of homage, endorsement, and succession is played out by both
Wordsworth and Tennyson with exemplary skill and economy in
this story. Tennyson cannot bear to speak to Wordsworth among the
women (to acknowledge 'the obligation which all Englishmen owed
to him'); within the male group Tennyson's homage, which is both
personal and representative, is paid both in public and in private, his
voice low, his emotion 'perceptible' but his actual words withheld;
Wordsworth's recognition, too, is given the same character, and later
expresses itself in the semi-public form of a letter which endorses
Tennyson without fanfare and explicitly connects this endorsement
with Tennyson's own expression of fealty. De Vere's coupling of the

two as 'Poet' and 'youthful compeer' strikes a chivalric note, Martin's
comment on the 'sceptre' and on Tennyson 'succeeding' Wordsworth
a dynastic one; but both are governed by an image of poetic power
being transferred in a male line of succession. But if Tennyson is
Wordsworth's 'youthful compeer', then 'The Lost Leader' records, as
'Childe Roland' will later do, the names of the 'lost adventurers his
peers': 'Shakespeare was of us, Milton was for us, | Burns, Shelley
were with us, — they watch from their graves!' (ll. 13–14). The
difference is that these names are the tale of Wordsworth's losses: he
has 'Got the one gift of which Fortune bereft us, | Lost all the others
she lets us devote' (ll. 3–4).

'Smooth Jacob still robs homely Esau', the narrator remarks
caustically at the end of 'The Flight of the Duchess'; Browning and
Tennyson figure as the smooth and hairy sons of Isaac–Wordsworth,
one blessed and one exiled.[16] 'The Lost Leader' accuses Wordsworth of
being 'lost' but also mourns Browning's loss of him. 'Hast thou not
reserved a blessing for me?' laments Esau; and Isaac replies that he will
end by breaking his brother's yoke (Genesis 27: 36–40). Browning is
Wordsworth's foundling, or abandoned child, or bastard (and Browning's early work is obsessed with lost or occluded heirs, like Sordello
gazing at the 'dismal father' on the tapestry). The image of Wordsworth in ll. 9–12 is unequivocally paternal, the tone is that of filial piety:

> We that had loved him so, followed him, honoured him,
>   Lived in his mild and magnificent eye,
> Learned his great language, caught his clear accents,
>   Made him our pattern to live and to die!

Followed, honoured, learned, pattern: perhaps these aren't comfortable words for a young poet; perhaps the poem registers a need for
creative autonomy which would necessitate the father's rejection
whether this rejection was justified or not. But the nature of the
justification remains important. To begin with, it is collective. The
personal pronouns governing the poem oppose *us* to *them*, an
opposition in which the 'he' of the first line has chosen the wrong
side. In adopting the second-person plural voice Browning is magnify-

---

[16] Tennyson's smoothness of versification and liking for medieval subjects are
perhaps relevant here; Aubrey de Vere records Wordsworth's admiration for Tennyson's 'stately' diction, and the Duke in 'The Flight of the Duchess' is, like Tennyson, a
'middle-age-manners-adapter'. But I don't know how to fit in the fact that Tennyson
was famously a rougher and hairier presence than Browning!

ing and depersonalizing his own anger and grief, making it the expression of a communal tragedy, the tragedy of all Wordsworth's sons. At the same time the 'we' who reproach Wordsworth embody the people whose cause he has betrayed, and also the community of readers who are identified as sympathizers with that cause.

There is, however, something problematic about this collective voice. It suggests that Wordsworth ought to have been at least 'of us', like Shakespeare, if not actually 'for us', like Milton.[17] He ought to have been marching in the 'van' with the 'freemen'. Yet such solidarity is not compatible with the kind of fatherhood or leadership which the speaker attributes to Wordsworth. A 'mild and magnificent eye' is associated with benign royalty, not democracy; to 'follow' such a leader is more than simply to march beside him at the head of the procession. The popular or radical cause has always been vexed by this problem of leadership; Romantic aesthetics, divided between the image of the poet as sublime prophet and common man, has a similar difficulty in accommodating the notion of genius to that of fellowship.[18] In Browning's imagination Wordsworth represents the intersection of politics and aesthetics at a crucial point of history. In 1843—the year Wordsworth became Poet Laureate—Browning was helping his friend R. H. Horne by suggesting mottoes or chapter headings for Horne's forthcoming survey of the literary scene, *A New Spirit of the Age*. His suggestion for Wordsworth was the following passage from Book X of *Paradise Lost*, in which Satan makes his entry to the council of the devils in Pandemonium after returning from his successful temptation of Adam and Eve:

> he through the midst unmarked,
> In show plebeian angel militant
> Of lowest order, passed; and from the door
> Of that Plutonian hall, invisible
> Ascended his high throne, which under state
> Of richest texture spread, at the upper end
> Was placed in regal lustre. Down a while
> He sat, and round about him saw unseen:
> At last as from a cloud his fulgent head
> And shape star bright appeared, or brighter, clad
> With what permissive glory since his fall

[17] The distinction is Browning's own, in a letter to Ruskin: see Woolford and Karlin: ii. 178.
[18] See Ch. 5 for a more detailed account of this division.

> Was left him, or false glitter: all amazed
> At that so sudden blaze the Stygian throng
> Bent their aspect . . .[19]

Satan–Wordsworth is here a king who disguises himself as a man of
the people; he does so in order to ascend his throne (the Laureateship)
and create a startling effect, because he is a showman as well as a
man of show; he has just returned from betraying mankind, not
serving it. The violent contempt which Browning must have felt at
Wordsworth's consummate hypocrisy is combined with the intensity
of his former admiration: the image of the star would connect
Wordsworth with Shelley's *Adonais*, for example, so that Wordsworth, like Keats, might be said to 'Beacon from the abode where
the eternal are', except that it's the wrong abode. Wordsworth is
stigmatized, somewhat unfairly, for being a bad leader, and for *not*
being what he is 'in show', a 'plebeian angel'; just as, in 'The Lost
Leader', Browning criticizes Wordsworth both for not being one of
'us' and for abandoning his children.

The speaker of 'The Lost Leader' situates himself as one of the
'freemen' and not a leader himself, and yet the sharpness of Browning's sense of Wordsworth's betrayal cannot but suggest a different
self-image. The radical egotist Chiappino, in Browning's play *A
Soul's Tragedy*, exclaims at the supposed betrayal of the cause by his
friend Luitolfo:

> You'll play, will you?
> Diversify your tactics,—give submission,
> Obsequiousness and flattery a turn,
> While we die in our misery patient deaths?
> We all are outraged then, and I the first!
> I, for Mankind, resent each shrug and smirk,
> Each beck and bend, each . . all you do and are,
> I hate!

> (i. 108–15)

Chiappino wants to pronounce his anathema as 'we', but can't help
shifting to 'I': 'I the first' tries to mean 'I'm the first one to be

<hr/>

[19] Browning's quotation is verbally accurate but has slightly different punctuation;
it omits l. 444. He underlines 'clad . . . glitter' and 'Stygian . . . aspect', commenting on
the latter phrase, 'As Jeffrey does in the reprint of his review of the Excursion: this is
too good a bit, I fear: take the kinder side of the matter and give him some or all of
your own fine sonnet'. Needless to say, Horne did not use the Milton lines.

outraged (on behalf of everybody)' but cannot avoid meaning 'it's I, principally, who am outraged': the 'plebeian angel militant' takes a grammatical turn into a figure who stands for 'Mankind', then takes their place and asserts his personal rivalry, injury, and hatred.

In February 1846—several months after the publication of 'The Lost Leader'—Elizabeth Barrett sent Browning a letter which she had recently received from Harriet Martineau, who had moved to Ambleside and was living in close proximity to Wordsworth. Martineau's letter portrays Wordsworth on the whole with affection and reverence, though affection is tempered by a wry acknowledgement of Wordsworth's personal foibles, and reverence by exasperation at some of his views. Browning's reaction to this letter is instructive: it takes on added heat from his strong dislike of Martineau (as an advocate of mesmerism, among other things) but it is mainly centred on the image of Wordsworth as, in Aubrey de Vere's words, 'the Poet whose great work was all but finished'. Here are the relevant extracts from Martineau's letter:

The Wordsworths are in affliction just now. His only brother died a few days ago; & a nephew here is dying & they have had accounts from their sick daughter-in-law in Italy. But, as you can well conceive, he can lose himself completely in any interesting subject of thought, so as to forget his griefs. His mind is always completely full of the thing that may be in it; & there he was on Wednesday, his face all gloom & tears at two o'clock from the tidings of his brother's death received an hour before, & lo! at three he was all animation, discussing the rationale of my extraordinary discourses (in the mesmeric state)—his mind so wholly occupied that he was quite happy for the time. . . . His conversation can never be anticipated. Sometimes he flows on in the utmost grandeur even you can conceive—leaving a strong impression of inspiration. At other times, we blush & are annoyed at the extremity of bad taste with which he pertinaciously dwells on the most vexatious & vulgar trifles. . . . I dare say you need not be told how sensual vice abounds in rural districts. Here it is flagrant beyond any thing I ever could have looked for; & here, while every Justice of the peace is filled with disgust, & every clergyman with (almost) despair at the drunkenness, quarrelling & extreme licentiousness with women,—is dear good old Wordsworth for ever talking of rural innocence, & deprecating any intercourse with towns, lest the purity of his neighbours should be corrupted! . . .

You know Wordsworth's affairs are most comfortable in his old age. His wife is perfectly charming & the very angel he should have to tend him. His life is a most serene & happy one, on the whole, & while all goes *methodically*, he is happy & cheery & courteous & benevolent,—so that one could almost worship him. But to secure this, every body must be punctual, & the fire must burn bright, & all go orderly,—his angel takes care that everything shall, as far as depends on her.   (Kintner: 461–2)[20]

Needless to say, the final image of Wordsworth dependent on his domestic angel was particularly offensive to Browning, who was contemplating a very different kind of union with Elizabeth Barrett, and it attracted especial scorn in his reply. After grudgingly praising Martineau for something she said earlier in her letter, he went on:

and *that* knowledge gets to seem a high point of attainment doubtless by the side of the Wordsworth she speaks of—for mine he shall not be as long as I am able! Was ever such a '*great*' poet before? Put one trait with the other—the theory of rural innocence—alternation of 'vulgar trifles' with dissertating with style of 'the utmost grandeur that *even you* can conceive' (speak for yourself, Miss M...!)—and that amiable transition from two o'clock's grief at the death of one's brother to three o'clock's happiness in the 'extraordinary mesmeric discourse' of one's friend. All this, and the rest of the serene & happy inspired daily life which a piece of 'unpunctuality' can ruin, and to which the guardian 'angel' brings as crowning qualification the knack of poking the fire adroitly—of this—what can one say but that— no—best hold one's tongue and read the Lyrical Ballads with finger in ear: did not Shelley say long ago 'He had no more *imagination* than a pint-pot' tho' in those days he used to walk about France and Flanders like a man—*Now* he is 'most comfortable in his worldly affairs' and just this comes of it! He lives the best twenty years of his life after the way of his own heart—and when one presses in to see the result of the rare experiment .. what the *one* alchemist whom fortune has allowed to get all his coveted materials and set to work at last in earnest with fire and melting-pot, what *he* produces after all the talk of him and the like of him—why, you get *pulvis et cinis* [dust and ashes]—a man at the mercy of the tongs and the shovel!   (Kintner: 464)

What is striking about this attack on Wordsworth when compared to 'The Lost Leader' is how completely it appears to ignore his political apostasy. Wordsworth figures here not as traitor, but as failure. And now the relationship is personal: Browning rejects the implied demand for allegiance exclusively on his own account: '*mine* he shall not be as long as I am able!' It is no longer a question of *us* and *them* but of *me* and *him*. The ground of this allegiance is

---

[20] I have silently expanded some of Martineau's contractions (e.g. 'extraor[y]', 'clergy[n]').

Wordsworth's greatness as a poet *and* as a man: in Browning's imagination the two are joined, and the depiction of Wordsworth as a selfish old fool is an allegory of his later work. (So politics does come in after all: for when Wordsworth 'walked around France and Flanders like a man' and wrote *Lyrical Ballads* he had not abjured his political faith; the mention of *Lyrical Ballads* is especially significant because it preserves the title of a collection which Wordsworth himself broke up, and one which contains the clearest evidence of his radical sympathies.) Two kinds of fire are contrasted in Browning's letter, that of poetry and that of the domestic hearth. The fire of poetry is an old Romantic topos, and so is its dying out. 'I am ashes where once I was fire, | And the bard in my bosom is dead', Byron wrote to the Countess of Blessington—that is one version of the sentiment, admittedly a cheap one. But Wordsworth is not even allowed this theatrical sigh: not only is his fire out, but Browning's alchemical metaphor implies a doubt about its very nature. As a metaphor for the imagination, alchemy is double-edged: it suggests either a transforming or a deceptive power, its practitioner (like Browning's own Paracelsus) may be a magician or a quack, its fire true 'glory' or 'false glitter'. We might *expect* an alchemist to end up with dust and ashes, rather than gold or the Philosopher's Stone, so that Wordsworth's ending up worrying about whether his domestic fire is burning brightly may not be such a bad outcome after all; but it turns out that this, too, is an allegory of his having the wrong kind of marriage. No wonder that when Browning came to write his great poem of married bliss and creative power he called it 'By the Fire-Side', and addressed it to 'my perfect wife, my Leonor'; sometimes I believe he was actually recalling this letter when he did so and having another surreptitious dig at Wordsworth. The old man is given no quarter for sitting by the fire in *his* 'life's November', because his angelic wife is an emblem and reward of his selfishness, not his inspiration; Browning is especially and cruelly funny in drawing out the hints of self-absorption in Martineau's account ('that amiable transition from two o'clock's grief at the death of one's brother to three o'clock's happiness in the "extraordinary mesmeric discourse" of one's friend') and yet he envies Wordsworth the creative opportunity which he has squandered, the isolation and devotion to the task which he has had twenty years to enjoy and whose fruit (like that which Satan and his devils are shortly to taste in the passage from *Paradise Lost* which Browning quoted to Horne) is dust and ashes. 'Dust and ashes! So you creak it, and I want the heart to scold', says the speaker of 'A Toccata of Galuppi's', another who ends up by a cold hearth. But it is one thing to mourn the transience of the body and its desires, another to mourn the transience of the soul, or its passage from one form of desire to another. In 'poking the fire adroitly' Mary Wordsworth waves Circe's wand and transforms Wordsworth (who used to 'walk about France and Flanders like a man') into 'a man at the mercy of the tongs and shovel'.

3

Sludgehood

An intellectual hatred is the worst . . .

(Yeats)[1]

'How Browning hates me!—and how I love him!'

(D. D. Home, attrib.)[2]

THE first encounter between Browning and Daniel Dunglas Home, the most famous medium of the nineteenth century, took place on 23 July 1855, at the house of Mr John Rymer, in Ealing. Home, born in Scotland, had been adopted by an aunt in America and had begun his career as a medium in the small towns of Connecticut and New York State where he was brought up. His reputation grew with the growth of the spiritualist movement, and in 1855 his patrons sponsored a European tour, partly on the grounds of health and partly to continue his spiritualist mission. The Rymers were English sympathizers who offered Home accommodation when he complained of the stress of London life.[3] The Brownings had, of course, heard of Home and Elizabeth Barrett Browning was eager to meet him. Besides her family, she wrote to her sister Henrietta, 'He's the most interesting person to me in England' (Huxley: 218).

The Brownings were familiar with the conduct of seances. The expatriate community in Florence was pullulating with mesmerism, table-turning, rapping, spirit-hands, voices, trances, levitation, and

---

[1] 'A Prayer for My Daughter', l. 57.

[2] Remark attributed to Home by Browning after the publication of 'Mr. Sludge, "the Medium"', according to William Allingham: Allingham and Radford: 102.

[3] For further information on Home, see his memoirs (Home 1863 and 1872; the latter reprints Home's account of the Ealing seance, first published in the *Spiritualist Magazine* in 1864). Jenkins is closely based on the foregoing and sympathetic to Home; Burton provides a more balanced account. Porter has the fullest account of the spiritualist circles in which the Brownings moved; for the seance at Ealing, see, besides accounts in the above, Phelps, and Miller 1957. The Brownings were introduced to the Rymers by their mutual friend Anna Jameson.

every conceivable variety of drawing-room paranormalia. Many of their friends and visitors were American, and America led the field in sensational accounts of spiritualist phenomena. Browning was a resolute sceptic and his wife as resolute a believer, but although they disagreed on the subject there is, until the Ealing seance, no suggestion of unease, let alone acrimony. Browning's attitude seems to have been one of humorous indulgence. At Bagni di Lucca in 1853 Elizabeth reported that their friend William Wetmore Story, had 'tried the "tables" for some twenty minutes—Under such disadvantages though.—for Robert just laughs & jokes—we had to turn him away after five minutes' (Landis: 200–1). She, too, could see the funny side of the craze. She wrote to Eliza Ogilvy shortly before leaving Florence for Bagni di Lucca: 'What are you reading, & writing, & thinking most of? Turning tables, like the rest of the world, & me in particular? Nobody here does anything else. . . . There's an engraving at the shop windows of an animated four legged pine, with the inscription ". . E pur si muove"' (Heydon and Kelly: 96–7).[4] In Browning's 'A Lovers' Quarrel', published in *Men and Women* in 1855 but written before the Ealing seance, the speaker sees such experiments as an aspect of erotic intimacy, where the playfulness of fantasy (communicating with the dead) gives way to real communion between the living:

> Try, will our table turn?
> Lay your hands there light, and yearn
>   Till the yearning slips
>   Thro' the finger tips
> In a fire which a few discern,
>   And a very few feel burn,
> And the rest, they may live and learn!
>
>   (ll. 43–9)

What, then, was it about the Ealing seance which precipitated Browning's hatred of Home? Is it a personal or an intellectual hatred which animates the poem he wrote in the winter of 1859–60, which he never showed to Elizabeth, and which he published in *Dramatis*

---

[4] The Italian phrase ('But it [the earth] does move') is the famous regretful murmur attributed to Galileo after his recantation. Elizabeth referred again to Galileo in her next letter to Mrs Ogilvy, from Bagni di Lucca, in which she writes of an enthusiastic conversation with friends on the subject of spiritualism: 'We stood up for our "new truths" . . side by side with Galileo, . . said somebody modestly' (p. 102).

Personae after her death—'Mr. Sludge, "the Medium"'? Indeed, is Home in fact the original of Sludge, as Browning biographers and scholars have almost universally assumed, and if he is, what process of transfiguration did he undergo?[5]

Browning's own account of the Ealing seance, the fullest and most immediate one we have, is contained in a letter to his friend Mrs Elizabeth Kinney written just two days after the event. It is a very long letter, and all accounts quote from it selectively—sometimes with the effect of seriously distorting its sense.[6] I give it here in full.

London, 13 Dorset St., July 25, '55.
Dear Mrs. Kinney,

I must give you, as I engaged to do, my experience of Mr. Home (as he now writes the name)[7] & his 'manifestations.' I shall be glad to get done with the matter. I & my wife went to Mr. Rymer's two evenings ago, on special invitation. At about 9 we were placed round a large table, as Mr. Home directed,—and the results were some noises, a vibration of the table, then an up-tilting of it in various ways, and then more noises, or raps, which were distinguished as the utterance of the family's usual visitor, the spirit of their child 'Wat' who died three years ago, aged twelve. They ceased presently, and we were informed that the circle was too large—it was lessened accordingly by the ejecting five individuals pointed out by the spirit —and the business was resumed, those remaining being Mr. Home, Mr. Rymer, Mrs. Rymer, ourselves, two lady-friends of the family, Miss Rymer, & Mr. Wilkie Rymer (son & daughter of our Host.) We had the same vibration, & upraising the table—a table-cloth, a few ornaments, and a large lamp were on it—all hands were visible. I don't know at all how the thing was done. Then Mrs. & Mr. Rymer were touched by what they recognized as the spirit of their child, & next my wife—whose dress, near the waist I saw slightly but distinctly uplifted in a manner I cannot account for—as if by some object inside—which could hardly have been introduced

---

[5] Goldfarb takes issue with the identification of Home with Sludge, arguing instead that the poem is based on a much more generalized knowledge of the spiritualist movement, and that Browning's real object of hatred is not in fact spiritualism but its credulous audience; not Sludge, but Horsefall. However, as Richard Kelly points out, a number of details relating both to the seance at Ealing and to Home's personality are repeated in the poem, for example the invocation of the dead child, the puzzle of objects not rolling off the table, the accordion-playing, and the medium's assumption of weakness or childishness.

[6] Elizabeth Jenkins, for example, quotes those parts of the letter in which Browning says that he cannot account for some of the phenomena he witnessed, but omits his unequivocal statement that he believed they could have been accounted for by proper investigation (p. 41). See also n. 11.

[7] Both the Brownings frequently wrote the name as 'Hume', which is how it was pronounced.

there without her becoming aware of it—this was repeated. The spirit then announced (by raps in answer to questions) that it would play on the accordion & show *myself* its hand,—all the raps seemed from or about the table—not the region outside us. The lamp was then extinguished, and all the light permitted came from the two windows thro' their muslin curtains —you could just distinguish any substance held up directly against them— not against the wall which divided them—but nothing of what was done *at the table*,—the night being cloudy. A hand appeared from the edge of the table, opposite to my wife & myself; was withdrawn, reappeared & moved about, rose & sank—it was clothed in white loose folds, like muslin, down to the table's edge—from which it never was separated—then another hand, larger, appeared, pushed a wreath, or pulled it, off the table, picked it from the ground, brought it to my wife,—who had left my side for the purpose of receiving it, at Mr. Home's desire, and had taken the chair by him,—and put it on her head—thence, at her request, it was carried, under the table, and given to me. I was touched several times under the table on one knee & the other,—and on my hands alternately (a kind of soft & fleshy pat) but not so that I could myself touch the object. I desired leave to hold the spirit-hand in mine, and was promised that favor—a promise not kept, however. Then Mr. Home took an accordion with one hand, held it below the table and sounds were produced and several tunes played—on it, I suppose,—but how, it is difficult to imagine—(there was light in the room for this experiment)—and I noted down, at the desire of the family, part of one air—but lost the thread, half-way through & did not recover it—it was a common-place air, *alla religiosa*, but played with expression enough—the spirit then promised to play on the instrument when in my own hand. I held it under the table as directed, & felt some pushes from beneath, which were ineffectual—I soon gave it up. The lights being away, the first hand pulled a small bell off the table, picked it from the floor & rang it. Another hand was held up, which opened & shut the fingers, turning itself as if to be seen.—I desired leave to touch it, but was refused (by the spirit). It was clothed to the *base*—(for one can't say *elbow*, where form was not distinguishable beneath the muslin-like drapery) and, like the other, kept close to the table. These performances were repeated several times—always in the wide space between Mr. Wilkie Rymer and Mr. Home—never in the open space of the room, tho' one hand crawled (as it were) up Mr. Home's shoulder, and, as I said, put the wreath on my wife, *how*, I was unable to see—but *under* the table their action was freer, apparently. Mr. Home observed that he supposed the hand with the wreath was that of a particular relation of my wife's—raps confirmed this opinion, the alphabet was put in requisition to discover the *name*—someone calling 'A.B.C.' &c. & the raps indicating the letter)—it was given successively as William, Frank, Charles, Henry—misses all. Hereupon Mr. Home went into a trance, & began to address Mr. Rymer, in the character of his dead child—in a sort of whisper, at first, to represent a child's voice, but with Mr. Home's own inflexions, peculiarities, and characteristic expressions—beginning 'Dear Papa,—is not God *good*, isn't he *lovely?*' &c. As this continued, by degrees Mr. Home's natural tones were resumed, the talk affected the parents, as you may suppose,—there was nothing in it pleasant to describe. Mr. Home next rose, saluted the company with upraised arms,—(we had light enough to see this) and began to speak, apparently in the character of 'the spirits' collectively,—instructing us on the legitimate objects of this work of investigation—and hardly can you conceive a poorer business—as for 'eloquence,' 'beauty,' 'poetry,' and so on,—I should be curious to know the meridian in which these qualities are attributed to such a holding-forth—nor did the speaker's sureness at all mend his matter. He said, in the course of it, that there had been four spirits over my wife's head pouring rays of glory from a sort of crown, or something and that 'we could have given their names but that you (my wife) were intently considering them, and would have called the answer thought-reading'—'There were other spirits present,' he said—'an old lady, Catherine, &c. &c.' It ended by his begging all to leave the room but the Rymer family to whom he (or they) had something to communicate—we retired for a quarter of an hour and were recalled,—the spirit having engaged, 'assisted by four strong spirits,' to lift the table, so that *I* might see the process—light was in the room—I looked under the table and can aver that it was lifted from the ground, say a foot high, more than once—Mr. Home's hands being plainly above it. It was tilted,—and the lamp remained—I am not sure whether there was anything remarkable in *that*,—its base being heavy, but on Mr. Rymer's remarking on the manner in which objects were 'held by the spirits on the table'—I called attention to the fact that a silver-pen rolled readily—the cloth notwithstanding—and said 'will the spirits now prevent the rolling of *this?*' on which Miss Rymer (who had gone into a trance also), replying as from the spirit, said 'Do not put that question! Have you not seen *enough?*'—and so all ended. On which I have to observe—first, that I believe in the honesty & veracity of the family—and in their absolute incompetence to investigate a matter of this sort. Next, in the impossibility of a stranger taking the simplest measure for getting at the truth or falsehood of the 'manifestations'—it was a family-party, met for family-purposes, and one could no more presume to catch at the hands (for instance) of what they believed the spirit of their child, than one could have committed any other outrage on their feelings. I heard that somebody who had been there two days before, and had told Mr. H. 'the hand is *yours*'—showed thereby his 'forgetting he was in a private house'—so I remembered it, you may be sure. Mr. Wilkie Rymer, the nearest to the hand, was more than once desired by Mr. H. 'not to look so closely'—& he refused to touch his brother's hand or drapery 'lest it might displease him'—why or wherefore,

I don't know. I asked if the hands were ever seen away from the table, &
Mr. Home—they were never so seen, tho' the family speak of spirits passing
the windows without, and other appearances. The great courtesy & kindness
of the family give the least possible desire to satisfy one's own curiosity at
their expense. I don't in the least pretend to explain how the table was
uplifted altogether—(the tilting & vibration do not seem inexplicable)—and
how my wife's gown was agitated—nor how the accordion was played.—
But light in some—& leave to investigate in others—of these cases—were
necessary to show whether they might not have been explained & easily. I
need not tell you if I was driven all the distance to the supernatural for my
first help! Had I not been counting, however, on the fulfilment of the
promise to 'place the hand in mine'—(the point for which I reserved myself)
I should have *tried* to get leave to touch & handle without hurting our host's
feelings. In the trance I would not believe tho' it had yielded a 'discourse' of
ten times the ability. I shall not much surprise you when I confess that my
wife believes in all the above, *but* the trance, which there was no getting
over. She suggests, however, explanations of various kinds, consistent with
Mr. H.'s integrity, (she thinks it was 'not unlike some dissenting sermons she
has heard' and I wish it may be so. On the whole, I think the whole
performance most clumsy, and unworthy anybody really setting up for a
'medium'.[8] I,—the poorest of mechanicians,—can fancy such an obvious
contrivance as a tube, fixed or flexible, under Mr. H.'s loose clothes & sack-
like *paletôt* & inordinate sleeves, which should convey some half a dozen
strings, & no more, to his breast,—for instance,—and work the three
fantoccini-hands, after these various fashions,—just as he did, and easily.[9]
There are probably fifty more ingenious methods at the service of every
'prestidigitateur'—I would also operate with lights on the table *always*
—challenge people to find out my tricks (as all good jugglers do) and leave
the 'trance' out altogether. Mr. H. says he is 'twenty,' but properly adds,
that he looks much older—he declares he has 'no strength at all' (why? even
if it were so!) and affects the manners, endearments and other peculiarities of
a very little child indeed—speaking of Mr. & Mrs. Rymer as his 'Papa &
Mama' & kissing the family abundantly—he professes timorousness, 'a love
of love'—and is unpleasant enough in it all—being a well-grown young
man, over the average height, and, I should say, of quite the ordinary bodily
strength—his face is rather handsome & prepossessing, and indicative of

[8] Notice that Browning places the term in quotation marks here as he does in the
title of 'Mr. Sludge, "the Medium"'.
[9] As Sludge puts it: 'Then, it's so cruel easy! Oh, those tricks | That can't be tricks,
those feats by sleight of hand, | Clearly no common conjuror's!—no, indeed! . . . Take
my word, | Practice but half as much, while limbs are lithe, | To turn, shove, tilt a
table, crack your joints, | Manage your feet, dispose your hands aright, | Work wires
that twitch the cutains, play the glove | At end of your slipper,—then put out the lights
| And . . . there, there, all you want you'll get, I hope!' (ll. 434–49).

intelligence,—and I observed nothing offensive or pretentious in his demeanour beyond the unmanlinesses I mention, which are in the worst taste—the family like the caresses, however, and reciprocate them, after a very unusual fashion. I ought not to omit that the sitting was conducted in exact conformity to Mr. Rymer's suggestions, which though polite were explicit enough,—that we should put no questions, nor desire to see anything but what the spirit might please to show us. I treated 'the spirit' with the forms & courtesies observed by the others, and in no respect impeded the 'developments' by expressing the least symptom of unbelief—and so kept my place from first to last. I should like to go again and *propose* to try a simple experiment or two, but fear it is already out of my power—my wife having told one of the party that I was 'unconvinced.'

You will observe that I simply speak of my own impressions—not of my wife's—much less those of many other persons reported to me; other people have their faculties and must see and judge for themselves. I only write this because you made me promise to do so—but this letter is intended solely for you—to be shown to anybody you please but on no account copied nor extracted from. I am not desirous of leaving on record so unwisely-spent an evening. I write at night, very rapidly, and am glad to get done with it. I don't answer anybody else's experiences—merely tell what happened to myself and what I think of it, and on review the exhibition seems the sorriest in my recollection. I dare say my wife will give you her own notion, which differs from mine in all respects; so are we constituted. I avoid adding a word on other subjects except that I am, with best regard to Mr. Kinney & your family,
Yours very faithfully ever,
Robert Browning.

The importance of this letter as an accurate account both of what took place at the seance and what Browning thought about it is, of course, directly linked to its closeness in time to the event. Home's own account first appeared in the *Spiritualist Magazine* in 1864, as a riposte to the publication of 'Mr. Sludge'; at exactly the same period Browning was giving William Allingham an equally biased account of the affair, and this bias seems to have increased with age.[10] The

[10] 'Sludge is Home, the Medium, of whom Browning told me to-day a great deal that was very amusing. Having witnessed a seance of Home's, at the house of a friend of B.'s, Browning was openly called upon to give his frank opinion on what had passed, in presence of Home and the company, upon which he declared with emphasis that so impudent a piece of imposture he never saw before in all his life, and so took his leave' (Allingham and Radford: 101). Browning's son Pen later wrote that he had heard his father 'repeatedly describe how he caught hold of his [Home's] foot under the table' (letter in *TLS*, 5 Dec. 1902, p. 365), an even less probable story. See also n. 16.

first part of the letter, describing the events at the seance itself, reads
like a legal deposition. It is formal and matter-of-fact in tone, exact
in its notation of time, place, and persons, and non-committal in its
phrasing ('we were informed that the circle was too large—it was
lessened accordingly by the ejecting five individuals *pointed out by
the spirit*' (my italics)). Browning carefully records the physical
conditions under which the phenomena took place (where people
were sitting, what light there was)[11] and scrupulously insists on his
inability to explain them. Here, however, there are traces of suppressed scepticism: 'I don't know at all how the thing was done', for
example, suggests that Browning thought the lifting of the table had
been 'done' somehow by Home. The rhetorical mask slips gradually
as the letter progresses; I imagine Browning had difficulty in wearing
it with complete gravity and self-control. There is revulsion in his
description of the feel of the spirit-hand, but it is contained within
the bounds of a parenthesis: '(a kind of soft & fleshy pat)'. He
permits himself a touch of sarcasm in remarking that the action of
the spirit-hands was 'freer, apparently' when under the table (where
they did not in fact 'appear'), and in his listing of the erroneous
names of the supposed 'particular relation' of Elizabeth—'misses all'
(which puns on the fact that they were all misters). 'Hereupon', in
the sentence beginning 'Hereupon Mr. Home went into a trance',
may imply that Home chose this moment in order to cover up his
failure to guess a correct name. But only at one point in this 'factual'
section of the letter does Browning openly allow his impression to
colour his report, in what he goes on to say about Home's 'trance'. I
shall come to this passage in a moment. After the trance came
Home's spiritual discourse, whose ' "eloquence," "beauty," "poetry,"

---

[11] With regard to the facts themselves there is only one serious discrepancy between
Browning's account and that of Home himself (first printed in the *Spiritualist
Magazine* in 1864, in the aftermath of the publication of 'Mr. Sludge' in *Dramatis
Personae*, and then in the second volume of his memoirs in 1872). This discrepancy
concerns the respective positions of Browning and his wife when the wreath was
placed on Elizabeth's head. Home says that Browning 'left his place and came and
stood behind his wife, towards whom the wreath was being slowly carried'; he says
nothing of requesting Elizabeth to change *her* place, and does not mention the wreath
being given to Browning afterwards, whether 'under the table' or not (neither, it must
be said, does Elizabeth herself mention this in her brief account of the seance, given to
her sister Henrietta in a letter of 17 Aug. 1855 (Huxley: 219–21)). I am inclined to
believe Browning's testimony here, partly because Home was writing his account nine
years on, and partly because he needed Browning to move from his place in order to
sustain the charge that Browning wanted the wreath to be placed on his own head (see
below).

and so on', seem to have afforded Browning a certain grim professional amusement.

So much for the factual part of the letter. Browning's interpretation
of what he witnessed, which occupies the latter portion, is much
more revealing. As to his disbelief in the authenticity of the phenomena, this is consistent with his known attitude; he had attended other
seances, had not been convinced before, and was in a good position
to judge this one 'the sorriest in my recollection'. He was clearly
confirmed in his scepticism by the semi-darkness in which several of
the phenomena took place, by the fact that the spirit-hand was
always within Home's reach, and by the broken promise to allow
him to hold the hand in his own, as well as by the nullity of the
trance (which he kindly recommends Home to dispense with in
future!). Although he states that he was unable to explain what took
place, he attributes this inability to the absence of 'light in some — &
leave to investigate in others — of these cases', and caustically rejects
a supernatural agency.[12]

Expressed in these terms, Browning's scepticism has nothing un-
remarkable in it, and might apply to any of the seances which he
attended, whether in England or Italy. The tone of his remarks about
both the Rymers and Home, however, is another matter. He seems
to have found Home's playing on the emotional attachment of the
Rymers to their dead child deeply offensive, though he implicitly
acknowledges that Home did not invent this communication (the
child's spirit is 'the family's usual visitor', and we know from other
accounts that his appearances began long before Home took up
residence).[13] What moved Browning in particular was Home's imper-
sonation of the child during his 'trance' and Home's own affectation
of 'the manners, endearments and other peculiarities of a very little
child indeed' in his behaviour towards his hosts. Browning treats the
incongruity of a 'well-grown young man' acting like a baby with
Dickensian scorn and suspicion: Home, proclaiming his own physical
weakness, 'timorousness', and 'a "love of love"', combines the

---

[12] Browning's statement contradicts that of Home, who claims that 'Mr. Browning
was requested to investigate everything as it occurred, and he availed himself freely of
the invitation' (Home 1872: 105).

[13] In 'Mr. Sludge, "the Medium"' the invocation of the spirit of a dead child is
explained as part of Sludge's technique for disarming rational investigation: 'Sludge
begins | At your entreaty with your dearest dead, | The little voice set lisping once
again, | The tiny hand made feel for yours once more ... A right mood for
investigation, this!' (ll. 471–9).

hypocrisy of Mr Chadband with the affectation of Mr Skimpole.[14] But behind the satire there is a real note of disgust and indignation in Browning's account of Home's 'unmanlinesses', which suggests that Home's transgression of natural boundaries (of age and gender) touched Browning in a way that he could not deal with either by humour or by an assumed objectivity.

Browning's response to the troubling instability of Home's persona is to insist on his own absolute maintenance of personal and social decorum.[15] Hence the deliberately restrained and formal language of the first, or evidential part of the letter (in contrast to Home's garbled discourse); hence the explanation that he would have considered trying to grab the spirit-hand an 'outrage' on the feelings of the parents (in contrast to Home's exploitation of those feelings); hence the elaborate conformity to spiritualist etiquette, as though it were a question of watching which knife and fork one's fellow-guests were using: 'I treated "the spirit" with the forms & courtesies observed by the others, and in no respect impeded the "developments" by expressing the least symptom of unbelief—and so kept my place from first to last.' Or, as Sludge puts it:

> Pray do you find guests criticize your wine,
> Your furniture, your grammar, or your nose?
> Then, why your 'medium?' What's the difference?
>
> (ll. 350–2)

Needless to say, Home used Browning's reticence at the time to

---

[14] The resemblance between Home and Skimpole is apparent in a description of him quoted by Jenkins: 'It seemed (to him) the most natural thing in the world that he should be cared for, cosseted and made the centre of things. He was always contentedly expectant to be carried smoothly and luxuriously along the road . . . his share in the adjustment of things was to be delightfully entertaining and gay, or sympathetic and sentimental, or worldly and sarcastic . . . but always genuine while the moment lasted . . . he appeared to regard unbelief in himself, or dislike, as a mysterious dispensation he could not try to account for' (p. 190). If the phrase 'love of love' is, as the quotation marks indicate, verbatim, it may be that Home (in the house of Rymer) was quoting Tennyson to Browning ('The Poet', l. 4). Browning's own description of the spirit-hand 'clothed in white loose folds, like muslin' may also (unconsciously?) recall Tennyson's description of the arm 'Clothed in white samite, mystic, wonderful' which rises out of the lake holding Arthur's sword Excalibur ('Morte d'Arthur' (1842), 31; the resemblance between the phrases is pointed out in Miller 1952: 185).
[15] In his letter to Miss de Gaudrion, which I discuss below, Browning wrote that he 'had some difficulty in keeping from an offensive expression of his feelings' during the evening.

argue that he had been convinced by the phenomena.[16] It is noticeable that Browning exonerates the Rymers, whose 'honesty & veracity' go along with their 'great courtesy & kindness'—though he can't quite get round their encouragement of Home's 'caresses', or the fact that Mr Rymer laid down the conditions under which the sitting was conducted, or that his daughter was also a practising medium whose sharp rebuke to Browning actually ended the sitting. In 'Mr. Sludge' he is not so generous: the evident protectiveness of the Rymers towards Home translates into bullying collusion in the behaviour of Hiram H. Horsefall and his like (see ll. 372–81). The intention is to isolate Home, to make him a social interloper. Browning is as concerned to show that Home is not manly, and not a gentleman, as that he is a false medium—or even to suggest an association between these things, so that unmanliness becomes an index of deceit.[17]

This aspect of the encounter has never been sufficiently stressed, and yet it has a significant bearing on 'Mr. Sludge', whose protagonist is a lower-class man of ambivalent gender who exploits the vanity and weakness of his social superiors. The episode of the wreath would have confirmed Browning in this view of Home, since it represented a patent and clumsy attempt at flattery. After the publication of 'Mr. Sludge', Home spread the story (which, with Sludge-like pusillanimity, he attributed to the Rymers) that Browning was jealous because the wreath had not alighted on *him* (Home 1872: 106). Even Home's defenders acknowledge the daftness of this suggestion, which, as Chesterton put it, 'is one of the genuine gleams of humour in this rather foolish affair' (Chesterton: 95). Browning's account of the incident in the letter is preoccupied with the fact that, in order for the wreath to be placed on Elizabeth's head, she was required to

[16] 'He expressed no disbelief; as indeed, it was impossible for any one to have any of what was passing under his eyes' (Home 1872: 106). Indeed, Home went so far as to say that 'Several times during the evening he [Browning] voluntarily and earnestly declared that anything like imposture was out of the question' (p. 105), which is as unlikely as Browning's own later statement to William Allingham that he had denounced Home as an impostor (see n. 10). In both cases a combination of wish-fulfilment and the lapse of time seems to have warped the account.

[17] Elizabeth was less troubled by Home's personal and social conduct than Browning. After the Brownings returned to Florence she heard rumours of 'some failure in his moral character', and admitted that he was 'weak and vain'. However, she insisted, 'his *mediumship* is undisproved, as far as I can understand. It is simply a physical faculty—he is quite an electric wire' (letter of 21 Feb. 1856, Kenyon 1898: ii. 226). Later on she was glad to hear that Home's 'manners, as well as morals, are wonderfully improved' (letter of 27 Mar. 1858, p. 280).

leave her place and sit next to Home (i.e. within his reach), whereas when it was subsequently 'given' to him, this was done under the table.

Elizabeth kept the wreath and hung it on her dressing table in Casa Guidi (where, some months later, Browning, in a fit of rage, flung it out of the window). To Henrietta she wrote unequivocally that 'at the request of the medium, the spiritual hands took from the table a garland which lay there, and placed it upon my head' (Huxley: 220). She added:

For my own part I am confirmed in all my opinions. To me it was wonderful and conclusive; and I believe that the medium present was no more *responsible* for the things said and done, than I myself was.   (p. 221)

That last statement has an unconscious irony which Browning brings out in 'Mr. Sludge': those who believe in spiritualism and who encourage the 'medium' to perform are, indeed, as responsible as he for what occurs. Just as Browning exonerated the Rymers from complicity with Home, so Elizabeth exonerates Home from responsibility for the inadequacies of his performance:

I think that what chiefly went against the exhibition, in Robert's mind, was the trance at the conclusion during which the medium talked a great deal of much such twaddle as may be heard in any fifth rate conventicle. But according to my theory (well thought-out and digested) this does not militate against the general facts. It's undeniable, and has been from first to last, that if these are spirits, many among them talk prodigious nonsense, or rather most ordinary commonplace.   (p. 220)

To Browning's disgust at Home's unmanliness we must therefore add alarm at his wife's credulity. Elizabeth repeated her assurance about Home's integrity in a letter to a Miss de Gaudrion, who had attended a seance at Ealing a few days after the Brownings with her fiancé, Frederick Merrifield. Merrifield was convinced that Home was a fraud, and Miss de Gaudrion wanted to know Elizabeth's opinion. Elizabeth again insisted that she could 'find no reason for considering the Medium in question responsible for anything seen or heard on that occasion'. With her letter she enclosed a note from Browning whose elaborate formality of address contrasts with the biting directness of its judgement on both Home and his wife:

Mr Browning did, in company with his wife, witness Mr. Hume's performances at Ealing . . . and he is hardly able to account for the fact that there can be another opinion than his own on the matter—that being that the whole display of 'hands,' 'spirit-utterances,' &c., were a cheat and imposture. Mr. Browning believes in the sincerity and good faith of the Rymer family, and regrets proportionably that benevolent and worthy people should be subjected to the consequences of those admirable qualities of benevolence and worth when unaccompanied by a grain of worldly wisdom—or, indeed, divine wisdom—either of which would dispose of all this melancholy stuff in a minute. Mr. Browning has, however, abundant experience that the best and rarest of natures may begin by the proper mistrust of the more ordinary results of reasoning when employed in such investigations as these, go on to an abnegation of the regular tests of truth and rationality in favour of those particular experiments, and end in a voluntary prostration of the whole intelligence before what is assumed to transcend all intelligence. Once arrived at this point, no trick is too gross—absurdities are referred to 'low spirits,' falsehoods to 'personating spirits'—and the one terribly apparent spirit, the Father of Lies, has it all his own way. Mr. Browning had some difficulty in keeping from an offensive expression of his feelings at the Rymer's; he has since seen Mr. Hume and relieved himself.—(*TLS*, 28 Nov. 1902, p. 356; repr. Burton: 28–9)[18]

In his letter to Mrs Kinney Browning wrote that he was unable to account for some of the phenomena he witnessed; but here what he is 'hardly able to account for' is the 'fact' of people's belief in spiritualism. He shifts the ground of argument from the medium's 'cheat and imposture' (which he takes for granted) to the willingness of 'the best and rarest of natures' to be duped. He himself 'accompanied' his wife, but she, like the Rymers to whom he ostensibly refers, was 'unaccompanied' by 'a grain of worldly wisdom'. It is this process of abnegation of reason which leads to the pun on the word 'apparent' (a stronger and angrier one than in his letter to Mrs Kinney). The devil, the 'Father of Lies', is 'terribly apparent' not when human beings conjure him, but when they perjure themselves. The 'voluntary prostration of the whole intelligence' which Browning

[18] The MS of this letter is not extant. I follow the *TLS* text, except for inserting 'Rymer' where it has blanks; Burton's text differs slightly, and, though it also derives from the holograph, is suspect (e.g. 'frustration' for 'prostration'). Browning's last remark refers to the occasion, shortly after the Ealing seance, on which Home, in company with Mrs Rymer, called on the Brownings at their lodgings in Dorset Street. Home's account of what took place—that Browning was rude (but not violent) to him, and told Mrs Rymer that he was 'exceedingly dissatisfied' with what he had witnessed at the seance, and that Mrs Browning was upset and apologetic—is probably closer to the truth than Browning's better-known version (as reported by William Allingham)—that he threatened to throw Home downstairs and that 'the Medium disappeared with as much grace as he could manage'. See Home 1872: 107 and Allingham and Radford: 101–2.

witnessed in the Rymers—and in Elizabeth—was a much more disturbing phenomenon than any amount of table-lifting or spirit-rapping. If he felt the same about the seances which he and Elizabeth attended in Italy, he may have consoled himself that these occasions were no more than parlour games played among their own social circle. Home's status as a professional medium, however, was another matter. It makes him into a diabolic seducer of 'the best and rarest of natures'; he is himself, by implication, the 'low' and 'personating' spirit on whose interference the medium blames his 'absurdities' and 'falsehoods'. The juxtaposition of high and low, the noble nature fouled by contact with the ignoble, explains the note of disgust in Browning's language, already vivid in the letter to Mrs Kinney and recurring here in the phrase 'relieved himself'. Several years later, Browning heard that his close friend, the sculptor William Wetmore Story, had refused to accept Home as a pupil but had been persuaded by a friend's recommendation to find him a studio: 'of course', he commented to Isa Blagden, 'Hume immediately wrote to England . . . that S[tory] *had* taken him as a pupil—it is Story's own business,—he chooses to take this dung-ball into his hand for a minute, and he will get more & more smeared' (McAleer 1951: 182–3).

As a seducer, Home's appeal lay in his childishness and affectation of helplessness. It gave him an unmanly power, which Browning was not surprised to see employed later in Home's career in his relations with a rich and elderly patron, Mrs Jane Lyon. Mrs Lyon planned to adopt Home as her son, gave him very large amounts of money, and made him her heir. Then she retracted her generosity and sued Home (successfully) for the return of the money. She claimed that he had persuaded her to give it to him by relaying spirit-messages from her dead husband. It seems probable that there was an erotic element in her attachment to him, and a mercenary one in his to her: at any rate Browning certainly believed so.[19] In a letter to Isa Blagden of 19 July 1867 (when the case was announced but had not yet come to trial), he wrote of Home's 'rascality' and 'how his own incredible stupidity as well as greediness wrought his downfall in the foolish old soul's estimation'; he also asserted that 'Hume wanted in the first place to marry Mrs Lyon', adding: 'There's a misfortune for dear Miss Hayes, Mrs Milner Gibson and such like vermin!' (McAleer 1951:

[19] Jenkins gives a full account of the Home–Lyon case, entirely from Home's point of view, but with many suggestive passages (pp. 180–222).

272–3).[20] The word 'vermin' links the dupes to the trickster; in an earlier letter to Isa Blagden, Browning had referred to Home himself as 'vermin' (p. 214). Elizabeth Barrett Browning may have been far removed in Browning's estimation from the silly adoring women who petted Home and were deceived by him, but this simply made her into a nobler class of victim, whose emotional and intellectual ruin Browning looked on with insupportable loathing. In another letter to Mrs Kinney, written in 1871, the loathing and disgust are as fresh as ever, and this time carry an explicit sexual charge: 'If I ever cross the fellow's path I shall probably be silly enough to soil my shoe by kicking him,—but I should prefer keeping that disgrace from myself as long as possible. Indeed I have got to consider such a beast as the proper associate and punishment of those who choose to shut their eyes and open their arms to bestiality incarnate' (DeVane and Knickerbocker: 199).[21] The materiality of Browning's epithets for Home ('dung-ball', 'vermin', 'beast', etc.) finds its way into the name of his fictional medium, Sludge, and becomes part of a network of allusions to dirt and bestiality in the poem. There is an ironic aptness in these degrading images, since the medium claims contact with a pure, immaterial, spirit-world.

Looking at the history of Browning's knowledge of, contact with, and language concerning Home, and applying that history in isolation to 'Mr. Sludge, "the Medium"', leads almost irresistibly to the conclusion that Browning saw in Home the quintessence of qualities which he associated with spiritualism itself (fraud, vulgarity, sexual perversion, even diabolic agency); and that the *tour-de-force* of the poem therefore consists in making the exponent of these qualities the spokesman, also, for their opposite. In other words, when Browning came to create the character of Sludge (as opposed to commenting on the character of Home) he took up the dung-ball and discovered in it a core of slimy truth, an authentic fallen awareness, even a debased poetics (or poetics of debasement). This is a traditional and

[20] Miss Hayes is unidentified, but along with Mrs Milner Gibson, a prominent society hostess, she is clearly stigmatized as one of Home's admirers and dupes. Home's seances at Mrs Milner Gibson's house (which included feats of levitation) attracted so much notoriety that when her husband, who was Secretary of the Board of Trade, rose on one occasion to make a speech in the House of Commons and began with the words 'I am a medium—' he was greeted with ironic laughter and applause (Jenkins: 113).
[21] Compare, for example, the last words of 'Now' (*Asolando*, 1889): 'arms open, eyes shut and lips meet!'.

powerful reading of the poem, but it rests on the assumption that Browning's personal hatred for Home sprang in the first instance from his hatred of spiritualism as a concept, and that the poem reflects this hierarchy of importance.

Yet the idea that Browning hated spiritualism sits oddly with his long-standing and generally sympathetic interest in the occult arts, fed by the large number of books on the subject in his father's library.[22] *Pauline* is prefaced by a quotation from the Renaissance mage Cornelius Agrippa, the hero of *Paracelsus* is an alchemist and occult philosopher, allusions to the 'Arab lore' of astrology and other magical arts are scattered throughout *Sordello*, the Gypsy who entrances the Duchess in 'The Flight of the Duchess' is clearly practising a form of mesmerism, and mesmerism itself provides the title of one of the poems of *Men and Women*.[23] The trail leads past 'Mr. Sludge' up to late works such as 'Pietro d'Abano', in which Browning returned to yet another Renaissance mage whom he had discovered and cherished in his youth.[24] As Chesterton says, Browning 'was the last man in the world to be intellectually deaf to a hypothesis merely because it was odd . . . Intellectually he may be said to have had a zest for heresies' (Chesterton: 92–3). In a memorable fancy, Chesterton added: 'If any one had told him of the spiritualist theory, or theories a hundred times more insane, as things held by some sect of Gnostics in Alexandria, or of heretical Talmudists in Antwerp, he would have delighted in those theories, and would very likely have adopted them' (p. 97; I discuss below Chesterton's own explanation for Browning's hatred of Home).

The occult offered Browning a symbolic vocabulary which, as Betty Miller points out, he made use of in *Sordello*, whose opening lines adjure the reader to 'only believe' in the poet in order for a

---

[22] See Dahl and Brewer: 104. Dahl and Brewer also give a useful estimate of Browning's likely knowledge of Hermetic and Neoplatonic ideas. The wilder shores of this subject are charted by Vivienne Browning, who contends that Browning was a Rosicrucian and that he was following a family tradition in being so: 'at least one Browning in every generation held a secret—an inherited esoteric knowledge of the early Christian mysteries'. Members of the family were also, it seems, 'personally involved in the medieval wars, the adventures giving rise to the Arthurian legends and the quest for the Holy Grail' (Browning: 15, 18). She concludes her book with an account of 'The Browning Hermetic Tradition in Australia'.

[23] For more on this background, and for a detailed discussion of 'Mesmerism', see Karlin 1989.

[24] See his translation of lines attributed to Abano and his comment to Elizabeth Barrett in a letter of 1845 (Woolford and Karlin: ii. 371–2).

hallucinated image of the poem's setting to 'appear' (Miller 1952: 186), and which presents the poet as a conjurer, whose audience is 'Summoned together from the world's four ends, | Dropped down from Heaven or cast up from Hell' (i. 32–3). The analogy between poetry and the occult is fully developed in Paracelsus, almost to the point of an allegorical design. Paracelsus's esoteric quest, in search of 'Mysterious knowledge, here and there dispersed | About the world, long-lost or ever-hidden' (i. 805–6), would have been as familiar to Shelley, Browning's precursor, as it was to be to his successor Yeats. But what is especially significant about Paracelsus is that Browning does not evade the issue of authenticity, either as it relates to the 'mysterious knowledge' itself, or to those who seek it out. On the contrary, the fact that Paracelsus is denounced as a quack and a sham magician is central to the poem. To many of his detractors, both contemporary and posthumous, Paracelsus was indeed 'Mr. Sludge, "the Medium"' (the inverted commas themselves testifying to the scorn with which his claim is regarded). The pattern of cheating, exposure, disgrace, and self-justification is worked out in both poems, but with quite different results. Paracelsus scornfully announces his fall from grace at Basle to Festus:

> Alack,
> 'Tis true: poor Paracelsus is exposed
> At last: a most egregious quack is he;
> And those he overreach'd must spit their hate
> On one who, utterly beneath contempt,
> Could yet deceive their topping wits.
>
> (iv. 53–8)

Like Sludge, Paracelsus despises his audience, whose 'topping wits' are no match for his. In Paracelsus's case his audience mistake a genius for an 'egregious quack', and in Sludge's case they are deceived into thinking an egregious quack a genius; but the distinction is really a matter of bias on Browning's part, since he chooses to defend one and not the other from accusations of dishonesty. At the end of the poem Browning printed an extract in translation from the entry on Paracelsus in a standard modern reference work, the *Biographie Universelle* (Paris 1822). This account gives a caustic picture of Paracelsus's intellectual and personal character: he 'displays everywhere an ignorance of the rudiments of the most ordinary knowledge', 'there is no proof of his having legally acquired the title of

Doctor', 'at Basil [i.e. Basle] it was speedily perceived that the new Professor was no better than an egregious quack', 'Paracelsus scarcely ever ascended the lecture-desk unless half drunk', 'He was accustomed to retire to bed without changing his clothes', and so on. As an example of how Browning dealt with such denigration, take the matter of Paracelsus's lack of formal education. In 'Mr. Sludge', Sludge's ignorance is both mocked and linked to his low social status (see, for example, ll. 309 ff.). In the case of Paracelsus Browning admits the fact of ignorance, but challenges its interpretation. Paracelsus does not lack 'ordinary knowledge', he deliberately *renounces* it. Festus, the voice of orthodoxy in the poem, is uneasy that Paracelsus intends to seek knowledge 'in strange and untried paths; | Rejecting past example, practice, precept' (i. 422–3) and adjures him to study the works of those who were 'famous in their day' and 'accept the light they lend' (ll. 579–80). But Paracelsus will have none of it:

> Their light! The sum of all is briefly this:
> They labour'd after their own fashion; the fruits
> Are best seen in a dark and groaning earth,
> Given over to a blind and endless strife
> With evils their best lore cannot abate.
> No; I reject and spurn them utterly,
> And all they teach.

(ll. 581–7)

Paracelsus's ignorance, in other words, is a manifestation both of Romantic radicalism (the rejection of the past) and Romantic sublimity (the solitary and aspiring genius).

Most of the criticisms levelled at the historical Paracelsus are similarly dealt with in Browning's poem. The one which most concerns us here, because it is the one which brings Paracelsus closest to Sludge, is that of egregious quackery, and the hatred which follows its exposure. Paracelsus experiences the same treatment from his erstwhile adorers at Basle as Sludge at the hands of his patron Hiram H. Horsefall. In both cases, wounded vanity 'spit[s] hate' at the detected cheat, and this reaction is depicted as, itself, a hateful instance of stupidity and hypocrisy. But how does Browning deal with the substance of the charge? In Sludge's case, it is clear that he *has* cheated; but in that of Paracelsus, Browning puts forward two defences which transform quackery into something else. He suggests, first, that what Paracelsus's audience saw as deceit was a reflection of their own incomprehension of his advanced ideas and methods, and, second, that these ideas and methods were indeed 'deceitful' in that they represented Paracelsus's failure to achieve his sublime aim of mastering the secret of all knowledge. Echoing Paracelsus's declaration in Book I that 'There is an inmost centre in us all | Where truth abides in fulness' (ll. 740–1), Festus acknowledges in Book III that a justification of Paracelsus's life would 'show within the heart, as in a shrine, | The giant image of Perfection' (ll. 861–2) even though this occult 'image' looks less than perfect to those outside. The genius disappoints his followers with a partial, obscure, and mystifying revelation, and yet this inadequacy is itself evidence of his genius. What appears in the arena of demonstration as trickery is a distortion of what, in the arena of the mind, appears as truth.

Paracelsus is thus able to accept, in the end, the hatred with which his 'exposure' as a quack is greeted in part because this hatred, too, fits the pattern of imperfect revelation.[25] Since he has 'done well, though not all well', 'men cannot do without contempt', and it is 'fit awhile | That they reject me, and speak scorn of me' (v. 881–4). Just as he himself is not really a quack, so those who think they have exposed him are not really Hiram H. Horsefalls, either: their 'hate is but a mask of love's', their 'poorest fallacies', like his own, are 'ambitious, upward tending' (ll. 861–7). With sweeping magnanimity, the poem views both the fallen idol and his deluded worshippers as victims of a noble, but impossible, aspiration towards perfection.

Why then should Home (and Sludge) not benefit from a similar magnanimity? In Chesterton's opinion, 'Browning's aversion to the spiritualists had little or nothing to do with spiritualism. It arose from a quite different side of his character—his uncompromising dislike of what is called Bohemianism' (Chesterton: 93). Comparing Browning's dislike of Home with his dislike of George Sand and her circle in Paris (about which he also disagreed with his wife), Chesterton acutely remarks that he 'objected not to an opinion, but to a social tone' (p. 94). There is surely a strong element of truth in this, but Chesterton is wrong, I think, to imply so clear a distinction between 'opinion' and 'social tone'. What seems to have animated Browning's hatred of Home is precisely the link between the two. If the medium is in any sense comparable to the poet, then what

---

[25] See also Ch. 5, where the hatred of Paracelsus by his followers is linked to a Romantic pattern of prophetic and poetic rejection.

Browning witnessed in Home was the poet's degradation, a kind of alchemy in reverse: the magical transformation of gold to dust and ashes. Home's social and sexual ambivalence, his tone of emotional aggression and strident, self-proclaimed weakness, his aping of filial and erotic bonds, gave his performance its peculiar resonance for Browning. He was a nightmare of what a poet might become, imprisoned by his patrons and forced by his dependence into feeding them the lies they craved.

'Mr. Sludge, "the Medium"' is the poem of this nightmare: it expresses Browning's hatred of Home, but also his understanding of what Home meant to him (there is a marked difference between this and 'sympathy'). The essence of 'Sludgehood' is the acceptance of a fate rejected in *Paracelsus*, the fate of becoming a half-man.[26] Sludge starts out as a real child, who rises from the gutter to find himself 'Sweet and clean, dining daintily, dizened smart, | Set on a stool buttressed by ladies' knees, | Every soft smiler calling me her pet' (ll. 269–71). But he never progresses from there: the condition of the petted child becomes a metaphor in which he is trapped and his real gifts betrayed and perverted:

> I've felt a child; only, a fractious child
> That, dandled soft by nurse, aunt, grandmother,
> Who keep him from the kennel, sun and wind,
> Good fun and wholesome mud,—enjoined be sweet,
> And comely and superior,—eyes askance
> The ragged sons o' the gutter at their game . . .
>
> .   .   .   .
>
> I've felt a spite, I say, at you, at them,
> Huggings and humbug—gnashed my teeth to mark
> A decent dog pass! It's too bad, I say,
> Ruining a soul so!
>
> (ll. 391–403)

In the list of female dandlers and spoilers one title is missing, that of *mother*: the women are all surrogates for this absent true nurturer, and Sludge depicts himself as, in a sense, truth's orphan, brought up

---

[26] Like Home, Paracelsus is accused of unmanliness: Browning's sources contained stories that he was castrated at the age of 3, or lost his virility by the bite of a pig. In his 'Note' on the poem Browning cited these stories, but dismissed them as a 'standing High-Dutch joke in those days at the expense of a vast number of learned men'; Paracelsus may forgo human love, but his search for knowledge, like that of Faust, is indisputably virile, and no question about his manliness is raised in the poem itself.

by liars.[27] This may also account for his repeated allusions to Hiram H. Horsefall's 'sainted mother', whose spirit he has been impersonating. He resembles another orphan, Fra Lippo Lippi, in his enforced subservience to social deceit (and in beginning his self-justifying monologue with someone's hand grasping his throat). The 'old schooling sticks' to Lippo: even as a grown man he can't escape the condition of a child. 'It's Art's decline, my son!' he hears his 'superiors' muttering, superiors to whom he is a son, only in name. Sludge, too, exemplifies 'Art's decline', in an even sharper and more frightening descent. It is Sludge who remains as a product of Browning's distilled hatred of Home—pure Sludge, at the bottom of the glass in which Browning saw his own face staring up at him.

[27] Though Browning claimed he had not read the first volume of Home's memoirs (Home 1863) before he wrote the poem, he may well have known that Home's natural parents had sent him away to America when he was 9.

4

Hatred and Creativity

What effects are generated by anger, hate, rage on the reader of literature? If love, kindness and placidity tend to elicit a reader's identifications, can fury and hatred form a demonic counterpart, absenting but by that very rejection haunting or hypnotizing her/him?

(Nicholas Royle)[1]

LET me return to the passage from 'One Word More' with which this book began.

> Dante once prepared to paint an angel:
> Whom to please? You whisper 'Beatrice.'
> While he mused and traced it and retraced it,
> (Peradventure with a pen corroded
> Still by drops of that hot ink he dipped for,
> When, his left hand i' the hair o' the wicked,
> Back he held the brow and pricked its stigma,
> Bit into the live man's flesh for parchment,
> Loosed him, laughed to see the writing rankle,
> Let the wretch go festering through Florence)—
> Dante, who loved well because he hated,
> Hated wickedness that hinders loving,
> Dante standing, studying his angel,—
> In there broke the folk of his Inferno.
> Says he—'Certain people of importance'
> (Such he gave his daily, dreadful line to)
> Entered and would seize, forsooth, the poet.
> Says the poet—'Then I stopped my painting.'

Browning invests Dante's actions with fiery creative force. His lulled, meditative tracing and retracing of the angel, which he is destined

---

[1] Royle: 76–7. Royle's immediate subject is George Douglas's story *The House with the Green Shutters*.

never to finish (and which brings him uncomfortably close to the despairing artistry of Andrea del Sarto), contrasts vividly with the swiftness and decisiveness of his writing: 'Back he held the brow . . . pricked . . . Bit . . . Loosed him, laughed . . . Let the wretch go'. And the complement of this creative energy is the moral authority which drives it. Dante's standing as a prophet, entitled to stigmatize the guilty, is taken for granted, as is the justness of his denunciations.[2] The source for this authority to hate and punish is, apparently, love, the visionary insight which allows Dante to 'hate wickedness which hinders loving'.

And yet, when you look closer, this celebration of creative power and moral authority has some disturbing features. The passage is structured around the notion of interruption. Browning interrupts his account of Dante's painting of the angel with a parenthesis describing Dante's composition of the *Inferno*—the 'daily, dreadful' task which Dante has, himself, interrupted in order to 'please' Beatrice. Then Dante's painting is interrupted by the very 'folk of his Inferno' (Browning characteristically uses an internal rhyme, 'In there *broke* the *folk*', like the squeak of a piece of chalk, to suggest the irritation of it). The subject of writing returns, breaks out of its parenthesis, and reimposes itself on the poet; moreover, it tries to do to him what he has been doing to it: the 'people of importance' attempt to 'seize . . . the poet', to capture him as he is in the habit of capturing them. And of course they succeed, though not perhaps in a way they expect. 'Says the poet—"Then I stopped my painting."' The line has an ominous ring for the 'people of importance' (reinforced, again, by a verbal device, the way in which '*Says* the poet' retaliates against the intention to '*seize* the poet'). Perhaps a few more of them are about to be pricked, bit, and sent festering off.

The passage seems unable to tear itself away from Dante's powerful hating. To this we need to add the extraordinary personal cruelty

---

[2] Dante had always had this authority for Browning: see, for example, *Sordello*, i. 349 ff., where Dante is described as 'relentless' in his absorption of the poetry of his precursor Sordello into the 'consummate orb' of his own work; Sordello's is the 'undercurrent' in 'the majestic mass | Leavened as the sea whose fire was mixt with glass | In John's transcendent vision', an image from Revelation (15: 2) which adds further prophetic and apocalyptic associations to Dante's work. Browning would certainly have known and admired Carlyle's elevation of Dante in *On Heroes and Hero-Worship*. He told Elizabeth Barrett that he had 'all of [Dante] in my head and heart' (letter of 3 May 1845, Kintner: 54).

of the writing. Browning anticipates by more than half a century Kafka's vision, in his story 'In the Penal Colony', of a punishment literally inscribed on the flesh of the victim, and does so not with horror but with sadistic relish. The idea of using 'the live man's flesh for parchment', of writing as a physically scarring and corrosive action, sits ill with the conventional piety which follows and which seems to be trying to cover up for it: 'Dante, who loved well because he hated, | Hated wickedness that hinders loving . . .' Hatred of sin is, indeed, a Christian injunction, but the abstract term 'wickedness' can't adequately cover the 'live man's flesh' or palliate, in particular, the laugh which Browning imagines for Dante: 'laughed to see the writing rankle, | Let the wretch go festering through Florence'.[3]

One further point needs to be made about the scene which Browning envisages here. It is radically incomplete. It imagines Dante as the writer not of the *Divine Comedy* (and certainly not of the *Vita Nuova*, from which the episode is in fact taken) but of the *Inferno* alone. It is as though the tender, the pathetic, and the redemptive sides of Dante's art have been displaced on to an activity —the painting of the angel—which is not only not 'natural' to Dante, but which is never fulfilled. The *Paradiso*, in particular—a text in which numerous angels figure—is obliterated, so that when Browning, in the next lines of the poem, addresses Elizabeth Barrett—

> You and I would rather see that angel
> Painted by the tenderness of Dante,
> Would we not?—than read a fresh Inferno.
>
>   (ll. 50–2)

—he is implicitly disallowing the answer 'yes, but there *is* a tender side to Dante, and plenty of angels, elsewhere in his work'. Browning forces us back to the vision of Dante as dynamic and potent in the work of hate, not love.

Everything in the Christian tradition, and the literary culture that derives from it, seems to go against the possibility that hatred might have a creative power. In *The Tempest*, Prospero warns Ferdinand and Miranda to remain chaste before their marriage; if they do not,

> No sweet aspersion shall the heavens let fall
> To make this contract grow; but barren hate,

---

[3] The last line has ghostly quotation marks around it, as though it were Dante's own contemptuous and dismissive remark.

> Sour-ey'd disdain, and discord, shall bestrew
> The union of your bed with weeds so loathly
> That you shall hate it both.
>
> (IV. i. 18–22)

The threat of barrenness is attached to hatred here (in fact the only thing that hatred breeds in these lines is hatred) and connects these lines with the ancient (pre-Christian) philosophical attributes of love and hatred as forces of attraction and repulsion, harmony and discord, union and separation.[4] In *Paradise Lost* Milton's account of the creation begins with 'Matter unformed and void':

> Darkness profound
> Covered th' abyss; but on the wat'ry calm
> His brooding wings the Spirit of God outspread,
> And vital virtue infused, and vital warmth
> Throughout the fluid mass, but downward purged
> The black tartareous cold infernal dregs
> Adverse to life . . .
>
> (vii. 233–9)

Human beings should ideally be 'infused' with 'vital virtue' and 'vital warmth', and 'purged' of their 'cold infernal dregs'; these terms, as Milton's language suggests, carry a complex of meanings ranging from the medical to the metaphysical. Hatred, 'adverse to life', makes its appearance in Eden immediately after the fall, when Adam and Eve quarrel over who is to blame:

> They sat them down to weep; nor only tears
> Rained at their eyes, but high winds worse within
> Began to rise, high passions, anger, hate,
> Mistrust, suspicion, discord, and shook sore
> Their inward state of mind, calm region once
> And full of peace, now tossed and turbulent . . .
>
> (x. 1121–6)

These 'high passions' undo the work of creation, which brought peace to the 'tossed and turbulent' region of Chaos; the 'high winds worse within' are opposed to the spirit or breath of God which infuses life.

---

[4] According to Empedocles, for example, the four elements of fire, air, water, and earth 'mingle and separate under the contrary impulses of Love and Strife to cause the arising and perishing of "mortal things"' (*Oxford Classical Dictionary*, 2nd edn.). See also Holbach's remarks on the relation between physical and moral or emotional properties quoted on pp. 10–11.

I do not mean to suggest that this model of creativity, in which
fertile love is opposed to sterile hatred, was the only one available to
Browning; on the contrary, the literary tradition in which he worked,
both classical and English, ranging from Aristophanes and Juvenal to
Pope, Swift, Blake, and Byron, offers plenty of examples of fecund
hatred, of hatred as a source of imaginative abundance, of hatred as
a manifestation of moral energy; in the late nineteenth century
Nietzsche theorized hatred as an explicit rejection of weak, humanis-
tic values.[5] Browning was aware of this counter-tradition; like Thackeray, he was both fascinated and appalled by the cruelty of writers
such as Swift, but he went further than Thackeray in his willingness
to 'participate in Sludgehood'. And if Browning's ultimate allegiance
is to the identification of creativity with divine love, there are many
poems nevertheless in which, as in the Dante passage of 'One Word
More', hatred is linked to creativity, whether artistic or other. In
Fifine at the Fair, Don Juan takes the creativity of hatred to be a
specifically masculine affair. Women may be inspired by the 'proud
humility of love' (l. 1319), but

> to obtain the strong true product of a man
> Set him to hate a little! Leave cherishing his root,
> And rather prune his branch, nip off the prettiest shoot
> Superfluous on his bough! I promise, you shall learn
> By what grace came the goat, of all beasts else, to earn
> Such favor with the god o' the grape: 't was only he
> Who, browsing on its tops, first stung fertility
> Into the stock's heart, stayed much growth of tendril-twine,
> Some faintish flower, perhaps, but gained the indignant wine,
> Wrath of the red press!
>
> (ll. 1330–9)

Juan's metaphor splits fertility itself into masculine and feminine,
strong and weak, fruit and flower; the 'true product of a man' is the

---

[5] Among early 20th-cent. writers, Lawrence, Yeats, and Kipling belong to this
counter-tradition; contemporary writers such as John Osborne and Kingsley Amis
have made their reputations as hate-inspired artists. Osborne, indeed, has attracted
more praise for his hate-filled memoirs than for most of his writing for the theatre; the
note of naughty excitement in many of the reviews of these memoirs perfectly
illustrates Hazlitt's contention 'that there is a secret affinity, a *hankering* after evil in
the human mind, and that it takes a perverse, but fortunate delight in mischief, since it
is a never-failing source of satisfaction' ('On the Pleasure of Hating', Hazlitt: xii. 128).

result of conflict and hostility,[6] an idea which Juan gives in a characteristically learned, fanciful, and perverse form. Vines are indeed pruned hard to encourage growth, but it would be a rash winegrower who grazed goats in his vineyard; Lemprière's *Classical Dictionary* (1827 edn.) tells us that the goat was sacrificed to Bacchus 'on account of the great propensity of that animal to destroy the vine'. Besides converting pest into helper, Juan also substitutes, for the classical association of wine with love and good humour, its biblical association with the wrath of God.[7]

These rhetorical shifts suggest both Juan's equivocation and Browning's. Two years before *Fifine at the Fair* was published, Browning had made a determined, but curiously unsuccessful, attempt to preserve the distinction between love and hate as separate and irreconcilable, with love as the creative and hate as the destructive force. In 1870 he wrote a sonnet, 'Helen's Tower', at the request of the Marquis of Dufferin, who had built a tower at Clandeboye in Ireland to commemorate his mother, Helen, Lady Dufferin.

> Who hears of Helen's Tower, may dream perchance
>   How the Greek beauty from the Scaean gate
>   Gazed on old friends unanimous in hate,
> Death-doomed because of her fair countenance.
> Hearts would leap otherwise at thy advance,
>   Lady, to whom this Tower is consecrate!
>   Like hers, thy face once made all eyes elate,
> Yet, unlike hers, was blessed by every glance.
>
> The Tower of Hate is outworn, far and strange:
>   A transitory shame of long ago,
>   It dies into the sand from which it sprang;
> But thine, Love's rock-built Tower, shall fear no change:
>   God's self laid stable earth's foundations so,
>   When all the morning stars together sang.

As in the passage from *Fifine at the Fair*, classical and Judaeo-Christian mythology and vocabulary struggle for supremacy in this poem. Browning begins by evoking Homer's great creation, and ends by quoting God's words to Job: 'Where wast thou when I laid the

---

[6] See the discussion of the 'strife/life' rhyme in Ch. 1.

[7] This classical association is well illustrated by the legend of Apollo softening the hearts of the three Fates by making them drunk with wine, on which Browning founded his poem 'Apollo and the Fates' (the prologue to *Parleyings*, 1887).

foundations of the earth? . . . When the morning stars sang together, and all the sons of God shouted for joy?' (Job 38: 4–7). The Old Testament text joins forces with the New Testament parable of the house built upon rock outlasting the house built upon sand (Matthew 7: 24–7) to triumph over the Greek legend, and to emphasize both the creative priority of love, and its continuing strength. Browning is of course right in implying that the actual citadel of Troy, if it ever existed, has 'long ago' been lost in the sands of Asia Minor (though it might be pointed out that Schliemann was beginning to dig it up again in the very year the poem was written), but this is emphatically not true of Homer's poetry. The Homeric texts are not 'outworn'; on the contrary, as Browning's own opening lines imply, it is they that have priority in the reader's mind. The Helen of the *Iliad* survives as an unchanging archetype of beauty and erotic power (in Browning's own *Fifine at the Fair*, for example, in ll. 210–17), while the Helen whom Browning celebrates in his sonnet triumphs over her rival only within the confines of the poem and thus, we might argue, does not triumph over her at all. If hatred is the motivating force of the Trojan War, then it has built itself a monument as enduring as love; to what else, after all, does Browning pay tribute in 'Development'? In that poem, too, the question of pleasure, which comes up so startlingly and disturbingly in the Dante passage of 'One Word More', is of crucial importance, as it is in many other poems by Browning where hatred is a topic.

We can see this equivocal creative alliance between hatred and pleasure in two poems where hatred is a central theme, 'Soliloquy of the Spanish Cloister' and 'Ixion'. I have chosen them for this reason, and because they are well matched: one early, one late; one comic, one tragic; one racy, colloquial, and rhymed, one lofty, solemn, and written in unrhymed classical elegiacs; one concerned with the perversion of the Christian religion, one with classical myth; one spoken by the hater, and one by the hated.

The conventional reading of 'Soliloquy of the Spanish Cloister', first published in *Dramatic Lyrics* (1842), takes this poem to be using the technique of dramatic monologue as a means of ironically revealing the speaker's warped passion and prejudice. The poem offers a critique of hatred, an insight into its workings which functions both as moral exemplum and as satire. A key part of the lesson would be that hatred defeats its own object: the speaker appears not only to be giving us an unintentional and unflattering self-portrait, but to be painting the very opposite picture of Brother Lawrence which his pettiness, malice, and jealousy imagine. As Iago says of Cassio in *Othello*, 'He hath a daily beauty in his life | That makes me ugly' (v. i. 19–20). Looking through the poem's distorted lens we 'correct' the image and see Brother Lawrence as kindly, good-humoured, unaffected; and that he has a kind of innocence, or holy simplicity. Other monks, apparently, consider him a saint—an opinion which causes the speaker to snort in disbelief. Brother Lawrence is a gardener, and his love of flowers and fruits is an emblem of his generous nature. The speaker, by contrast, is introverted, malicious, and mean-minded. His religion is a matter of empty formalism, which Browning treats in the same style of rollicking anti-Catholic satire that shows up in 'The Tomb at St. Praxed's' with the Bishop's references to 'the blessed mutter of the mass' and 'Good strong thick stupifying incense-smoke' (ll. 81, 84). 'Soliloquy of the Spanish Cloister', too, might have been designed to appeal to the anti-Tractarian movement in England in the 1840s, when Protestant attacks on Catholic ritualism and formalism were at their height:

> When he finishes refection
> > Knife and fork across he lays
> Never, to my recollection,
> > As do I, in Jesu's praise.
> I, the Trinity illustrate,
> > Drinking watered orange-pulp;
> In three sips the Arian frustrate;
> > While he drains his at one gulp!
>
> (ll. 33–40)[8]

Brother Lawrence's artless manners and healthy appetite show up the speaker's meaningless gestures, the trappings and suits of a merely external piety (or perhaps the symptoms of his obsessive neurosis). And yet, what catches my eye here is also that sparkling detail of the 'watered orange-pulp'. It speaks of a whole world of diluted, unsatisfying experiences, a world in which the speaker feels his physical senses thwarted and confined. The pleasures of the flesh

---

[8] The meaning of this relates to the Arian heresy, named after the 4th-cent. theologian Arius who denied the divinity of Christ and therefore challenged the doctrine of the Trinity. Needless to say, the issue would not have been a live one for Brother Lawrence and his fellow-monks, given that the poem has a contemporary setting ('my scrofulous French novel', l. 57).

are denied to him, except through the eye and the imagination—but in this sense the speaker is an artist, and his eye is 'alive', noticing in a way that Brother Lawrence's is not.

> Saint, forsooth! While brown Dolores
>   Squats outside the Convent bank,
> With Sanchicha, telling stories,
>   Steeping tresses in the tank,
> Blue-black, lustrous, thick like horsehairs,
>   —Can't I see his dead eye grow
> Bright, as 'twere a Barbary corsair's?
>   That is, if he'd let it show.
>
> (ll. 25–32)

With a slight twist of perspective, the speaker might turn into another lover of the flesh, another monk who rejects the sterility of his imposed vocation, but whom readers are invited rather to admire than to unmask, the painter Fra Lippo Lippi; and, like Lippi, the speaker of the 'Soliloquy' has a beady eye for the gradations of hierarchy in a small, enclosed community:

> Oh, those melons! If he's able
>   We're to have a feast; so nice!
> One goes to the Abbot's table,
>   All of us get each a slice.
>
> (ll. 41–4)

More important, the speaker shares with Lippi a 'rage' which, though it has very different effects, springs from the same cause, that of physical longing and immersion in the life of the body:

>   so I swallow my rage
> Clench my teeth, suck my lips in tight, and paint
> To please them—sometimes do, and sometimes don't,
> For, doing most, there's pretty sure to come
> A turn—some warm eve finds me at my saints—
> A laugh, a cry, the business of the world—
> (*Flower o' the peach,*
> *Death for us all, and his own life for each!*)
> And my whole soul revolves, the cup runs o'er,
> The world and life's too big to pass for a dream,
> And I do these wild things in sheer despite,
> And play the fooleries you catch me at,
> In pure rage!
>
> (ll. 242–54)

A biblical allusion sums up Lippi's ironic sense of his predicament; a biblical pun suggests his response to it. By 'the cup runs o'er' he means that the constraints of his life are too much for him; his cup is a cup of bitterness, like that which Jesus prays to be spared (Matthew 26: 39), although the original of the phrase, 'my cup runneth over' (Psalms 23: 5), expresses the fulfilment and excess of pleasure for which he yearns. The 'warm eve' is the evening, but also the figure of Eve, warm with life; for, as Lippi says only a few lines further on, in condemnation of the world's hypocrisy:

> You tell too many lies and hurt yourself.
> You don't like what you only like too much,
> You do like what, if given you at your word,
> You find abundantly detestable.
> For me, I think I speak as I was taught—
> I always see the Garden and God there
> A-making man's wife—and, my lesson learned,
> The value and significance of flesh,
> I can't unlearn ten minutes afterward.

> (ll. 261–9)[9]

What the speaker sees in the garden of the Spanish cloister is Brother Lawrence busily unlearning this lesson; for Brother Lawrence is an obedient and contented artist, whereas his hater is a Romantic dissident from the orthodox aesthetic of love. Brother Lawrence's benign creativity—watering, tending, trimming—is set against the speaker's malignant rhetorical flourishes, his savage mimicry of Brother Lawrence's meek and mild mannerisms.

> At the meal we sit together:
>   *Salve tibi!* I must hear
> Wise talk of the kind of weather,
>   Sort of season, time of year:
> *Not a plenteous cork-crop: scarcely*
>   *Dare we hope oak-galls, I doubt:*
> *What's the Latin name for 'parsley'?*
>   What's the Greek name for Swine's Snout?

> (ll. 9–16)

---

[9] Browning had made the creation of Eve the basis for a simile in *Sordello*: 'just-tinged marble like Eve's lilied flesh | Beneath her Maker's finger when the fresh | First pulse of life shot brightening the snow' (i. 413–15).

The lines are alive with observation, and give pleasure to us despite —or perhaps even because of—their transparent unfairness. Hatred, rancour, envy, and repression have become the speaker's resources, even the basis of an aesthetic. He could hardly have studied Brother Lawrence more intimately had he been, not his 'heart's abhorrence', but his lover.[10]

The poem begins and ends with a brutish snarl—from 'Gr-r-r —there go, my heart's abhorrence!' to 'Gr-r-r—you swine!'—and other references to 'Swine's Snout' and 'thick like horsehairs' stress the speaker's low, animal nature. But then, 'You understand me,' says Fra Lippo Lippi confidingly, 'I'm a beast, I know' (l. 270). We find this engaging; in fact, we mentally translate Lippi's self-deprecating remark into the equivalent of 'I'm only human, I have physical appetites'. I am not suggesting that the speaker of the 'Soliloquy' makes the same appeal to us as Lippi; but I would argue that his warped sense of fun is rooted in the same frustrations, that our enjoyment of the poem is linked, in a way we are perhaps reluctant to admit, to a kind of sympathy (even if that sympathy is not the same as fellow-feeling), and that his energy of hatred is a creative force similar to Lippi's 'pure rage'.

The conflict between Brother Lawrence and his hater may be thought of in moral terms as a conflict between good and evil, or in aesthetic terms (as I have suggested) as one between the art of obedience and the art of rebellion. Behind Brother Lawrence stands the unfallen Adam, gardening in Paradise; behind his hater (much reduced from his grand original, admittedly) stands Milton's Satan— like the speaker of the 'Soliloquy' a leering, jealous voyeur,[11] but also (for Shelley, Blake, and others) an embodiment of radical energy. In traditional moral terms the energy of Satan is purely negative and destructive. Brother Lawrence makes things grow; his adversary ('Satan' means 'adversary') rejoices when 'his lily snaps' (l. 24) and keeps his flowers 'close-nipped on the sly' (l. 48). The art of goodness, we might say, is 'primary', authorized by God, and belongs to a hierarchical design (the melons divided according to rank); that of

---

[10] In Part III of *Paracelsus*, Paracelsus and Festus argue about whether love is blind to the faults of that which it loves. Festus argues that 'love is never blind; but rather | Alive to every the minutest spot | That mars its object, and which hate (supposed | So vigilant and searching) dreams not of' (iii. 838–41).

[11] 'Aside the Devil turned | For envy, yet with jealous leer malign | Eyed them askance' (*Paradise Lost* iv. 502–4).

evil is 'secondary', in Harold Bloom's terms 'anxious' or 'belated'.[12] Another way of putting it would be to say that Brother Lawrence's art is an unconscious expression of divine love, whereas that of the speaker is racked by consciousness, the root of all evil. Brother Lawrence either prattles innocently or says nothing; his inner life, if he has one, is ruthlessly disregarded, while that of the speaker takes centre-stage. If it is the human mind we are interested in, then the speaker has our attention.

The same is true of 'Ixion', a poem first published over forty years after 'Soliloquy of the Spanish Cloister', in *Jocoseria* (1883). Ixion, a legendary king of Thessaly, is not a savoury character in Greek myth, and it is typical of Browning to have taken up his case. The *Oxford Classical Dictionary* (2nd edn., 1970) calls him 'the Greek Cain'. He murdered his father-in-law so barbarously that no one would purify him except Zeus, whom he repaid, in Oxford's quaint phrase, by 'attempting the chastity of Hera'. Zeus deceived Ixion by substituting a cloud-image for the real Hera (from this union, according to some accounts, came the Centaurs), and then punished him by binding him to a wheel of fire revolving eternally in Hades. Needless to say, in Browning's poem these events are selectively recorded and given different values. There is no mention of Ixion's murder (or of the Centaurs); Ixion represents fallible humanity, Zeus absolute power, and the poem argues that unless such power is joined to love it deserves not worship but defiance.

'Browning's real object in *Ixion*', DeVane states flatly, 'is to set himself squarely, once and for all, against the belief in perpetual vindictive punishment by the gods' (DeVane: 470). This has been the prevailing view, according to the Yale/Penguin edition, which adds the rider that there might be 'some irony in Ixion's protests' (Pettigrew and Collins: ii. 1088).[13] As to the last point, it doesn't square with F. J. Furnivall's account of Browning's pre-publication reading of the poem: 'his voice became impassioned, his proof shook in his

---

[12] An echo of the Spanish cloister turns up in Andrea del Sarto's very Bloomian image for his life's decline: 'The last monk leaves the garden; days decrease | And autumn grows, autumn in everything' (ll. 44–5).

[13] Clyde Ryals protests that the poem 'is surely more complicated' in that it 'makes a statement more about man's existence on earth than about his afterlife' (Ryals: 183). I do not agree that the conclusion follows the premiss. But Ryals goes on to make an observation as shrewd as it is seemingly incongruous: that the account of Ixion's sufferings may reflect Browning's feelings about his treatment by the critics (p. 184). I discuss this topic in the next chapter.

hands, and he was almost like one inspired as he proclaimed the triumph of the suffering tortured Man over the tyrant God' (Peterson: 199). But if not irony, then there is something more disturbing still, and it concerns the relation of Browning's poem to a famous precursor, Shelley's *Prometheus Unbound*. Shelley's poem opens with a speech in which Prometheus laments his suffering and proclaims his superiority to Jupiter, his tormentor:

> Monarch of Gods and Daemons, and all Spirits
> But One, who throng these bright and rolling worlds
> Which Thou and I alone of living things
> Behold with sleepless eyes! regard this Earth
> Made multitudinous with thy slaves, whom thou
> Requitest for knee-worship, prayer, and praise,
> And toil, and hecatombs of broken hearts,
> With fear and self-contempt and barren hope.
> Whilst me, who am thy foe, eyeless in hate,
> Hast thou made reign and triumph, to thy scorn,
> O'er mine own misery and thy vain revenge.
> Three thousand years of sleep-unsheltered hours,
> And moments aye divided by keen pangs
> Till they seemed years, torture and solitude,
> Scorn and despair, — these are mine empire: —
> More glorious far than that which thou surveyest
> From thine unenvied throne, O Mighty God!
>
> (i. 1–17)

Ixion clearly resembles Shelley's Prometheus in his endurance of an unjust punishment, his poignant evocation of his suffering, and his assertion of a moral victory over the arbitrary power that crushes him. But his opening lines also swerve away from this Shelleyan model, a difference marked first by the difference in genre, and second by a flamboyant rhetorical figure:

> High in the dome, suspended, of Hell, sad triumph, behold us!
>   Here the revenge of a God, there the amends of a Man.
> Whirling forever in torment, flesh once mortal, immortal
>   Made — for a purpose of hate — able to die and revive,
> Pays to the uttermost pang, then, newly for payment replenished,
>   Doles out — old yet young — agonies ever afresh;
> Whence the result above me: torment is bridged by a rainbow, —
>   Tears, sweat, blood, — each spasm, ghastly once, glorified now.
>
> (ll. 1–8)

Prometheus addresses Jupiter directly (even though he is not present), and the usual dramatic conventions apply: the spectator or reader 'eavesdrops' on the scene. The effect is to emphasize the dialectical nature of drama, its aptness for oppositions and confrontations. Prometheus and Jupiter are framed in an enmity so absolute that it can never be resolved; indeed, it was part of Shelley's deliberate purpose, as he explains in the Preface, to change the received version of the myth, in which Prometheus bargains with Jupiter for his release. But Ixion is the speaker of a monologue, not a character in a drama; if he addresses anyone other than the reader it is himself (no other interlocutor is posited), and what he says is not 'behold me' but 'behold *us*'—that is, himself *and* Zeus. 'Here the revenge of a God, there the amends of a Man': what is at issue in 'Ixion' is a relationship *between* God and Man, in which 'God' is figured as the principle of suffering itself, *through* which Man triumphs; it is not, as in Shelley, a question of *rejecting* a cruel and hateful divine authority, but of refiguring it as the very condition of human existence.

Prometheus goes on to emphasize his difference from Jupiter by abjuring his earlier curse, pronounced when Jupiter first imposed his punishment. If the reader had felt any doubt as to the referent of 'eyeless in hate' in l. 14, it soon becomes clear that it applies to Jupiter alone: Prometheus manages (in true Shelleyan fashion) both to pity Jupiter and not to spare him:

> What ruin
> Will hunt thee undefended through wide Heaven!
> How will thy soul, cloven to its depths with terror,
> Gape like a hell within! I speak in grief,
> Not exultation, for I hate no more,
> As then ere misery made me wise. The curse
> Once breathed on thee I would recall.
>
> (i. 53–9)

Jupiter gets no credit for inflicting this 'misery', of course; it is not as though he and Prometheus are partners in the latter's achievement of 'wisdom'. In saying 'I hate no more', Prometheus is distancing himself even further from Jupiter, the persistence of whose hate is precisely the theme of the opening lines. 'Eyeless' turns out to mean blind: Jupiter's hatred has defeated its own object, as hatred is traditionally said to do.

In 'Ixion', too, hatred creates, destroys, and re-creates Ixion in an apparently endless, sterile cycle; but what hatred is simultaneously creating is the means, eventually, of its own transcendent defeat. The punishment inflicted on Ixion *generates* the rainbow of his suffering. The image of the rainbow makes a powerfully distorted allusion to the rainbow in Genesis. There it signified God's own Promethean renunciation of his curse on mankind: 'And the bow shall be in the cloud; and I will look upon it, that I may remember the everlasting covenant between God and every living creature of all flesh that is upon the earth' (Genesis 9: 16). Ixion's rainbow is not an external phenomenon, but, in an image fully as Kafkaesque as that of flesh as parchment in 'One Word More', 'flesh become vapour through pain'. At the end of the poem the image returns as the sign of mankind's triumph over a hateful and hating deity whose action, nevertheless, is a *necessary* part of the process of redemption. The hell in which Ixion suffers turns out to be life itself, the 'poor human array, | Pride and revenge and hate and cruelty' (ll. 108–9), and escape is a matter not of negation but of understanding. At the end of the poem Ixion has a vision of the 'influence, high o'er Hell, that turns to a rapture | Pain—and despair's murk mists blends in a rainbow of hope' (ll. 115–16), and sees himself rising 'past Zeus to the Potency o'er him'. This vision replaces the ascent of Demogorgon in *Prometheus Unbound* which signals Prometheus' liberation and inaugurates the reign of love, the kingdom of heaven on earth. But in Browning's version the 'Purity all-unobstructed', which Ixion glimpses beyond the universe of pain made by Zeus 'for a purpose of hate', remains visionary and unattained because that is the only way in which it can give a value to human life which is more than the cheap consolation of orthodox religion.

It is with the appearance of this second divine principle that 'Ixion' signals its relation to another precursor poem, in this case one of Browning's own. In 'Caliban upon Setebos' (first published in *Dramatis Personae*, 1864) Caliban posits the existence of two deities, one a creator, Setebos, the other the 'Quiet' beyond him. Like Zeus, Setebos, who dwells in 'the cold o' the moon' (l. 2), has made the world 'for a purpose of hate', and for the same reason: 'He hated that He cannot change his cold | Nor cure its ache' (ll. 32–3), in other words he hates his own exile from the world he makes. The poem differs radically from 'Ixion' in that the 'Quiet', the 'something over Setebos | That made Him' (ll. 129–30), is not a focus for human aspiration, but is distant and self-absorbed:

> There may be something quiet o'er His head,
> Out of His reach, that feels nor joy nor grief,
> Since both derive from weakness . . .
>
> .   .   .   .   .   .
>
> This Quiet, all it hath a mind to, doth.
> 'Esteemeth stars the outpost of its couch,
> But never spends much thought nor care that way.
> It may look up, work up,—the worse for those
> It works on! 'Careth but for Setebos
> The many-handed as a cuttle-fish,
> Who, making Himself feared through what He does,
> Looks up, first, and perceives He cannot soar
> To what is quiet and hath happy life;
> Next looks down here, and out of very spite
> Makes this a bauble-world to ape yon real,
> These good things to match those as hips do grapes.
>
> (ll. 132–48)

Caliban may lack a classical education, but the deity who 'feels nor
joy nor grief', who 'is quiet and hath happy life', is Epicurean, and
the god who 'Makes this a bauble-world to ape yon real' has been
reading Plato. Caliban's dualism may also be seen as a variant of the
Gnostic idea (itself derived from Plato) in which material creation is
the work of an inferior deity, the Demiurge, above whom is a
supreme, remote, and unknowable Being.[14] Gnosticism held that the
material world was evil, but Caliban's view is more ambiguous: one
of the most interesting things about the poem is the way in which
Caliban combines the idea that Setebos made the world out of
'spite', or in frustrated imitation of the 'real' one, with the most
sensuous, concrete, and, so to speak, 'loving' evocation of that
world:

> Yon otter, sleek-wet, black, lithe as a leech;
> Yon auk, one fire-eye in a ball of foam,
> That floats and feeds; a certain badger brown
> He hath watched hunt with that slant white-wedge eye
> By moonlight; and the pie with the long tongue

---

[14] See the entry on Gnosticism in the *Oxford Dictionary of the Christian Church*
(2nd edn., rev., 1983). Browning's interest in Gnostic ideas dates back to *Paracelsus*:
see Woolford and Karlin: i. 105. Plato's Demiurge appears in the *Timaeus* as a
craftsman who makes the world in accordance with the ideal Forms: since he is a god,
he 'must be entirely good and free from envy or malice' (Irwin: 112), i.e. the exact
opposite of Setebos.

That pricks deep into oakworts for a worm,
And says a plain word when she finds her prize,
But will not eat the ants; the ants themselves
That build a wall of seeds and settled stalks
About their hole—He made all these and more,
Made all we see, and us, in spite: how else?

(ll. 46–56)

'Caliban upon Setebos' was probably written in the winter of 1859–
60, soon after the publication of *Origin of Species*, and there is
evidence that Browning was responding to the debate over Darwin's
book (Pettigrew and Collins: i. 1158). A Darwinian emphasis on the
'struggle for existence' (creatures eating others or defending themselves from being eaten) is of the very essence of the poetry here,
which seems to propose not a horrified recoil from Tennyson's
'Nature, red in tooth and claw' (*In Memoriam* lvi. 15) but an
embrace of it. Compared to this rich and strange world, the world
of the 'Quiet' seems alien and indifferent. 'This Quiet, all it hath a
mind to, doth' suggests a creativity as self-contained as the syntax
which describes it. The 'Quiet' may possess 'happy life', but this
very possession renders it suspect. Freedom from human 'weakness'
is also an incapacity, a failure to be human. Browning, I think,
intended the relation between Zeus and the 'Potency o'er him' in
'Ixion' to remodel that between Setebos and the 'Quiet'. Caliban
lacks the imagination to comprehend (literally to get his mind
around) his own suffering: not for him the rainbow which signifies
a perpetually renewed hope of transcendence, but a final immersion
in the physical world, as he bows to the storm of Setebos's anger.
By concluding the poem with a tempest, Browning may be alluding
to the opening of Shakespeare's play, an allusion which would
further emphasize Caliban's superstitious primitivism. And yet,
though Setebos, in Caliban's 'Natural Theology', hates the world
that he has made, and rules it as a cruel, arbitrary despot, the
poem offers a counterweight to this hatred in Caliban's own
'many-handed' grasp of his environment, the sharpness of his perceptions, the lyric and rhythmic pleasures of his speech.[15] 'Ixion'
in comparison has a pallid, strained, intellectual power, but not
the power to make us see. The organic metaphor which governs
Caliban's monologue—'Letting the rank tongue blossom into

[15] The influence of Shakespeare's Caliban, of course, is strong in all these features.

speech' (l. 23)—would have no place in Ixion's mythological and theatrical 'set'.

Despite these differences, 'Caliban upon Setebos' and 'Ixion' are united in casting doubt on the existence of an absolute divide between creative love and barren hatred. Browning had raised this issue over twenty years before 'Caliban upon Setebos', though in a very different form, in the second episode of *Pippa Passes* (1841).[16] This episode concerns a plot against the young French sculptor Jules by his fellow art-students, led by the mediocre English painter Lutwyche. (Lutwyche's sinister euphemism for it is a 'piece of friendly vengeance'.) By means of forged letters they persuade Jules that a beautiful, rich young girl, Phene, is an admirer of his art and has fallen in love with him. Because of her family's purported opposition, Jules (who has never seen Phene) agrees to an epistolary courtship and clandestine marriage with her.[17] She is in fact an 'artist's model' (that is, a prostitute), procured through a pimp called Natalia. The episode opens with the group of students gathered outside Jules's house, waiting for him to arrive back from the church with his bride, who is then to reveal her real identity.

Why does Lutwyche (he maintains he is no more than a 'spokesman' for the group, but it is clear that he is the prime mover of the plot) hate Jules and wish to destroy him? The answer is that his attitude to Jules is the same as that of the speaker of 'Soliloquy of the Spanish Cloister' to Brother Lawrence. The two main differences

---

[16] The bulk of *Pippa Passes* consists of four separate dramatic episodes, linked by Pippa's 'passing' by the site of each episode during her holiday ramble around the town of Asolo. These four episodes do not, however, correspond to the four 'parts' of the work, each of which is divided into two scenes (in Parts I and II a scene in verse followed by one in prose; in Part III two verse scenes; in Part IV a prose scene followed by verse). The first episode occupies only the verse scene of part one, the second (the one I am discussing) occupies the prose scene of Part I and the verse scene of Part II, the third occupies the prose scene of Part II and the first verse scene of Part III (the second verse scene is free-standing), and the fourth occupies only the prose scene of Part IV (its verse scene functions as the epilogue). The fourth episode contains a reprise of the second, when the Bishop reads a letter from Jules the sculptor written after the denouement of his confrontation with Phene. It is only at this point that we realize that the Bishop has been Jules's artistic patron.

[17] Four years after the publication of *Pippa Passes* (1841), did the Jules–Phene episode resonate in the minds of both Browning and Elizabeth Barrett when they began their own secret courtship correspondence? Browning remained interested in forged love-letters: they form part of Guido's plot against Pompilia and Caponsacchi in *The Ring and the Book*.

are generic (this is a drama and not a dramatic monologue, so we get to hear Jules's side of the story), and thematic: since Jules and Lutwyche are both artists their conflict can be openly staged as an *aesthetic* antagonism. Lutwyche hates Jules *as an artist*.

In 'Soliloquy of the Spanish Cloister' Brother Lawrence is seen only in the refraction of the speaker's gaze; he is, in a sense, shielded from our judgement. In *Pippa Passes* we are able to compare what Lutwyche says about Jules with what Jules says himself. Lutwyche's image of Jules is that of a callow, vain, stuck-up, priggish youth: 'this strutting stone-squarer', he calls him (i. 311), who views his fellow-students as 'dissolute, brutalized, heartless bunglers' (i. 315–16) and whose pretentious attitude both to art and women is ripe for puncturing. Here is Lutwyche ('1 Student'), first caricaturing Jules's behaviour in the 'Model-Gallery' (gallery of plaster casts) of Canova's sculpture at Possagno, and then mocking his determination to keep himself sexually pure:

he marches first resolvedly past great works by the dozen without vouchsafing an eye: all at once he stops full at the *Psiche-fanciulla*—cannot pass that old acquaintance without a nod of encouragement—'In your new place, beauty? Then behave yourself as well here as at Munich—I see you!'—Next posts himself deliberately before the unfinished *Pietà* for half an hour without moving, till up he starts of a sudden and thrusts his very nose into . . I say into—the group—by which you are informed that precisely the sole point he had not fully mastered in Canova was a certain method of using the drill in the articulation of the knee-joint—and that, even, has he mastered at length! Good bye, therefore, to Canova—whose gallery no longer contains Jules, the predestinated thinker in marble!

    5 Student. Tell him about the women—go on to the women.

    1 Student. Why, on that matter he could never be supercilious enough. How should we be other than the poor devils you see with those debasing habits we cherish? He was not to wallow in that mire, at least: he would love at the proper time, and meanwhile put up with the *Psiche-fanciulla*.

(i. 354–78)[18]

Lutwyche is evidently unjust, but, as with the speaker of the

---

[18] 'Psiche-fanciulla' (Psyche as a young girl) is the name of a statue by Canova which exists in several versions; the one dating from 1793 was the one Jules would have seen in Munich. The plaster cast at Possagno was in fact of the head only. The legend of Cupid and Psyche has an obvious relevance to the relationship between Jules and Phene, a relevance which Browning somewhat heavy-handedly emphasized in one of his numerous revisions to this part of *Pippa Passes*: see Woolford and Karlin: ii. 68.

'Soliloquy', hatred stimulates his powers of observation. His picture of Jules as the young genius has a ring of malicious truth about it, especially his 'readings' of Jules's gestures (the familiar nod to Psyche, the nose-scraping scrutiny of the *Pietà*). Browning means us to understand, I think, both that Jules *is* a genius, and that his behaviour is provocative to the 'bunglers' who surround him; that, in the 'dissolute' community of art-students whom Browning draws here from the life, Jules's high-mindedness, ambition, and dedication to his art might make anyone want to bring him down a peg.

What happens when, in the following scene, we hear Jules himself? Lutwyche's account is both confirmed and rebutted. Phene (who is going to turn out as different from Lutwyche's expectations as from Jules's) stands silently in front of her new husband while he rhapsodizes about her (and about himself). His exalted sense of himself and his vocation are much in evidence (he boasts to Phene of his skill, he points out works in his studio for her to admire, he even asks her, since she is Greek, to read out one of his favourite passages of Homer).[19] He wonders aloud whether his life will be the same now that Phene is to share it:

> O, my life to come!
> My Tydeus must be carved that's there in clay,
> And how be carved with you about the chamber?
> Where must I place you? When I think that once
> This room-full of rough block-work seemed my heaven
> Without you! Shall I ever work again—
> Get fairly into my old ways again—
> Bid each conception stand while trait by trait
> My hand transfers its lineaments to stone?
> Will they, my fancies, live near you, my truth—
> The live truth—passing and repassing me—
> Sitting beside me?
>
> (ii. 13–24)

At first (l. 15) it looks as if Jules is worried that Phene's presence 'about the chamber' will distract him from his work (by making love, or lunch); then in the next line he seems to be considering her as an *objet d'art* which, on reflection, doesn't fit the rest of the

---

[19] The passage, *Odyssey*, xxii. 8, concerns the killing of Antinous, the leader of Penelope's suitors, by Odysseus; it may ironically represent the vengeance Lutwyche is about to inflict on Jules, or prefigure the vengeance which Jules will inflict on Lutwyche (though this does not in fact come about).

decor; only in ll. 22–4 does it become clear that Jules has (as you might expect) an *intellectual* anxiety about Phene's effect on him. This anxiety pertains to his idea of his own creativity, the idea which makes him, if not deserving of Lutwyche's hatred, then at least vulnerable to his satire.

It is an idea close to that of Aprile in *Paracelsus*, who, as sculptor, planned to 'carve in stone, or cast in brass, | The forms of earth' (ii. 369–70). Jules's aesthetic — 'Bid each conception stand while trait by trait | My hand transfers its lineaments to stone' — is, as he comes to realize, essentially imitative and deadening.[20] The mastery which Lutwyche identifies as Jules's ambition is one which rests on his ability to outdo his predecessors, and which is linked, also, to manipulation (in the literal as well as figurative sense) of his materials and subjects:

> But of the stuffs one can be master of,
> How I divined their capabilities
> From the soft-rinded smoothening facile chalk
> That yields your outline to the air's embrace,
> Down to the crisp imperious steel, so sure
> To cut its one confided thought clean out
> Of all the world; but marble! — 'neath my tools
> More pliable than jelly . . .
>
> (ll. 79–86)

Jules's boast of his proficiency brings him in one sense close to Caliban's notion of the 'Quiet': 'This Quiet, all it hath a mind to, doth', a perfection not admirable because not human. In another sense Jules can be seen as *avoiding* a fully human life: this is the burden of Lutwyche's insinuation that his ardour is self-directed, and his art a form of masturbation, a means of deferring real sexual encounters ('he would love at the proper time, and meanwhile put up with the *Psiche-fanciulla*').[21] Certainly mastery and sexuality are con-

---

[20] Compare the different implication of the first lines of 'Popularity' (1855): 'Stand still, true poet that you are, | I know you; let me try and draw you'. There the speaker's desire to capture the likeness of the 'true poet' is humble rather than self-serving.

[21] It is worth noting at this point the Keatsian luxuriance of Jules's language. This is not the only possible Keats connection: Browning could have been told by friends who had known Keats (for example Leigh Hunt) of the practical joke played on Keats's brother Tom by Charles Wells, who forged love-letters from a mysterious French lady. Keats believed that the deception hastened his brother's death. But Jules eventually turns the Keatsian tables on Lutwyche: see p. 103.

nected: chalk and steel seem typecast in terms of gender as female ('soft-rinded') and male ('imperious'); marble's submissiveness is also erotic, particularly since earlier in Jules's speech it is a simile for Phene herself, whom Jules compares to 'my very life's-stuff, marble' (l. 66).[22]

But at this point we may become aware of an unstated, a subterranean connection between Jules and Lutwyche. For Lutwyche, too, is interested in mastery, though his ambition takes a different form and follows a different aesthetic principle. All along Lutwyche has seen himself as the *author* of a cruel comedy of manners, whose 'characters', Jules and Phene, have their parts scripted and are not expected to deviate from them. Lutwyche is the author of Phene's supposed love-letters, and of the 'verses' which she is to recite (when Jules lets her get a word in) to reveal the trick that has been played on him. His method is devious and indirect—you might say, dramatic, like that of the author who creates and undoes him.[23] But like Jules he thinks of his materials as 'pliable as jelly' and exults in his power to mould them. Lutwyche is Jules's dark twin: he hates him because of likeness, not difference.

This symbolic reversal or undoing (of antagonism into desire, desire into antagonism) becomes explicit in the long speech written by Lutwyche for Phene to recite. The speech begins:

> The Bard said, do one thing I can—
> Love a man and hate a man
> Supremely: thus my lore began.
> Thro' the Valley of Love I went,
> In its lovingest spot to abide;
> And just on the verge where I pitched my tent
> Dwelt Hate beside—
> (And the bridegroom asked what the bard's smile meant
> Of his bride.)
> Next Hate I traversed, the Grove,
> In its hatefullest nook to dwell—
> And lo, where I flung myself prone, couched Love
> Next cell.
>
> (ll. 128–40)

---

[22] See the quotation from *Sordello* in n. 9 above. Compare also 'The Tomb at St. Praxed's': 'mistresses with great smooth marbly limbs' (l. 75).

[23] Lutwyche has not counted on Phene stumbling over her lines and ad libbing, nor, of course, could he anticipate Pippa's 'passing' at the climax of the scene and causing a radical change of mind in Jules. These are features of Browning's script, not his; for poor Lutwyche turns out to be a character himself in a drama not of his devising.

In the *Poems* of 1849, where *Pippa Passes* (and especially this episode) appeared in a heavily revised version, Browning changed the opening in a clumsy attempt to portray Lutwyche as motivated by envy and a sense of his own inferiority.[24] In the process, by changing one conjunction, he dislocated the subtlety of Lutwyche's designs on Jules:

> I am a painter who cannot paint;
> In my life, a devil rather than saint,
> In my brain, as poor a creature too—
> No end to all I cannot do!
> Yet do one thing at least I can—
> Love a man, or hate a man
> Supremely . . .

Not only do the first four lines make Lutwyche seem banal and untypically self-pitying, but the change from 'Love a man *and* hate a man' to 'Love a man, *or* hate a man' restores exactly the distance between the two feelings which the first edition text elides. Lutwyche both loves *and* hates Jules: that is why his plot takes the form of an erotic deception, the loathing counterpart of a courtship.[25] The 'valley' and 'grove' are features of the same landscape of feeling: as Lutwyche concludes, in his search for

> The Hate of all Hates, or the Love
> Of all Loves in its glen or its grove,
> —I find them the very warders
> Each of the other's borders.
> So most I love when Love's disguised
> In Hate's garb—'tis when Hate's surprised
> In Love's weed that I hate most . . .
>
> (ll. 166–72)

The logic of this is clear: if Lutwyche claims to hate Jules, then he

---

[24] The revisions can be followed in full in Woolford and Karlin: ii. 62–4.

[25] Not all Browning's revisions were as clumsy. Phene's preamble to her recital of Lutwyche's verses is considerably expanded in 1849, and in the course of it she hints to Jules that the plot against him has a perverted sexual element. When she was receiving her instructions from Lutwyche and the others she had observed 'On every face, so different in all else, | The same smile girls like us are used to bear, | But never men, men cannot stoop so low; | Yet your friends, speaking of you, used that smile, | That hateful smirk of boundless self-conceit | Which seems to take possession of this world, | And make of God their tame confederate, | Purveyor to their appetites'.

must love him; his love is certainly 'disguised | In Hate's garb'. The 'pure' form of each passion turns out to be the sign, not of itself, but of its opposite. The further implication is that Jules, as Lutwyche's true love, must respond to his courtship of hate: and this is just what he does, until Pippa's unexpected intervention. As Phene's speech draws to a close, Jules interrupts her, impatient to show that he has grasped the point: 'Lutwyche—who else! But all of them, no doubt, | Hated me' (ll. 180–1); he then expresses his intention to fight duels with 'all fifteen of them' (l. 193) until either he or they are dead.

How is Jules rescued from Lutwyche's loathing embrace? Technically by Pippa's song; but what, in him, does her song release? For an answer we need to return to the flawed aesthetic to which Jules subscribes. He shares with Lutwyche an obsession with mastery, with control of his 'stuff', but there is also a subtler link between them. After the denouement of his scene with Phene, Jules, as we discover near the end of the poem, in the course of the fourth episode, writes a letter to his patron, the Bishop. In this letter he renounces sculpture altogether (of which there was no hint in the second episode—on the contrary).[26] He says in the letter (the Bishop is reporting his words):

'He never had a clearly conceived Ideal within his brain till to-day. Yet since his hand could manage a chisel he has practised expressing other men's Ideals—and in the very perfection he has attained to he foresees an ultimate failure—his unconscious hand will pursue its prescribed course of old years, and will reproduce with a fatal expertness the ancient types, let the novel one appear never so palpably to his spirit: there is but one method of escape—confiding the virgin type to as chaste a hand, he will paint, not carve, its characteristics.' (iv. 45–55)

The fixity of the 'ancient types' is related to that of the 'conceptions' whose lineaments Jules had seen himself transferring to stone. He now realizes that these types belong to an equally static set of 'Ideals'; the forms of classical sculpture are a kind of permanent intellectual allegory. Of the sculptures which he points out to Phene in his studio, three are figures from classical mythology (Tydeus, Psyche, Hippolyta), and one (the 'Almaign Kaiser') is a modern

---

[26] Although he breaks the statues in his studio and says to Phene that he is going to 'begin art afresh', he immediately adds: 'Shall I meet Lutwyche [i.e. in a duel], | And save him from my statue's meeting him?' (ll. 234–5), implying that he plans to continue as a sculptor.

version of a classical model; as for the anonymous Greek 'praiser', who has a more Romantically expressive form, this turns out to have been commissioned by Lutwyche, in one of 'Phene's' forged letters.

Jules's art is therefore imprisoned by a 'fatal expertness', a position which exactly corresponds to Lutwyche's view of him: for Lutwyche, remember, notices and mocks Jules's obsession with technical accomplishment. None of Browning's 1849 revisions is so incomprehensible as the one word he inserted in Lutwyche's sneer that Jules believes himself to be 'the predestinated thinker in marble'. In 1849 this reads 'the predestinated novel thinker in marble', but 'novel' is just what Jules is not. He is 'predestinated' both to the mechanical reproduction of 'other men's Ideals', and (so Lutwyche believes) to playing his part in another man's plot.[27]

Moreover, Jules's letter acknowledges Lutwyche's cleverness in tying together erotic and aesthetic weaknesses: the metaphor of the 'virgin type' and the 'chaste hand' remembers Lutwyche's original mockery of Jules for refusing to indulge in 'debasing habits'. The sexual debasement which Jules claimed to reject was all the time present in his art: he and Lutwyche were, after all, wallowing in the same mire. But Jules recuperates the purity which Lutwyche had exposed as false; he 'begins art afresh' (l. 234) and takes his place as a primary, not secondary, artist, as a creator, not a follower: in relation to both his art and his love for Phene, he will not simply 'produce form out of shapelessness' but 'evoke a soul | From form' (ll. 217–19). Jules's final, visionary words to Phene seal this resolution:

> Like a god going thro' his world I trace
> One mountain for a moment in the dusk,
> Whole brotherhoods of cedars on its brow—
> And you are ever by me while I trace
> —Are in my arms as now—as now—as now!
> Some unsuspected isle in the far seas!
> Some unsuspected isle in far off seas!

> (ll. 237–43)

---

[27] The word 'predestinated' ties in with the theme of Providence and free will which runs throughout *Pippa Passes*, and in particular glances at Pippa's words in the prologue (repeated at the end of the epilogue), the keynote of the whole work: 'each but as God wills | Can work—God's puppets, best and worst, | Are we; there is no last nor first'. For Browning's own commentary on these lines, see Woolford and Karlin: ii. 27.

Poor Lutwyche, spying from the balcony! Like Milton's Satan, he sees 'these two | Imparadised in one another's arms', the difference being that the 'sight hateful, sight tormenting' is the outcome of his temptation rather than the prelude. Eden lies ahead of the lovers, in the flight to a new world, 'unsuspected' both because they will be secure from intrusion, and as a symbol of the new art which Jules will practise, and which will not have been foreshadowed (and overshadowed) by the art of the past. The syntax of the first three lines allows two readings: either the mountain whose outline Jules traces in the dusk is like a god, or else the god is Jules himself.[28] The doubleness expresses Jules's new-found artistic vision and pride, a pride Lutwyche can no longer accuse of being morally and aesthetically suspect.

The example of the Jules–Phene episode of *Pippa Passes* suggests that hatred as creative force is linked to the perceived likeness between the passions of hate and love, and that the limit of this likeness is defined by the fixed conception of the passions themselves. A change in the order of ideas, the setting in motion of a new dynamic, may break the perspective from which hatred and love seem aspects of the same condition.

---

[28] Browning wantonly 'clarified' the passage in 1849: 'Like a god going through his world there stands | One mountain . . . And you are ever by me while I gaze'.

5

Being Hated

'Till Block-heads blame, and Judges praise,
The Poet cannot claim his Bays;
On me, when Dunces are satyrick,
I take it for a Panegyrick.
Hated by Fools, and *Fools to hate*,
Be that my Motto and my Fate.

(Swift)[1]

Or being hated, don't give way to hating,
And yet don't look too good, nor talk too wise . . .

(Kipling)[2]

I HAVE argued that the artist as hater figures strongly in Browning's poetry, and that there is a connection between hatred and creativity in his aesthetics; but there is another side to this question, and it concerns the hatred of which the artist is himself the object. In 'One Word More' Browning argues that all artists yearn for a private art in which to express their personal feeling, an art that is not also the instrument of their public mission. And the reason is again to do with hatred, though this time it is not the hatred with which the artist writes, but that with which he is received by his public. Browning's image here is not (or not apparently) Dante, but Moses, an embittered prophet who guides his thankless people through the wilderness:

He who smites the rock and spreads the water,
Bidding drink and live a crowd beneath him,
Even he, the minute makes immortal,
Proves, perchance, his mortal in the minute,

---

[1] 'To Doctor D - - - - y [Delany]', ll. 167–72. Swift revised 'Block-heads' to 'Criticks' in his copy of *Miscellanies* (1732).
[2] 'If—', ll. 7–8.

Desecrates, belike, the deed in doing.
While he smites, how can he but remember,
So he smote before, in such a peril,
When they stood and mocked—'Shall smiting help us?'
When they drank and sneered—'A stroke is easy!'
When they wiped their mouths and went their journey,
Throwing him for thanks—'But drought was pleasant.'
Thus old memories mar the actual triumph;
Thus the doing savours of disrelish;
Thus achievement lacks a gracious somewhat

.   .   .   .

For he bears an ancient wrong about him,
Sees and knows again those phalanxed faces,
Hears, yet one time more, the 'customed prelude—
'How should'st thou, of all men, smite, and save us?'
Guesses what is like to prove the sequel—
'Egypt's flesh-pots—nay, the drought was better.'

(ll. 74–95)[3]

Browning has creatively misread the source of this episode (in
Exodus 17 and Numbers 20). There the children of Israel do indeed
complain to Moses that he has led them into a wilderness to die of
thirst, but they do not show ingratitude when he does something
about it. (The person who is angry with Moses *after* the miracle is
God, because 'ye believed me not, to sanctify me in the eyes of the
children of Israel'.) Browning also introduces an element of recur-
rence ('So he smote before, in such a peril') not present in the
original; the effect is to make the biblical episode an archetype of the
relation between prophet/poet and people/audience, enabling Browning to speak of an 'ancient wrong', a grievance inherent in and
inseparable from the very nature of artistic production.[4] The word
'smote' connects prophecy to poetry (as in Tennyson's 'Locksley
Hall', l. 33: 'Love took up the harp of life, and smote on all the
chords with might', or Kipling's poem 'When 'Omer Smote 'Is
Bloomin' Lyre') and reminds us of familiar complaints about the
ingratitude meted out to poets, succinctly put in Thomas Seward's

[3] As with the Dante passage, the passage about Moses is anticipated in *Sordello* (iii.
800 ff.) where Browning criticizes the fashion for smooth, trivial verse, 'while awk-
wardly enough your Moses smites | The rock'; the contrast between the rough-but-real
and the facile-but-spurious is profoundly Carlylean.
[4] The exasperation with which the prophet hears 'one time more' the people's
reproaches contrasts with the tender insistence of the lovers' 'one word more'.

famous couplet: 'Seven wealthy towns contend for Homer dead, |
Through which the living Homer begg'd his bread'.

Elements of the passage about Dante with which I began this
book, and which comes earlier in the poem, are repeated here, but
with significant transformations. Dante's 'people of importance'
become the 'crowd beneath' the poet; again there is a violent action
('smiting'), but this time it is healing and redemptive; there is hatred,
but it flows now not from the poet towards those he stigmatizes, but
from his audience, those he is trying to help, towards him. At this
point Dante re-enters the picture, since he was famously a victim of
the ingratitude of his fellow-countrymen, and had indeed become for
the generation of Romantic poets who were Browning's precursors
an image of the artist who is exiled and persecuted as a reward for
his genius.[5]

We now have a double picture of the prophet/poet as both hater
(of 'wickedness') and hated (by his, if not wicked, then ignorant and
stupid audience). What is common to both images is the poet's
superiority to those about whom, or for whom, he writes. This state
of mind is one side of a Romantic dualism which Browning inherited,
a split in Romantic notions of the artist's role and status. Is the poet
a privileged figure, endowed with divine insight, separated from the
common run of mankind? Or is the poet, in Wordsworth's famous
phrase from the Preface to *Lyrical Ballads*, 'a man speaking to men',
in whose qualities 'is implied nothing differing in kind from other
men, but only in degree'? If the former, then poets have the authority
to behave as Browning shows Dante behaving; and the obverse of
this power is that they will themselves be stigmatized by an uncompre-
hending and hostile public. They will be exalted, but alienated. But if
the latter, then poets should be rewarded with the fellowship and
solidarity of mankind, only they must come off the mountain to
get it.

Clearly Browning's Dante and Moses belong in the prophetic

---

[5] The *locus classicus* is Byron's *The Prophecy of Dante*, published in 1819, which
contains such passages as the following: 'Oh Florence! Florence! unto me thou wast |
Like that Jerusalem which the Almighty He | Wept over, "but thou would'st not"; as
the bird | Gathers its young, I would have gather'd thee | Beneath a parent pinion,
hadst thou heard | My voice; but as the adder, deaf and fierce, | Against the breast that
cherish'd thee was stirr'd | Thy venom' (i. 60–7). Dante himself gave warrant for this
view: in the *Inferno*, for example, Brunetto Latini tells him that 'that ungrateful,
malignant people [of Florence] . . . will make itself an enemy to thee for thy good
deeds' (xv. 61–4). See also *Paradiso*, xvii. 46 ff.

BEING HATED97

camp. Together they form a composite and representative figure
—representative not just of the prophet/poet, but of the visionary
in any field of action. The pattern of exaltation and rejection is at its
most intense and clear in a short poem from *Men and Women*, 'The
Patriot', where its subject is politics: the anonymous 'patriot' of the
title,[6] who had led a successful popular revolution the year before, is
now on his way to the scaffold, hated and reviled by the very people
who had cheered him:

> I go in the rain, and, more than needs,
>   A rope cuts both my wrists behind,
> And I think, by the feel, my forehead bleeds,
>   For they fling, whoever has a mind,
> Stones at me for my year's misdeeds.

(ll. 21–5)

'More than needs': the pathos of this laconic, concrete detail is
complicated by the fact that such vengeful excess springs from the
excess of the crowd's fervour a year ago, and that in turn was a
response to the patriot's own unmeasured ambition. He had 'leaped
at the sun, | To give it my loving friends to keep' (ll. 11–12). 'The
Patriot' is subtitled 'An Old Story', but the implication is not just
that those who aspire to do good or render service to their fellow-
men are invariably rewarded by ingratitude; that would align it with
Kipling's later, and simpler, version:

> Take up the White Man's burden—
>   And reap his old reward:
> The blame of those ye better,
>   The hate of those ye guard.

Kipling's poem has the ruler and ruled as natural antagonists; Browning's, more disturbingly, concerns the ingratitude of the patriot's
'loving friends', and suggests that there is something *in his aspiration
itself* which prompts such treatment.

'The Patriot' opens with a famous line, 'It was roses, roses, all the
way', recalling the patriot's triumphant entry into the city, an entry
which also recalls that of Christ into Jerusalem (Matthew 21). If

---

[6] The term 'patriot' here implies a radical reformer, not simply a lover of one's
country, as in *A Soul's Tragedy*, ii. 409–12: 'both great parties in the state, the
advocators of change in the existing system of things, and the opponents of it, patriot
and anti-patriot'.

Christ is the archetype of the visionary destined to be hated and executed, it is because he represents in extreme form the Romantic dualism of divine mission and human solidarity. It is an unresolvable dualism, unless you embrace one of two great Christian heresies, the Arian (denying the divinity of Christ) or the Gnostic (denying his humanity). The stern figure who rejects Satan in the wilderness, treats the Pharisees with contempt, chases the moneylenders from the temple, speaks of bringing 'not peace, but a sword' and of the terror of the last days, seems to stand behind and authorize the Dante and Moses of 'One Word More', though he lacks either Dante's rancour or Moses' bitter self-consciousness. But the hatred which Christ attracts is also, in its excessive cruelty, a function of his proclaimed mission, the 'appropriate' payment for his exalted status. Christ's gospel of love ('Love your enemies, bless them that curse you, do good to them that hate you, and pray for them which despitefully use you and persecute you', Matthew 5: 44) is forcefully acted out in his own person, and with the vital addition that the 'enemies' are those to whom he offered salvation. The Good Shepherd is savaged by his sheep.[7]

Of the characters in Browning's major poetry it is Paracelsus, one of the earliest, who most corresponds to this Christ-like pattern, and most clearly suggests the difficulties and contradictions which Browning saw in it. Browning's Paracelsus (who is nominally based on the real sixteenth-century alchemist and physician) has a genius-complex of intractable proportions. Not only does he know himself to be cleverer than his fellows; not only does he feel himself born to be one of mankind's great benefactors and redeemers; but he believes that his ambition is divinely sanctioned, and that he is in direct, instinctive communication with the will of God. What he lacks is 'love', defined in the poem as sympathy and fellowship with other human beings, a consciousness of sharing their lot—of being 'a man speaking to men'. On the contrary, Paracelsus describes himself, in a phrase of striking economy and psychological acuteness, as longing 'To trample on yet save mankind at once' (i. 469), and sees himself as a saviour of mankind who

---

[7] It is this which distinguishes the pattern from another favourite Romantic myth (which also interested Browning), that of Prometheus/Satan/Faust; for here the aspiring visionary is defeated not by those he tries, or purports, to benefit, but by the supreme power which he defies.

        would withdraw from their officious praise,
        Would gently put aside their profuse thanks,
        Like some knight traversing a wilderness,
        Who, on his way, may chance to free a tribe
        Of desert-people from their dragon-foe;
        When all the swarthy race press round to kiss
        His feet, and choose him for their king, and yield
        Their poor tents, pitch'd among the sand-hills, for
        His realm; and he points, smiling, to his scarf,
        Heavy with rivel'd gold—his burgonet,
        Gay set with twinkling stones—and to the east
        Where these must be display'd . . .

                                        (i. 480–91)

The opposition of 'savage' and 'civilized' imagery (which belongs
more to nineteenth-century ideas about Africa than to sixteenth-
century tales of chivalry) works metaphorically here: the 'swarthy
race', that is the general run of mankind, are emblematically 'dark'
because of their ignorance and live in primitive conditions because of
the poverty of their mental horizons; similarly the knight's finery is
emphasized rather than his weaponry, because such luxury is a
marker of privilege and apartness. What Paracelsus completely fails
to realize, at the outset of the glorious career he plans for himself, is
that, after initially pressing round to kiss his feet, the 'swarthy race'
are going to turn round and side with the dragon. But by the time we
meet him in Part III of the poem, installed to popular acclaim as
professor of chemistry at Basle University, his tone has completely
changed. His lofty disdain of mankind has sharpened into overt
contempt, and he explicitly anticipates being 'exposed' as a quack
and hounded from his post—which does indeed happen.[8] He tells
his one friend and confidant, Festus, an exemplary tale of how he
saved the life of a powerful prince in the face of religious and
medical prejudice and superstition, only to be rewarded by ingratitude and having to flee for his life on suspicion of being a sorcerer.
Mankind are irredeemable fools: 'gull who may, they will be blind! |
They will not look nor think' (iii. 200–1). Prophet and people are
here at their sharpest point of antagonism. But Paracelsus, though he
is rejected and hated for wanting to do good and bring enlightenment,
is (until the very last part of the poem) the reverse of Christ-like,

---

[8] See Ch. 3 for discussion of a different aspect of this episode.

both in his lovelessness and in his inability to bear his fate. The ingratitude of those whom he is trying to help and teach rankles with him, as it does with Moses in 'One Word More'; he bears the 'ancient wrong' about him with a vengeance.

The consequence of this is that Paracelsus develops a remarkable thesis about hatred, that he comes close, at one point in the poem, to making hatred his gospel. About to flee Basle in disgrace, he expresses his contempt for his persecutors: 'I could not spare them | The pleasure of a parting kick', he declares, and Festus replies approvingly: 'You smile: | Despise them as they merit!' Paracelsus goes on:

> If I smile,
> 'Tis with as very contempt as ever turn'd
> Flesh into stone: this courteous recompense,
> This grateful . . . Festus, were your nature fit
> To be defiled, your eyes the eyes to ache
> At festering blotches, eating poisonous blains,
> The ulcerous barky scurf of leprosy
> Which finds a man and leaves a hideous thing
> That cannot but be mended by hell fire,
> I would lay bare the heart of man to you,
> Which God cursed long ago — which devils have made
> Their pet nest and their never-tiring home.
> O, sages have found out that man is born
> For various ends — to love, to know. Has ever
> One stumbled in his search on any signs
> Of a nature in him form'd to *hate*? To *hate*?
> If that be man's true object which evokes
> His powers in fullest strength, be sure 'tis hate:
> Yet men have doubted if the best and bravest
> Of spirits can nourish him with hate alone.
>
> (iv. 132–51)

'Were your nature fit . . . I would lay bare . . . ulcerous barky scurf of leprosy . . . mended by hell fire': the language here has a curious ancestry in the words of the Ghost in *Hamlet*, who tells Hamlet that he comes from Purgatory, where he is

> confin'd to fast in fires
> Till the foul crimes done in my days of nature
> Are burnt and purg'd away. But that I am forbid
> To tell the secrets of my prison-house,

> I could a tale unfold whose lightest word
> Would harrow up thy soul . . .
>
> (I. v. 11–16)[9]

Later in the scene the Ghost describes how Claudius poisoned him
by means of a 'leperous distilment', so that 'a most instant tetter
bark'd about, | Most lazar-like, with vile and loathsome crust | All
my smooth body' (ll. 63–73). Browning makes the physical symptoms
of poisoning into attributes of spiritual corruption, the consequence
of the 'foul crimes done in my days of nature'; indeed, in Paracelsus's
bitter judgement it is human nature itself which is the 'prison-house'
whose 'secrets' must be kept from the uninitiated. Yet in hating his
enemies Paracelsus is also hating himself. The autobiographical form
of the Ghost's tale in *Hamlet* combines with the sliding, ambiguous
referents of Paracelsus's own speech in such a way that, by the end
of the passage, the hatred which he expresses for the corrupted
hearts of those who have turned against him is indistinguishable
from hatred of his own.[10] And as the Ghost, for all his apparent
restraint in not telling Hamlet about the 'secrets of [his] prison-
house', actually does tell him a secret which has the same horrifying
effect on him, so Paracelsus, apparently restraining himself from
exposing the generous and sympathetic Festus to the full vision of
the heart's corruption, in effect spares him nothing.

Paracelsus's exaltation of hatred sounds, and is, unbalanced; its
hidden cause is his inability to tolerate the hatred which has been
directed against him, and which he had once boasted to Festus of
provoking (just as he proves unable to live without the human love
to which he had professed himself indifferent).[11] This hatred is of
two kinds, one fantasized and the other real: first, the antagonism of
his intellectual precursors, in whose footsteps he disdains to follow;[12]

[9] There is another echo of *Hamlet* shortly before this passage (iv. 118): Paracelsus
sarcastically reports that when his popularity as a teacher began to fade there was 'a
vast flourish about patient merit | Obscured awhile by flashy tricks', the phrase
'patient merit' deriving of course from the 'To be or not to be' soliloquy: 'the spurns |
That patient merit of th' unworthy takes' (III. i. 73–4).

[10] Browning reinforced this doubleness in revision: from 1849 l. 144 read 'sages
have discovered we are born', 'him' in l. 147 was changed to 'us', and 'man's' and
'His' in two following lines to 'our' and 'Our'. The effect is that Paracelsus more
clearly implicates himself in his statements about human nature.

[11] This is what differentiates Paracelsus from Don Juan in *Fifine at the Fair*, whose
praise of hatred is self-aware and self-possessed.

[12] Compare Jules's rejection, in *Pippa Passes*, of the 'fatal expertness' of traditional
art.

second, the hatred of his contemporaries, including those who had
been his students and followers. On his deathbed in Part V of the
poem, he raves in his delirium at his 'wise peers':

> Only observe: why fiends may learn from them!
> How they talk calmly of my throes — my fierce
> Aspirings, terrible watchings — each one claiming
> Its price of blood and brain; how they dissect
> And sneeringly disparage the few truths
> Got at a life's cost; they too hanging the while
> About my neck, their lies misleading me,
> Their dead names brow-beating me. Wretched crew!
> Is there a reason for your hate? My truths
> Have shaken a little the palm about each brow?
>
> (v. 159–68)

Of course Paracelsus's precursors cannot literally hate him, but there
is a powerful psychological truth in his taking personally, so to
speak, their presence in his mind. Having proclaimed himself their
adversary, he now suffers from his isolation, but at least he can
rationalize their hatred as the result of jealousy of his achievements.
This consolation is denied to him in the case of his contemporaries,
whose hatred strikes him Lear-like, naked and without protection:

> Ha, what? spit at me, and grin and shriek
> Contempt into my ear — my ear which drank
> God's accents once, and curse me? Why men, men,
> I am not form'd for it; those hideous eyes
> Will be before me sleeping, waking, praying;
> They will not let me even die: spare me, spare me
> Sinning or no, forget that, only spare me
> That horrible scorn; you thought I could support it,
> But now you see what silly fragile creature
> I am. I am not good nor bad enough,
> Not Christ, nor Cain, yet even Cain was saved
> From hate like this: let me but totter back,
> Perhaps I shall forget those jeers which creep
> Into my very brain, and shut these scorch'd
> Eyelids, and keep those mocking faces out.
>
> (v. 292–306)

I think Browning had Keats in mind when he wrote these lines.
Earlier in the scene Paracelsus speaks of the 'hooting' of those who
believe he has been exposed as a quack (v. 146); this, and the word

'fragile' (v. 299), occur in Shelley's famous attack, in the preface to
Adonais, on the *Quarterly Review*'s treatment of Keats, whose
'genius . . . was not less delicate and fragile than it was beautiful . . .
The poor fellow seems to have been hooted from the stage of life.'
Jules, in *Pippa Passes*, uses the same insult against his rival Lutwyche,
who really *is* mediocre: he looks forward to Lutwyche's eventual
downfall as 'A wretched dauber men will hoot to death' (ii. 221).[13] In
1865 Browning wrote to Julia Wedgwood:

I believe Keats *did* have death accelerated, if not induced, by that criticism.
He did not put finger in eye, nor bully[14]—but certainly felt strongly, what we
feel strongly: don't believe a man of average sensibility is ever insulted by a
blackguard without suffering enough: despise it? yes,—but you feel the slap
in the face, too: and, in this case, to feel anything unduly, was to spill the
fast-lessening life: 'the seeds of death were in him already,' say the foolish
people:—why quicken them under a melon-glass then? . . . Don't suppose
that joking about such a person's pestle & mortar, & so on, did not drop
hell fire on the sore-place.   (Curle: 128–9)[15]

For Paracelsus, however, the matter does not rest there. His anguish
at the 'hell fire' meted out to him does not lead him to die, as
Browning believed Keats had died, in a mood of 'irritability' which
'almost amounted to madness'.[16] On the contrary, Paracelsus comes
out of his delirium to embrace, in the last part of the poem, the
necessity of his suffering as part of the vision of human progress with
which he ends his life. He tells Festus:

> As yet men cannot do without contempt—
> 'Tis for their good, and therefore fit awhile
> That they reject me, and speak scorn of me;
> But after, they will know me well: I stoop
> Into a dark tremendous sea of cloud,
> But 'tis but for a time; I press God's lamp
> Close to my breast—its splendour, soon or late,
> Will pierce the gloom: I shall emerge one day.
> (v. 882–9)

[13] See p. 88, n. 21.
[14] 'Put finger in eye' means to cry, from the old nursery rhyme 'Cry, baby, cry; put
your finger in your eye'; Browning may be recalling *The Comedy of Errors*: 'no longer
will I be a fool, | To put the finger in the eye and weep' (II. ii. 202–3). 'Bully' here has
the sense of 'bluster'.
[15] I have slightly corrected Curle's text by reference to the facsimile of the manuscript between pp. 128 and 129.
[16] Browning's information (in the same letter to Julia Wedgwood) came from
Joseph Severn, who cared for Keats in his last illness.

The image of men's hatred and misprision as 'a dark tremendous sea of cloud' both naturalizes and elevates Paracelsus's suffering, and the verb 'I stoop' is finely poised between voluntary and involuntary motion. Paracelsus is reconciled to the fate he cannot avoid (the poem in which he speaks these lines is, of course, the site of his re-emergence). The lines look forward to 'Popularity', published twenty years later in *Men and Women*, where the 'true poet', though 'named a star' by the speaker, is similarly occluded and similarly promised a glorious return:

> My star, God's glow-worm! Why extend
>   That loving hand of His which leads you,
> Yet locks you safe from end to end
>   Of this dark world, unless He needs you—
> Just saves your light to spend?
>
> His clenched Hand shall unclose at last
>   I know, and let out all the beauty.
> My poet holds the future fast,
>   Accepts the coming ages' duty,
> Their present for this past.
>
>   (ll. 6–15)

The subject of 'Popularity' is in fact Keats, who is named in the last line of the poem. Browning takes Paracelsus's argument a stage further: the poet's lack of recognition is providential, part of a divine plan to make the best use of his genius; God's 'loving hand' is simultaneously a 'clenched Hand', both a guiding and restricting force. Nothing is said of the price exacted by the poet's own labour (Paracelsus's 'fierce | Aspirings, terrible watchings'), and nothing about his suffering: the implication that God's plan necessitated Keats having hell fire dropped on him is ignored. Indeed, Paracelsus's active stooping, his pressing God's lamp close to his breast, shrinks in 'Popularity' to the poet being held passively in God's hand, led and 'locked safe' in 'this dark world', a phrase which nods politely, which barely glances, at Paracelsus's 'dark tremendous sea of cloud'.

Must artists expect to be hated in their lifetime? 'Popularity' seems to flinch from the idea, preferring to think of its poet as neglected or obscured from view; but in other places Browning maintained the position he takes in *Paracelsus*, 'The Patriot', and 'One Word More'.

In relation to *Paracelsus*, indeed, he created a myth of its critical reception in which he plays a Keatsian role. He wrote to Elizabeth Barrett in September 1845 of 'the reviews & newspapers that laughed my "Paracelsus" to scorn ten years ago' (Kintner: 200), and repeated the allegation three months later, contrasting his poem's treatment with that accorded to a play by Thomas Noon Talfourd:

> my own 'Paracelsus,' printed a few months before, had been as dead a failure as 'Ion' a brilliant success . . . until Forster's notice in the 'Examiner' appeared, *every* journal that thought worth while to allude to the poem at all, treated it with entire contempt . . beginning, I think, with the 'Athenaeum' which *then* made haste to say, a few days after its publication, 'that it was not without talent but spoiled by obscurity and only an imitation of—Shelley!' . . . and that first taste was a most flattering example of what the 'craft' had in store for me . . . out of a long string of notices, one vied with its predecessor in disgust at my 'rubbish,' as their word went . . . (Kintner: 312)[17]

Browning held tenaciously to this view, which is at best misleading: *Paracelsus*, as his first biographer Mrs Orr rightly says, may not have given Browning 'his just place in popular judgement and public esteem', but 'it compelled his recognition by the leading or rising literary men of the day' (Orr: 83). Alfred Domett recorded in his diary in 1872 that Browning 'considers that he was not acknowledged much by the public till the generation succeeding ours. I suppose he knows best—but should have thought his reputation had grown gradually from 1835, or the time of publication of *Paracelsus*, the genius of which was most cordially recognized and welcomed by a *good many* of his own contemporaries' (Horsman: 55).

Browning's memory of a 'long string of notices' rubbishing the poem, which is simply false in relation to *Paracelsus*,[18] is much more accurate applied to *Sordello*, which really did bring down on its author a storm of abuse and ridicule; Browning was clearly remembering this when, in *Pippa Passes* (published a year after *Sordello*), he

---

[17] Browning's singling out of the *Athenaeum* is particularly ironic in the light of his letter to its editor, Norman MacColl, in 1876, in which he recalls the anonymous review of *Pauline* 'which gratified me and my people far beyond what will ever be the fortune of criticism now' (Hood: 172).

[18] Besides the brief notice in the *Athenaeum* which Browning paraphrases, there were three reviews of *Paracelsus* before the one in the *Examiner*; none was favourable, but none was brutal or unduly scornful. The reviews are reprinted in Kelley and Hudson: iii. 347 ff.

put into the mouth of the dissolute Bluphocks a mock-epitaph for a failed masterpiece: 'Here so and so, the mammoth, lies, Fouled to death by butterflies' (i. 290–1). The name 'Bluphocks' is said to have been derived from the *Edinburgh Review*, which was bound in a cover of blue and fox, and had been responsible among other things for printing Jeffrey's notorious review of Wordsworth's *The Excursion* (the one beginning 'This will never do').[19] The connection is suggestive. Wordsworth had reacted to Jeffrey's review very much along the lines of Browning's comment about being 'insulted by a blackguard' ('despise it? yes,—but you feel the slap in the face, too'): he wrote to Catherine Clarkson, 'You cannot scower a spot of this kind out of your mind as you may a stain out of your clothes' (Gill: 306). And in the *Essay, Supplementary to the Preface* of 1815, a work which I believe profoundly influenced Browning's whole conception of poetry, Wordsworth defended himself against Jeffrey's attack by arguing that it was a perverse tribute to his genius, that he, Wordsworth, was one of the 'select Spirits for whom it is ordained that their fame shall be in the world an existence like that of Virtue, which owes its being to the struggle it makes, and its vigour to the enemies whom it provokes'. In a 'hasty retrospect of the poetical literature of this Country for the greater part of the last two Centuries', Wordsworth then sought to prove that every great writer without exception had been neglected, slighted, or worse on their first appearance, and that this was almost an essential attribute of original genius.

Perhaps, therefore, Browning had an interest in representing *Paracelsus*, his first acknowledged publication, as having been 'laughed to scorn'. It would align him with Keats, with Wordsworth, and with the great poets whom Wordsworth saw as submitting to a law of deferred poetical gratification. This is the consolation which Christ offered to his disciples: 'If the world hate you, ye know that it hated me before it hated you. If ye were of the world, the world would love his own: but because ye are not of the world, but I have chosen you out of the world, therefore the world hateth you' (John 15: 18–19). And yet the logic of this view is sad as well as hopeful. It implies that poets face their immediate, contemporary audience as antagonists, that the relationship is at least one of difficulty and at worst one of

[19] The explanation of Bluphocks's name is given in Edward Berdoe's *Browning Cyclopaedia* (1892), 351; its source is F. J. Furnivall, who may have got it from Browning himself.

outright rejection. John Woolford has shown that Browning was not only aware of this problem, but made strenuous efforts to resolve it; he wanted to write popular works, and was disappointed (and bewildered) at the repeated failure of his attempts up to *The Ring and the Book*.[20] But this is only one side of the picture; on the other the idea persists obstinately in Browning's writing that the true poet should expect his audience (and in particular his critics) to be ignorant, ungrateful, and hostile—in fact, to hate him.

As it happens, the clearest and angriest expression of this idea was prompted by an argument over the poem 'Popularity' itself. The argument was with Ruskin, who wrote to Browning after Dante Gabriel Rossetti, in his enthusiasm, had thrust *Men and Women* on him and forced him to stay up all night reading it.[21] Ruskin's insults were veiled in good humour and sparkled with wit, but they were sharp enough for all that. He called the poems of *Men and Women* 'absolutely and literally a set of the most amazing Conundrums that ever were proposed to me . . . I look at you every day as a monkey does at a cocoanut, having great faith in the milk—hearing it rattle indeed—inside—but quite beside myself for the Fibres.' He chose 'Popularity' to comment on in detail (it 'touches the matter in hand') and ridiculed its abruptness, its compression, its elliptical syntax, and especially its rhetoric. Quoting the first two lines ('Stand still, true poet that you are, | I know you; let me try and draw you'), he inquired: 'Does this mean: literally—stand still? or where was the poet figuratively going—and why couldn't he be drawn as he went?' He objected to 'locks you safe' in l. 8: 'How does God's hand lock him; do you mean—keeps him from being seen?—and how does it make him safe. Why is a poet safer or more locked up than anybody else? I go on—in hope.' He did, and got carried away somewhat: the letter gets funnier, but also more wounding. When Browning compares the poet to a fisherman bringing to land the shells from which Tyrian dye was extracted, Ruskin bursts out: 'Now, where are you going to—this is, I believe pure malice against *me*, for having said that painters should always grind their own colours.' He pounced on ll. 49–50 ('The bee goes singing to her groom | Drunken and overbold'): 'I thought there was only one Queen-bee and she was never out o'nights—nor came home drunk or disorderly.'

[20] See ch. 2, 'The Problem of Audience', in Woolford 1988.
[21] For Ruskin's letter, see DeLaura: 324–7; for Browning's reply, see Collingwood: 8. 199–202.

Browning defended himself vigorously against these specific charges (his gloss on 'Stand still' is an exemplary piece of practical criticism), but faced with the attitude from which Ruskin's objections sprang he could do no more than blankly oppose his own: 'We don't read poetry the same way, by the same law; it is too clear. I cannot begin writing poetry till my imaginary reader has conceded licences to me which you demur at altogether.' The issue goes deeper than this, however; for it implies that such readers might exist, even if Ruskin was not one of them. But Browning, with an eloquence as unguarded as Ruskin's, went on:

Do you think poetry was ever generally understood—or can be? Is the business of it to tell people what they know already, as they know it, and so precisely that they shall be able to cry out—'Here you should supply *this* —*that*, you evidently pass over, and I'll help you from my own stock'? It is all teaching, on the contrary, and the people hate to be taught. They say other-wise,—make foolish fables about Orpheus enchanting stocks and stones, poets standing up and being worshipped,—all nonsense and impossible dreaming. A poet's affair is with God, to whom he is accountable, and of whom is his reward: look elsewhere, and you find misery enough. Do you believe people understand *Hamlet*? The last time I saw it acted, the heartiest applause of the night went to a little by-play of the actor's own—who, to simulate madness in a hurry, plucked forth his handkerchief and flourished it hither and thither: certainly a third of the play, with no end of noble things, had been (as from time immemorial) suppressed, with the auditory's amplest acquiescence and benediction. Are these wasted, therefore? No—they act upon a very few, who react upon the rest: as Goldsmith says, 'some lords, my acquaintance, that settle the nation, are pleased to be kind.'

Browning's language, alive with scorn, picks out the indignity of diminishing *Hamlet* to 'a little by-*play* of the actor's own', and remembers Hamlet himself instructing the player not to 'saw the air too much with your hand' (III. ii. 5–6). The example leads him into an extraordinary and extreme metaphor: Goldsmith's aristocratic patrons become a figure for the *intellectual* elite, whose understand-ing is alone of importance to poets, since it is this élite who will dictate their standing with the wider public. (I think we can take it that the Goldsmith metaphor works through time as well as in the present: Shakespeare's fame is determined by 'a very few' in each age.) In a letter Browning wrote soon afterwards to his publisher Edward Chapman, reacting bitterly to the adverse reviews of *Men and Women*, the notion of the élite comes up again, this time with the added twist that Browning complains of their *not* 'settling the nation' as they should:

As to my own Poems, they must be left to Providence and that fine sense of discrimination which I never cease to meditate upon and admire in the public: they cry out for new things and when you furnish them with what they cried for, 'it's *so* new,' they grunt. The half-dozen people who know and could impose their opinions on the whole sty of grunters say nothing to *them* (I don't wonder) and speak so low in my own ear that it's lost to all intents and purposes.   (DeVane and Knickerbocker: 92–3).[22]

Browning now finds himself in the same position as Wordsworth in the *Essay*: he is driven by the pressure of critical incomprehension to abandon thoughts of brotherhood or fellowship with his readers, in favour of an uncompromising, and tragic, doctrine of poetic singularity. The example of Orpheus, cited by Browning as a 'foolish fable' of 'poets standing up and being worshipped', is doubly foolish in view of Orpheus's eventual fate; far from enchanting his readers ('stocks and stones' in Browning's sardonic adaptation of the myth), the poet is more than likely to be torn to pieces by them.

Browning's insistence that poetry is 'all teaching' and that 'the people hate to be taught' returns us to the identification of the poet with Moses and with a prophetic, and therefore unpopular, mission. It is not just 'people' (most people, people in general) who hate to be taught, but '*the* people': the definite article stresses the poet's relation to a collective audience, a tribe, a nation. It is the collective voice which Browning records in 'One Word More', murmuring against its saviour: 'How should'st thou, of all men, smite, and save us?' But it is against the critics, the tribunes of the people, that the fiercest of his polemic is directed. Their hatred of being taught, in Browning's

[22] One of the reticent half-dozen was, ironically enough, Ruskin himself: as Browning put it to Chapman in the same letter, this 'layer-down of law in matters of art' had only just got around to publishing his fulsome praise of 'The Tomb at St. Praxed's' (in vol. iv of *Modern Painters*), eleven years after the poem's appearance; and, Browning went on, 'nobody will snip that round into a neat little paragraph, and head it "Ruskin on Browning," and stick it among the "News of the Week," "Topics of the Day," as the friendly method is!' (p. 93). If this was a hint to Chapman it had no effect; his lack of energy and initiative eventually led to Browning's change of publisher. As for adverse criticism, Browning believed that it had more effect on literature than on art: commenting on the poor reception of one of his son Pen's paintings, he wrote: 'how harmless is all such criticism when a picture is once fairly hung up and open to view for the next month or more! In the case of a *book*—the ill word may possibly *shut up* its contents altogether from the reader of the criticism, if he believes it fair and good' (McAleer 1966: 104).

representation of it, seems more like real hatred than, say, a lazy disinclination, and triggers in him a corresponding hatred. It can be seen in the animal and insect imagery which he constantly uses to describe them. Already, in *Sordello*, the critic Naddo is 'busiest of the tribe | Of genius-haunters—how shall I describe | What grubs or nips, or rubs, or rips—your louse | For love, your flea for hate' (ii. 821–4).[23] Browning's contemptuous reference, in his letter to Chapman about *Men and Women*, to the 'whole sty of grunters', is echoed in another to the same correspondent: 'don't take to heart the zoological utterances I have stopped my ears against at Galignani's of late. "Whoo-oo-oo-oo" mouths the big monkey—"Whee-ee-ee-ee" squeaks the little monkey and such a dig with the end of my umbrella as I should give the brutes if I couldn't keep my temper, and consider how they miss their nuts and gingerbread!' (DeVane and Knickerbocker: 85).[24] Furious at the review of *Dramatis Personae* in the *Edinburgh Review*, he wrote to Julia Wedgwood: 'I had fancied that the bug-holes of that crazy old bedstead were plugged-up at this time of the day,—but no, here is the nastiness on one again! or rather off already, for to smash it would make things worse' (Curle: 103).[25] Twenty years later, in the poem 'Of Pacchiarotto, and How He Worked in Distemper', Browning compares his critics to geese 'born to cackle and waddle | And bite at man's heel as goose-wont is' (ll. 566–7). His own two pet geese were called 'Edinburgh' and 'Quarterly'. In a letter of 1887 professing indifference to criticism the same simile comes up: 'I have had too long an experience of the inability of the human goose to do other than cackle when

[23] The louse/flea parallel probably recalls Johnson's refusal to distinguish between the poetical merits of Derrick and Smart: 'Sir, there is no settling the point of precedency between a louse and a flea'.

[24] Galignani's was a publishing house in Florence whose reading room received copies of foreign newspapers and journals. 'Nuts and gingerbread' refers to the trivial commonplaces and decorative language of conventional verse with which Browning refuses to 'treat' his readers.

[25] This review, by William Stigand, also took a retrospective look at Browning's career by considering the 3-vol. *Poetical Works* of 1863 along with *Dramatis Personae*, a fact which added to Browning's annoyance: 'The clever creature rummages over my wardrobe of thirty years' accumulation, strips every old coat of its queer button or odd tag and tassel, then holds them out, "So Mr B. goes dressed now!"—of the cut of the coats, not a word.' John Woolford, however (in Shattock and Wolff: 123–5), points out that Stigand's review itself attracted criticism in other journals, in keeping with a change in the way periodical criticism was viewed in the 1860s. Browning's ideas about such criticism were formed in the 1830s and 1840s, when the genre was more partisan, more self-serving, and more viciously personal.

benevolent, and hiss when malicious; and no amount of goose criticism shall make me lift a heel at what waddles behind it' (Griffin and Minchin: 259).

The 'human goose' singled out for kicking in 'Of Pacchiarotto' was Alfred Austin, Poet Laureate in succession to Tennyson (an elevation Browning luckily did not live to see). Austin is travestied as the mediocre painter Pacchiarotto in the first part of the poem; in the concluding section Browning does all but print his name. He presents his critics as a band of musical chimney-sweeps come to 'serenade' him on May morning, and sends them packing with the threat that his housemaid will fling a chamber-pot over them from the upstairs window. He then alludes directly to Austin:

> While as for Quilp-Hop-o'-my-thumb there,
> Banjo-Byron that twangs the strum-strum there—
> He'll think, as the pickle he curses,
> I've discharged on his pate his own verses!
> 'Dwarfs are saucy,' says Dickens: so, sauced in
> Your own sauce . . .
>
> No, please! For
> 'Who would be satirical
> On a thing so very small?'—PRINTER'S DEVIL.
>
>   (ll. 529–34 and Browning's footnote)[26]

The mockery of Austin's height was denounced by the *Examiner* as a 'gross assault': 'common feeling for several generations has discountenanced attacks upon a rival's natural defects of body as being brutal and unmanly' (Hood: 362). But Browning did not feel discountenanced: he defended himself, in a letter to Edmund Gosse, by means of a disingenuous play on the literal and metaphorical senses of 'little':

One particular piece of blackguardism . . . could only save its author from a kicking by the charitable hope that he was too small for that treatment. I never was unlucky enough to set eyes on the man: if he *is* physically as well as morally and intellectually a dwarf—you may be sure I should have considered him a pygmy had his stature been that of Goliath. But I really meant nothing except to enliven my visionary dance of chimney-sweeps by a grotesque monkey-image . . . and it seems that one fillip more than avenges fifty flea-bites. . . . What man of the ordinary size ever yet ducked down so

[26] The 'Printer's Devil' is (Browning would have thought) Swift, in 'Doctor Delany's Villa', though modern scholarship attributes this poem to Sheridan.

low,—hooted from his hiding at what he presumed to call his 'fellows,'—and then tried to stand on tiptoe by their side, as a 'poet,' just as if
nothing had happened?   (Hood: 175–6)[27]

It would be hard to believe that Browning's jibes were the result of a
coincidental choice of epithet; whether he had met Austin or not
makes no difference to what was a matter of common knowledge in
literary circles. But in any event the question is settled by a letter to
his brother-in-law George Barrett written over a year before the
publication of the poem, in which the prose equivalent of the passage
in 'Pacchiarotto' is found, with additional sarcasms on 'my little bug
of an Austin' (Landis: 300). The coarseness of Browning's justification
follows naturally from that of the original insult, but it is curious to
set alongside it his indignation at the personal attacks on Keats—like
Austin a small man, who 'stood tip-toe upon a little hill' and had the
impertinence to believe himself a poet. 'Don't suppose that joking
about such a person's pestle & mortar, & so on, did not drop hell
fire on the sore-place.' Is Browning justified in dropping hell fire on
Austin's sore-place because Keats's pretension was right and Austin's
wrong?

I should add that almost all Browning's earliest recorded mentions
of Austin contain allusions to his size. He calls him 'a filthy little
snob' and a 'little fool' in a letter to Isa Blagden in 1870, and tells a
humiliating anecdote about him which concludes: 'Off went the
"blighted being" in such a rage as never entered into a flea on a
dog's back at the first sprinkle of Scotch snuff bestowed upon him as
a notice to quit' (McAleer 1951: 332). Two years later Alfred Domett,
recently returned from New Zealand, asked Browning who Austin
was: ' "A scurvy little fellow who always abuses me" was the reply'
(Horsman: 67).

To another correspondent Browning emphasized that his attack
on Austin was linked to a larger design: 'He has been flea-biting me
for many years past in whatever rag of a newspaper he could hop
into . . . I don't mind leaving on record that I had just that fancy
about the people who "forty years long in the wilderness" criticized
my works' (Griffin and Minchin: 260).[28] The reference to 'forty
years' is close to being literally exact (in 1876 it was forty-three years

---

[27] Browning gave Mrs Fitzgerald the same explanation, in virtually the same words
(McAleer 1966: 36).

[28] He made the same point in the letter to Mrs Fitzgerald mentioned in the

since the publication of *Pauline*) but that, of course, is not its main significance: it takes us back to the Moses allusion in 'One Word More', to the poet as prophet slighted by his people. We can now see a connection between the imagery of littleness, of fleas and bugs, and the prophet 'bidding drink a crowd *beneath* him'. Artists who look down on their public may *represent* criticism as 'flea-biting', but this very fact suggests that they *feel* it as something different. Browning's stored-up vengeance comes from a deep sense of injury, and yet the injury could only be as deep as his own self-image allowed. In 'Of Pacchiarotto' he mocks his critics for believing they could serve notice on him to quit his poetical premises:

> Mine's freehold, by grace of the grand Lord
> Who lets out the ground here,—my landlord:
> To him I pay quit-rent—devotion;
> Nor hence shall I budge, I've a notion,
> Nay, here shall my whistling and singing
> Set all his street's echoes a-ringing
> Long after the last of your number
> Has ceased my front court to encumber . . .
>
> (ll. 510–17)

As Browning told Ruskin twenty years before, 'A poet's affair is with God, to whom he is accountable, and of whom is his reward'. This proclamation of god-given status accounts for the ambivalence with which Browning treats the harsh criticism he received. It was galling to be hated, but it was also uplifting. And the artist's own hatred is then, itself, sanctified. In the Mosaic gesture of *smiting* the rock to release the living water lurk other Biblical smitings, in which prophets themselves may put on the mantle of God's hatred. The 'crowd beneath', if we trace the darkest thread of this connection, may remind us of the 'mad people' in *Sordello* whom the great warrior Salinguerra remembers 'smiting' in the course of a bloody skirmish at Vicenza:

> the edge,
> Use the edge—shear, thrust, hew, melt down the wedge,
> Let out the black of those black upturned eyes!
> Hell—are they sprinkling fire too? the blood fries

preceding note: 'I always intended, for the benefit of my successors, to leave on record some memorial of my feeling for the authorities who have sate in judgment on me this long while'.

> And hisses on your brass gloves as they tear
> Those upturned faces choaking with despair.
>
> (iv. 705–10)

The repetition of 'upturned' is as important here as the surging violence of the verbs. This is 'dropping hell-fire on the plague-spot' with a vengeance, except that the tables are turned and it is now the 'crowd beneath' who are 'sprinkled'. In what might be a nightmare image of the mutual hatred of prophet and tribe, they look up to him and are well and truly smitten.

6

Perfect Hatred

And I hope that you die
And your death'll come soon
I will follow your casket
In the pale afternoon
And I'll watch while you're lowered
Down to your deathbed
And I'll stand o'er your grave
'Til I'm sure that you're dead . . .

(Bob Dylan)[1]

Private reasons great or small
Can be seen in the eyes of those that call
To make all that should be killed to crawl
While others say don't hate nothing at all
Except hatred.

(Bob Dylan)[2]

Do not I hate them, O Lord, that hate thee? and am not I grieved with those that rise up against thee? I hate them with perfect hatred: I count them mine enemies.

(Psalms 139: 22)

THERE are many instances of righteous hatred in the Bible, especially in the Old Testament. It can take the form of hating a specific sin, as in Exodus 19: 21 ('men of truth, hating covetousness'), or of hating wickedness generally, as in Psalms 97: 10 ('Ye that love the Lord, hate evil') and Amos 5: 15 ('Hate the evil, and love the good'). 'Wisdom', in the book of Proverbs, declares: 'The fear of the Lord is to hate evil: pride, and arrogancy, and the evil way, and the froward

---

[1] 'Masters of War' (*The Freewheelin' Bob Dylan*, Columbia 1963).
[2] 'Its Alright, Ma (I'm Only Bleeding)' (*Bringing It All Back Home*, Columbia, 1965).

mouth, do I hate'. These abstractions are given vivid physical correlates in the same book, in verses which tell us that God himself is a hater:

These six things doth the Lord hate: yea, seven are an abomination unto him: a proud look, a lying tongue, and hands that shed innocent blood, an heart that deviseth wicked imaginations, feet that be swift in running to mischief, a false witness that speaketh lies, and he that soweth discord among brethren.   (6: 16–19)

God also hates, among other things, human sacrifice (Deuteronomy 12: 31) and robbery for burnt offerings (Isaiah 61: 8); he hates and despises the feast days and solemn assemblies of the sinful Israelites (Amos 5: 21), abhors the excellency of Jacob and hates his palaces (Amos 6: 8). Naturally enough (if you accept that the Old Testament God, at any rate, isn't the sort to turn the other cheek), he hates those who hate *him*: 'for I the Lord thy God am a jealous God, visiting the iniquity of the fathers upon the children unto the third and fourth generation of them that hate me' (Exodus 20: 5, a gloss on the second commandment). Like God's anger, to which it is of course closely connected, God's hatred (and that felt by the righteous who take his part) is a persistent motif in the Bible; it is as though it bears no relation to the equally strong condemnation of hatred as a manifestation of human wickedness.

It may be argued that hatred of sin is not the same thing as the sin of hatred. Browning or his characters sometimes enjoin the former in a thoroughly conventional way: Don Juan, with the air of stating a truism, says in *Fifine at the Fair* that 'Life means—learning to abhor | The false, and love the true' (ll. 1513–14); in *La Saisiaz*, similarly, we read of 'life's lesson, hate of evil, love of good' (l. 285); in 'Development' Browning says that one of the things he learned from Homer was that his 'aim should be to loathe, like Peleus' son, | A lie as Hell's Gate' (ll. 100–1).[3] The trouble with these formulas is that they deal in abstractions. What happens when the 'false' and the 'evil' are embodied in people, classes, or nations? Aneurin Bevan got into trouble for saying: 'No amount of cajolery, and no attempts at ethical and social seduction, can eradicate from my heart a deep burning hatred for the Tory Party ... So far as I am concerned they are lower than vermin.'[4] The second part is the give-away, moving

[3] 'Peleus' son' is Achilles, but there is in fact no reference in the *Iliad* to his hatred of lying.

[4] Speech at Manchester, 4 July 1948.

from a class to its members, and suggesting that such hatred may be in itself an abstracting or dehumanizing process. Bevan's resistance to 'ethical and social seduction' also implies that we are constantly being seduced away from righteous hatred, instead of *into* it. 'Dear Bathurst', Dr Johnson told Mrs Piozzi, 'was a man to my very heart's content: he hated a fool, and he hated a rogue, and he hated a whig; he was a very good hater.' The triplet fool–rogue–whig seems meant to suggest an ascending order of hatefulness, but the third term, wittily substituting a political for a moral antagonism, springs an ambush on the reader and asks him not for righteous endorsement ('good hater' = 'hater of evil') but for laughing tolerance of the gruff old Tory's prejudices ('good hater' = 'hater of things I dislike'). We know, too, that Johnson's hatred of whigs did not mean 'hatred of every person who is a whig': Boswell's elaborate account of the meeting he arranged between Johnson and Wilkes is designed precisely to make this point, but it also implicitly suggests the moral quandary in which we may find ourselves if we hate on principle. 'Have you a fundamental moral objection to killing?' the judge asks the conscientious objector in James Michie's comic and fearful poem 'Dooley is a Traitor', to which the doomed wag replies:

'No objection at all, sir,' I said.
'There's a deal of the world I'd rather see dead—
Such as Johnny Stubbs, or Fred Settle or my last landlord, Mr. Syme.
Give me a gun and your blessing, your Honour, and I'll be killing them all
   the time.
But my conscience says a clear no
To killing a crowd of gentlemen I don't know.
Why, I'd as soon think of killing a worshipful judge,
High-court, like yourself (against whom, God knows, I've got no grudge—
So far), as murder a heap of foreign folk.
If you've got no grudge, you've got no joke
To laugh at after.'

(ll. 9–19)[5]

Dooley's joking evasion of abstract moral categories rests on a head/ heart division which is as absolute in its own way as the morality he rejects: called upon to join the 'fight | Against wrong ideas on behalf of the Right' and to 'help to destroy evil ideas', he replies 'I couldn't

---

[5] The text is from Philip Larkin's *Oxford Book of Twentieth-Century Verse*.

find it in my heart to be unkind | To an idea'. His position is the exact counterpart of Swift's, who, in a letter to Pope, attempts with equal playfulness to make this distinction between classes and individuals: 'I have ever hated all nations, professions and communities, and all my love is toward individuals; for instance, I hate the tribe of lawyers, but I love Counsellor Such-a-one, Judge Such-a-one: so with physicians—I will not speak of my own trade—soldiers, English, Scotch, French, and the rest. But principally I hate and detest that animal called man, although I heartily love John, Peter, Thomas, and so forth' (29 September 1725).

Does it help, then, to be forthrightly personal?

> Here lies the Earl of Leicester
> Who governed the estates
> Whom the earth could never living love,
> And the just heaven now hates.

This epitaph, attributed to Ben Jonson in a nineteenth-century collection which Browning may have seen,[6] is nothing if not pre-emptive: it expresses its author's confidence more than it commands the reader's assent, and its moral effect is to call into question the author's idea of what a heaven's for. If hatred itself is a sin, then it, too, may be righteously hated. Tennyson wrote that the poet is 'Dowered with the hate of hate' ('The Poet', l. 3); in one of the epigraphs to this chapter, Bob Dylan tells us—or says that 'others' tell us—to 'hate nothing at all | Except hatred'—although another epigraph comes from a famous paean of hatred by him. These paradoxes return us to the question of language: of whether the same word, 'hatred', can contain different meanings in separate compartments.

At times Browning shows righteous hatred in a subtler and more complex light than is suggested by the examples I have given. A morbid light, in the case of 'Childe Roland to the Dark Tower Came', where a retributive theology governs the landscape: the speaker is repelled by the sight of a 'stiff blind horse . . . Thrust out past service from the devil's stud . . . I never saw a brute I hated so— | He must be wicked to deserve such pain' (ll. 76–84).[7] Taking a vengeful God's part is not, however, always associated in Browning's work with spiritual sickness or derangement. In *Sordello*, after describing the appalling crimes of the thirteenth-century Italian warlords

---

[6] Tissington, *Collection of Epitaphs* (1857).
[7] See the discussion of 'Childe Roland' in Ch. 11.

Ecelin III and his brother Alberic ('Kings of the gag and flesh-hook, screw and whip') Browning reflects with apparent coolness on their equally appalling fate, especially that of Alberic:

> Ecelin perished: and I think grass grew
> Never so pleasant as in valley Rù
> By San Zenon where Alberic in turn
> Saw his exasperated captors burn
> Seven children with their mother, and, regaled
> So far, tied on to a wild horse, was trailed
> To death through raunce and bramble-bush: I take
> God's part and testify that mid the brake
> Wild o'er his castle on Zenone's knoll
> You hear its one tower left, a belfry, toll—
> Cherups the contumacious grasshopper,
> Rustles the lizard and the cushats chirre
> Above the ravage . . .

(vi. 773–85)

Ecelin gets just two words, though Browning certainly knew the old chronicles which would have told him how, at the siege of Milan, 'being wounded and made a prisoner, he tore open the lips of his wound, that he might die as cruelly as he lived' (cited in Woolford and Karlin: i. 762). Ecelin's lips are sealed here; and is Browning really saying that he views with equanimity, or worse, the burning alive of Alberic's family and his own death by torture?

The main historical source for the events, Giambattista Verci's *Storia degli Ecelini*, gives a long account which includes Alberic's pathetic farewell speech to his wife and children and a rhetorically heightened account of his death-scene; Browning's treatment is almost flippant (Alberic, as a gourmet of torture, is 'regaled' by his suffering). Yet it happens that we know from sources outside the poem that Browning was profoundly affected by his knowledge of this event, and that the landscape he describes, which is near to his beloved Asolo and which he first saw during his trip to Italy in 1838, haunted him all his life. (Indeed, the 'one tower left' of Alberic's stronghold, the first appearance in Browning's poetry of this central symbolic motif, leads directly to Childe Roland's Dark Tower.)[8] Katharine Bronson records that during the last year of his life he

[8] Ruined towers and other structures in Browning's poetry include the turret where Luigi and his mother meet in the third episode of *Pippa Passes*, the 'strange square black turret' on one of the isles of the siren in 'England in Italy' (l. 219), the 'single

would point out San Zenone to visitors as 'scene of the most fearful tragedy in all history', and that 'If his listener seemed interested he would relate in a few fiery sentences the story of Alberico, betrayed in his last stronghold; how the Trevisani determined to extirpate the race of Eccelini from the earth, and how, to this end, they destroyed Alberico, his wife, and five children, by tortures too terrible to describe' (Meredith: 129).[9] Mrs Bronson also relates that, when Browning revisited the 'one tower left', he looked over the 'wild land at the foot of the eminence' and said: 'Just think of Alberico tied to the heels of his horse, dragged to death over those sharp rocks and stones!' Browning's fascination with the manner of Alberic's death has a literary as well as historical origin: it echoes the death of Hippolytus, dragged to death by his own horses after his father Theseus cursed him. The emotion which Browning suppressed in this passage returns in full force in a poem written soon after *Sordello*, 'Artemis Prologuizes'. There Browning makes full use of Verci, of Euripides' *Hippolytus*, and of Ovid's *Metamorphoses* in the description of Hippolytus' death.[10]

Hippolytus, of course, is innocent, but if this accounts for the difference in tone it would make Browning like Childe Roland: Alberic 'must be wicked to deserve such pain'. The answer seems rather to lie in Browning's phrase 'I take God's part' (which means both 'I am on God's side' and 'I take God's part *on me*', 'I act for God').[11] To what does Browning 'testify'? Not to the righteousness of the Trevisani's remorseless hatred, or the pity and terror of Alberic's punishment; Browning, like God, takes the long view. We have come a long way from the Carlylean impulse, so evident at the start of the poem, to 'single out | Sordello, compassed murkily about | With ravage of six long sad hundred years' (i. 7–9), to this tender and ironic evocation of natural beauty and fertility 'above the ravage'. The site of hatred and suffering modulates through time to this 'one tower left', in an anticipation of 'Love Among the Ruins'; and the

little turret that remains' in 'Love Among the Ruins' (l. 37), the 'old tomb's ruin' in 'Two in the Campagna' (l. 14), and, also in the Roman Campagna, the 'old malicious tower' mentioned by the Pope in *The Ring and the Book* (x. 626). See Ch. 11 for further discussion of some of these occurrences.

[9] Mrs Bronson's 'five children' is an error: see Woolford and Karlin: i. 763.

[10] Lines 39–61; for the literary allusions, see Woolford and Karlin: ii. 109–10.

[11] The Biblical text to which Browning alludes here is Moses' cry in Exod. 32: 26, 'Who is on the Lord's side?', the prelude to a massacre of idolaters. Browning uses it again in *The Ring and the Book* v. 1549 and x. 2099.

question of the poet's engagement with the passions of the past, his
justification of necessary or gratuitous cruelties, is deflected into a
question about the question, thrown at the reader:

> . . . and the cushats chirre
> Above the ravage: there, at deep of day
> A week since, heard I the old Canon say
> He saw with his own eyes a barrow burst
> And Alberic's huge skeleton unhearsed
> Five years ago, no more: he added, June's
> The month for carding off our first cocoons
> The silkworms fabricate—a double news,
> Nor he nor I could tell the worthier. Choose!
>
> (vi. 784–92)

Against the grotesque intrusion of the past is set the busy, contented,
prosperous life of the present. But the choice we are offered between
them is an invidious one, for the news is 'double' in a double sense.
The two 'items', symbols of death in life and life in death (since the
cocoon is a symbol of the dead awaiting resurrection), are bound to
each other. Neither has meaning without the other. Taking God's
part here means not aligning oneself with divine wrath, but with the
action of time over which God presides.

It is typical of Browning not just to have returned to this subject in a
later poem, but to have thought about it from a quite different angle.
'The Heretic's Tragedy' (published in *Men and Women*, 1855) also
concerns an evil potentate who is tortured and executed to popular
acclaim. But those who 'take God's part' in this 'Middle-Age Interlude' are in a very different position from that of the poet-narrator of
Sordello. Browning seems to be looking back at his earlier self and
taking polemical issue with it.

The 'interlude' is both a popular commemoration of the event of
du Bourg-Molay's execution, and a sermon on it. The sermon is
based on a thoroughly orthodox Christian idea, that God's hatred of
sin is the exact counterpart of his love and mercy: as the 'Abbot
Deodaet' says at the start,

> Give both the Infinites their due—
> Infinite mercy, but, I wis,
> As infinite a justice too.
>
> (ll. 6–8)

In du Bourg-Molay's case, infinite justice demands retribution for the 'Unknown Sin' he has committed; and the poem describes how, while being burned alive, he has the presumption to call on the name of the Saviour he had insulted and profaned: "'Tis John the mocker cries, Save thou me!' (l. 53). He has 'made God's menace an idle word' (l. 54), believing that, when it came down to it, God wouldn't have the heart to punish him; he is proved wrong. Just as God's love takes love to its infinite potentiality, so his wrath takes hatred to its ultimate consummation:

So, as John called now, through the fire amain,
  On the Name, he had cursed with, all his life—
To the Person, he bought and sold again—
  For the Face, with his daily buffets rife—
Feature by feature It took its place!
  And his voice like a mad dog's choking bark
At the steady Whole of the Judge's Face—
  Died. Forth John's soul flared into the dark.

SUBJOINETH THE ABBOT DEODAET
  God help all poor souls lost in the dark!

(ll. 80–7)

This is how the poem ends, but not at all how it has gone on; readers who know the poem will realize that the account I have given of it is very one-sided. The last lines, with their indignant emphasis, their passionate severity, and with that sudden touch of tenderness at the close, suggest that while Browning may not agree with the theology being expounded (any more than with Bishop Blougram's) he is allowing it to speak 'sincerely' for itself. It is, after all, true to the Dante of 'One Word More', who 'loved well because he hated'. But what are we to make of these lines, which come earlier in the poem?

In the midst is a goodly gallows built;
  'Twixt fork and fork, a stake is stuck;
But first they set divers tumbrils a-tilt,
  Make a trench all round with the city muck,
Inside they pile log upon log, good store;
  Faggots not few, blocks great and small,
Reach a man's mid-thigh, no less, no more,—
  For they mean he should roast in the sight of all.
CHORUS
  We mean he should roast in the sight of all.

Good sappy bavins that kindle forthwith;
   Billets that blaze substantial and slow;
Pine-stump split deftly, dry as pith;
   Larch-heart that chars to a chalk-white glow;
Then up they hoist me John in a chafe,
   Sling him fast like a hog to scorch,
Spit in his face, then leap back safe,
   Sing 'Laudes' and bid clap-to the torch.
CHORUS
   Laus Deo—who bids clap-to the torch.

John of the Temple, whose fame so bragged,
   Is burning alive in Paris square!
How can he curse, if his mouth is gagged?
   Or wriggle his neck, with a collar there?
Or heave his chest, while a band goes round?
   Or threat with his fist, since his arms are spliced?
Or kick with his feet, now his legs are bound?
   —Thinks John—I will call upon Jesus Christ.
[*Here one crosseth himself.*

(ll. 19–44)

In these lines there is little of the nobility of hatred—little, indeed, of
the Abbot Deodaet. Instead, the spirit of medieval Catholicism—
naïve, jovial, savage—appears at the sardonic behest of a mid-
nineteenth-century liberal Protestant, who is both horrified and fascinated by its relish for cruelty. Perhaps there is a dig at Ruskin's
praise of medieval workmanship and its relation to religious faith in
the way these pious butchers display their knowledge and apprecia-
tion of the different qualities of the wood used for the fire. Certainly
the precision of the detail, the neatness of the arrangements, and the
gusto with which they are carried out, are deliberately incongruous
and offensive.

Is Browning making fun of religious hatred by showing its link to
grotesque barbarity? This reading would be supported by covert and
ironic links between John and Christ (both executed for blasphemy,
both spat upon and reviled by the mob) and by placing alongside the
sadistic enjoyment of the victim's helplessness in ll. 39–43 Browning's
delighted account of the Leveller John Lilburne's behaviour: 'who,
when pilloried, or carted rather, "did justify himself to all men,"
whereon they gagged him and tied his hands lest he should gesticulate
and explain something by that; "yet did he protest against them by a

stamping with his feet," to the no small comfort of his stout heart, I warrant' (Kenyon 1906: 118–19).[12] Browning loved such cramped, expressive gestures: he wrote to Elizabeth Barrett, at around the same period as this letter, of watching a member of the audience at a performance of Beethoven's *Fidelio* unable to express his admiration with his whole body because of the crush around him, but managing to raise an arm above the crowd: 'and this arm waved and exulted as if "for the dignity of the whole body,"—relieved it of its dangerous accumulation of repressed excitability' (Kintner: 156–7).[13] Denied the language of the body, John's 'accumulation of repressed excitability' finds an inward expression: his appeal to Christ is thus an appeal *from* the crowd to God, an appeal which, again, we might expect Browning to treat with sympathy.[14]

We might therefore conclude that the poem has a moral aim of its own—'religious hatred, especially communal religious hatred, is a corrupting and hateful phenomenon'—which counters the moral expressed *within* the poem, that of God's righteous and remorseless justice. But this would be to ignore the sublimity of the ending, from which all traces of hateful enjoyment have disappeared; it would also be to ignore the more disturbing possibility that the poem invites us to share in the very emotions it condemns. We are left with an inconsistent and unstable text, where the direction of our sympathy is unclear or subject to violent alternations. In order to understand why Browning might have designed such an outcome we need to go back to the poem's initial premiss, the historical fiction on which it is founded.

Browning's prefatory 'editorial' note speaks of the 'interlude' being a 'glimpse of the burning of Jacques du Bourg-Molay . . . as

[12] Browning had already alluded to this incident, in an earlier letter to Domett, as an image of his own writing: 'wishing you to consider these scratches but as so many energetic "kickings of the feet" (such as those by which John Lilburne "signified his meaning" when they gagged his jaws at the pillory)' (p. 108).

[13] The quotation is from *Macbeth*, v. i, the dialogue between the doctor and Lady Macbeth's waiting-gentlewoman as they watch her sleep-walking: 'What a sigh is there! The heart is sorely charg'd. | I would not have such a heart in my bosom for the dignity of the whole body.' That a phrase associated with guilt and murder should have occurred to Browning when he wanted to describe an opera-lover's irrepressible enthusiasm raises a question about the doubleness or interchangeability of the terms *love* and *hate* in Browning: see Ch. 8.

[14] Fear of the mob was never as strong in Browning as in other Victorian writers (such as Dickens or Tennyson), but the idea of an individual being tortured to death by an exultant multitude may have touched another nerve in him, that of the artist's martyrdom by an ignorant and cruel public.

distorted by the refraction from Flemish brain to brain, during the course of a couple of centuries'. The process of time, therefore, has the reverse effect to that in *Sordello*: it has 'distorted' the nature of the real historical event, and has therefore displaced the object of attention from that event to its representation. If *Sordello* is a meditation on history, 'The Heretic's Tragedy' is a meditation on fiction: doubly so, indeed, because Browning has made up the 'document' itself, and because within that document history has been transformed into fiction by a process of 'refraction'. This process also takes place in *The Ring and the Book* (yet another poem about the execution of a wicked aristocrat). The story of Guido's trial and execution follows the same pattern of temporal erosion, and as in 'The Heretic's Tragedy' what is left is a text: 'Ever and ever more diminutive . . . Dwindled into no bigger than a book' (i. 669–71). But the crucial difference is that the textual residue, the Old Yellow Book, is *not* invented, but is, as Browning continually insists, 'pure crude fact', the fragment from which the poet can 'calculate . . . the lost proportions of the style' (i. 677–8). In 'The Heretic's Tragedy' no such calculation is desired: what interests Browning here is the grossness of the refraction itself.

Jacques du Bourg-Molay was the last Grand Master of the Order of the Knights Templars, which was suppressed in 1313 by Pope Clement V on the orders of King Philip IV of France. Whether the charges (of heresy, simony, sorcery, etc.) against du Bourg-Molay and many other Templars were true or not, they were simply the pretext for the purge; the real reason was that Philip coveted the Order's enormous wealth. In fact, when he was first brought to the stake du Bourg-Molay recanted his confession, which had been extracted from him by torture; he was taken back to prison, but almost immediately brought out again and executed. He died as innocent a Grand Master of the Order of the Knights Templars as it was possible to be in that venal age—Dante's age.

To begin with, then, the 'glimpse' afforded by the poem of this event is 'distorted' in the fundamental sense that it accepts a falsehood as true. Again the contrast with both *Sordello* and *The Ring and the Book* is striking: these are works where a Carlylean confidence and energy informs the act of historical resurrection, such that Browning can affirm, at the outset of *The Ring and the Book*, that after his first reading of the Old Yellow Book he grasped the truth of the story:

> The life in me abolished the death of things,
> Deep calling unto deep: as then and there
> Acted itself over again once more
> The tragic piece. I saw with my own eyes
> In Florence as I trod the terrace, breathed
> The beauty and the fearfulness of night,
> How it had run, this round from Rome to Rome . . .

(i. 520–6)

The poet's insight *restores* life to the original event, which then acts *itself* before him: he depicts himself as an eyewitness to the events, a spectator of the drama, and (in the other sense of *seeing*) an interpreter of both. In 'The Heretic's Tragedy' such confidence is burlesqued by the numerous mistakes of fact perpetrated by the author of the 'interlude', Master Gysbrecht, whose knowledge of scripture is as hazy as his grasp of historical chronology:

> John, Master of the Temple of God,
>   Falling to sin the Unknown Sin,
> What he bought of Emperor Aldabrod,
>   He sold it to Sultan Saladin—

(ll. 10–13)

The 'Unknown Sin' really is unknown—the capitals make it out to be something tremendously demonic, like the 'blasphemy against the Holy Ghost', the one sin which cannot be forgiven (Matthew 12: 31–2); but it isn't that, and in any case John would have had difficulty committing it with Aldabrod, who never existed (he is a sort of composite 'Emperor of the West'), or Saladin, who died many years before du Bourg-Molay was born. If there is 'truth' here, it is not to be looked for in the facts, but in the verse: in the nursery-rhyme thump and jingle which are at the heart of what the prologue, with an unwitting pun, calls Master Gysbrecht's 'conceit'. And yet the same conceit modulates into the tragic affirmation of the last stanzas; Browning seems to want us to accept that the truth of the poem is inextricable from its falsehood, that its taking of God's part cannot be separated from its hateful relish for the consequences.

In this sense the heart of the poem is the vision of the infernal rose which is vouchsafed to John in cruel fulfilment of his prayer. The Latin title of the interlude is 'Rosa Mundi; seu, fulcite me floribus' (Rose of the World; or, comfort me with flowers); it taunts John with his pathetically mistaken hope that God will prove to be

merciful and loving: 'Why else is the same styled, Sharon's rose? |
Once a rose, ever a rose, he saith' (ll. 60–1).[15] Browning almost
certainly knew the apocryphal biblical story of Zillah, the Jewish
maiden falsely accused of devil-worship and condemned to be burned,
who was saved by the miraculous transformation of the stake into a
rose-tree bearing red and white roses, the first to appear on earth
since the Fall. He also had in mind, I think, the ending of Tennyson's
'Vision of Sin', where, in answer to the cry 'Is there any hope?', 'on
the glimmering limit far withdrawn | God made Himself an awful
rose of dawn'. What happens to John is the inverse of Zillah's
miraculous rescue, and the inverse, too, of Tennyson's distanced
majesty: John's stake turns into a rose that represents both his own
intolerable physical agony and God's rejection of him:

> Ha ha, John plucks now at his rose
>   To rid himself of a sorrow at heart!
> Lo, — petal on petal, fierce rays unclose;
>   Anther on anther, sharp spikes outstart;
> And with blood for dew, the bosom boils;
>   And a gust of sulphur is all its smell;
> And lo, he is horribly in the toils
>   Of a coal-black giant flower of Hell!
> CHORUS
>   What maketh Heaven, that maketh Hell.
>
>   (ll. 71–9)

The last line reflects on the poet whose 'affair is with God' as well as
God himself; taking God's part means such an exposure to hatred, to
such a laugh as begins the stanza, to such a gloating exclamation as
ends it: 'a coal-black giant flower of Hell!' The reader, too, is
'horribly in the toils' of the poem which springs this ambush. What
the chorus says is both a profound truth about God's justice, and an
unacceptable endorsement of human hatred.

The example of both *Sordello* and 'The Heretic's Tragedy' would
imply, albeit in very different ways, that Browning is sceptical (in his
poetry, at least) of the concept of moral or righteous hatred, and that
this connects to a more general scepticism about human motives and

---

[15] The allusion is to S. of S. 2: 1: 'I am the rose of Sharon, and the lily of the
valleys'; it does not in fact refer to Christ in the traditional allegorical reading, but to
the Church.

moral action. 'The Heretic's Tragedy' further suggests that such scepticism is not in itself simple-minded. It is not merely a question of stripping away the disguise of righteous hatred and exposing something unpleasantly human underneath. In two plays published in 1846, *Luria* and *A Soul's Tragedy*, personal hatreds and resentments do disguise themselves as disinterested moral imperatives; in neither does the process of exposing the disguise conduct matters to a straightforward moral conclusion. As Don Juan says, in *Fifine at the Fair*, 'Each has a false outside, whereby a truth is forced | To issue from within' (ll. 1510–11).

In *Luria*, Braccio, the 'commissary' of Florence, suspects the Moorish mercenary Luria of plotting to overthrow the state after his victory in the war against Pisa. Domizia, who pretends to be in love with Luria, hopes he will fulfil Braccio's prediction: she wants to destroy Florence because her own father and brothers were formerly accused of treason in similar circumstances. Puccio, Luria's deputy, hates him for having superseded him as commander. No wonder Luria's confidant, Husain, describes the Florentines as a 'hating people' (ii. 105), though he himself hates Florence and urges Luria, when the time comes, to rape the city ('She lies now at thy pleasure—pleasure have!', iv. 168). But how do these characters see themselves? Puccio purports to view Luria as 'This Moor of the bad faith and doubtful race' (i. 39; 'bad faith' punningly suggests that a heathen must be untrustworthy), and furthermore as a mere 'boy' of 'untried sagacity' and 'Raw valour' (i. 40–1). On this professional scepticism he bases his willingness to supply Braccio with an account of Luria's 'Errors and oversights . . . petulant speeches, inconsiderate acts' (i. 166–70). Braccio isn't fooled; he knows that Puccio's actions are not high-minded, but spring from his 'pale discontent'. Puccio's later protestations that he didn't realize that his information would be used against Luria (iii. 143–9) sound rather hollow.

Braccio's own case is more complex. An intellectual who fears and hates men of action, he projects his hatred into a universal doctrine. Believing that 'there's one thing plain and positive; | Man seeks his own good at the whole world's cost' (i. 132–3), he believes as a matter of course that soldiers will attempt to take over the state if they are given the chance. But beneath this unexceptionable political doctrine, which the experience of our own century would do little to refute, lies the feeling which Braccio confides to Lapo, his secretary—

            pray God I hold in fit contempt
This warfare's noble art and ordering,
And, — once the brace of prizers fairly matched,
Poleaxe with poleaxe, knife with knife as good, —
Spit properly at what men term their skill . . .

                    (i. 50–4)

— a feeling for which he is able to find ennobling abstractions:

Brute-force shall not rule Florence! Intellect
May rule her, bad or good as chance supplies, —
But Intellect it shall be, pure if bad,
And Intellect's tradition so kept up
Till the good comes . . .

                    (i. 190–4)

Braccio displays the deep-founded resentment of a 'poor scribe' (as he later calls himself with dubious modesty) towards 'plumes and tags and swordsman's-gear' (i. 200); his subtlety and coldness are played off against Luria's guileless generosity. Their relationship has something in common with that of Lutwyche and Jules in *Pippa Passes*: like Lutwyche, Braccio is cynical and manipulative, but unlike him he also has a coherent ethical justification for his actions. Are we to think of Braccio as a hypocrite, disguising his compulsive antagonism towards Luria and everything that he represents with a cloak of civic virtue? Elizabeth Barrett didn't think so; she thought that Braccio's long speech in Act III, justifying his actions on behalf of Florence as an ideal of the city-state, was 'very subtle and noble—one half forgives Braccio in it'.[16] The juxtaposition of 'noble' and '*half* forgives' acutely registers Elizabeth Barrett's understanding of the difficulty here. She recognizes an inherent ambivalence or instability in our judgement of human motivation, one which operates even more strongly in the case of Domizia.

Domizia does not disguise her hatred of Florence from herself: like the speaker of 'The Laboratory' she plays with the idea that its very intensity gives it an immaterial power:

Well, Florence, shall I reach thee, pierce thy heart
Thro' all its safeguards? Hate is said to help—
Quicken the eye, invigorate the arm,
And this my hate, made of so many hates,

---

[16] From Elizabeth Barrett's critical notes on the manuscript, now in the library of Wellesley College; quoted in Woolford and Karlin: ii. 415.

Might stand in scorn of visible instrument,
And will thee dead . . .

(ii. 1–6)

In Act III, when Luria discovers Braccio's plot against him, and
realizes simultaneously that Domizia has been leading him on,
Domizia is willing to admit both that her hatred of Florence is a
personal matter, and that she has used Luria, while despising him, as
an instrument of vengeance:

> I am a daughter of the Traversari,
> Sister of Porzio and of Berto both.
> I have foreseen all that has come to pass:
> I knew the Florence that could doubt their faith,
> Must needs mistrust a stranger's — holding back
> Reward from them, must hold back his reward.
> And I believed, that shame they bore and died,
> He would not bear, but live and fight against —
> Seeing he was of other stuff than they.

(iii. 285–93)

Although Domizia is speaking *to* Luria here, she uses the third
person, as though she could not bear to touch him; the same racial
disdain infects the phrase 'other stuff than they'. But in Act IV
Domizia exhorts Luria to punish Florence from altogether more
noble motives: she compares him to Julius Caesar, the legendary
founder of Florence, and other 'famous men of old'; no more about
his being of 'other stuff' than her relatives, he is now the standard-
bearer for all humanity:

> Go on to Florence, Luria! 'Tis man's cause!
> But fail thou, and thy fall is least to dread!
> Thou keepest Florence in her evil way,
> Encouragest her sin so much the more —
> And while the bloody past is justified,
> The murder of those gone before approved,
> Thou all the surelier dost work against
> The men to come, the Lurias yet unborn,
> That, greater than thyself, are reached o'er thee
> Who giv'st the vantage-ground their foes require,
> As o'er my prostrate House thyself wast reached!
> Man calls thee — God shall judge thee: all is said!
> The mission of my House fulfilled at last!

And the mere woman, speaking for herself,
Reserves speech; it is now no woman's time.

(iv. 235–47)

Again showing her mastery of grammatical nuance, Domizia denies
that she is 'speaking for herself' by putting herself in the third
person, distancing her personal motives from those which relate to
'The mission of my House'. Personal feeling is gendered as female,
whereas the male voice is impersonal and abstract: the passage
begins by embracing 'man's cause' and ends by denying 'woman's
time'. Wearing a mask of impersonal authority, Domizia addresses
Luria as 'thou' (hitherto it has always been 'you'), elevates private
motives into public duties, and alters the historical frame so that her
family history takes its place in a larger cycle involving the interest of
'men to come'. It is a weakness in the play that we never find out
how much of this Domizia herself believes; but as with Braccio it is
not clear that we are invited simply to reject it as a transparent
hypocrisy. Perhaps personal hatred has indeed given Domizia an
insight into the mechanism of power politics by which states like
Florence exploit and betray their servants.[17] On the other hand, the
rhetoric of 'this my hate, made of so many hates' is hard to reconcile
with 'The mission of my House'.

The problem of a character whose hatreds are displayed as part of
a moral design is even more sharply posed by the case of Chiappino
in *A Soul's Tragedy*. Chiappino is a revolutionary whose hatred of
tyranny and injustice turns out to be inextricably involved with his
own frustrated desire for power. In the first part of the drama
(written in blank verse) he is shown awaiting the news that a last
appeal against his banishment from the city of Faenza has been
turned down by the ruling Provost. The appeal is being made by
Chiappino's lifelong friend Luitolfo. While he waits (in Luitolfo's
house, and in the company of Luitolfo's bride-to-be, Eulalia), Chiappino makes a savage attack on his friend's lukewarm liberalism in
contrast to his own intransigent refusal to compromise with the
system. Ironically mimicking the townspeople's praise of Luitolfo,
Chiappino calls him

> A happy-tempered bringer of the best
> Out of the worst; who bears with what's past cure

[17] The play's theme of collective ingratitude links it to the topic of the hatred
suffered by the artist which I discuss in Ch. 5.

And puts so good a face on't—wisely passive
Where action's fruitless . . .

(i. 65–8)

His own way has been the opposite:

True, I thank God, I ever said 'you sin,'
When a man did sin: if I could not say it,
I glared it at him,—if I could not glare it,
I prayed against him,—then my part seemed over;
God's may begin yet—so it will, I trust!

(i. 85–9)

The mention of God is not accidental, and neither is the echo, once again, of Browning's gesticulating hero, John Lilburne.[18] Chiappino's self-image is that of a persecuted prophet, who has God on his side but nobody else; and, like Braccio and Domizia, he has a grand abstraction to back him up. Speaking of the willingness of reformers like Luitolfo and Eulalia to placate tyranny rather than fight against it, he denounces their obsequiousness and flattery, while 'we [the common people] die in our misery patient deaths' and declares himself the partisan of 'Mankind' (i. 110–13). His allusion to 'patient deaths' aligns him with Sordello, whose radical humanism is fired by the appalling sights he witnesses at the siege of Ferrara: 'that rabble's woes, | Ludicrous in their patience as they chose | To sit about their town and quietly | Be slaughtered' (v. 249–52). But the parallel does Chiappino no good: his vulnerability is signalled in the excess and self-regard of his rhetoric. Sure enough, in the second part of the play (written in prose) he will renege on 'Mankind' as soon as he is offered the opportunity to be on the receiving end of the obsequiousness and flattery. The plot turns on Chiappino's falsely taking credit for the 'assassination' of the Provost (which was in fact attempted by Luitolfo, and resulted only in the Provost being slightly injured and running away). Elevated by popular acclaim after the successful 'revolution', Chiappino gradually comes round, guided by the wily papal legate Ogniben, to accepting the post of Provost for himself. Ogniben enters Faenza to quell the disturbance 'laughing gently to himself', and reflecting that he has 'known three and twenty leaders of revolts' (ii. 93–5). He certainly proves too much for Chiappino: at

---

[18] See above, pp. 123–4.

the end of the play, just as Chiappino is about to be confirmed as the
new Provost, Ogniben unmasks, humiliates, and dismisses him to the
exile he was facing when the play opened, uttering the famous
concluding quip, as Chiappino, like an undeserving Keats, is hooted
from the stage of life, 'I have known *Four*-and-twenty leaders of
revolts!'

What then of Chiappino's righteous hatred of oppression and
injustice? Are we to see it as nothing more than a sham? The
problem is compounded by Chiappino's relationship with Eulalia, to
whom he declares his love in Part I. Despite the fact that he is doing
so behind his 'friend' Luitolfo's back, Chiappino's tormented revelation of his long-standing desire has a real pathos and dignity:

> You knew it, years ago;
> When my voice faltered and my eyes grew dim
> Because you gave me your silk mask to hold—
> My voice that greatens when there's need to curse
> The people's Provost to their heart's content,
> —My eyes, the Provost, who bears all men's eyes,
> Banishes now because he cannot bear!
>
> (i. 128–34)

Chiappino's private, suppressed love for Eulalia is linked, as these
lines suggest, to his public 'cursing'.[19] And he is nowhere more
ignoble in Part II than in his easy, unfaltering explanation to Eulalia
of why he is abandoning her along with his political principles:

Eulalia. So the love breaks away too!

Chiappino. No, rather my soul's capacity for love widens—needs more
than one object to content it,—and, being better instructed, will not persist
in seeing all the component parts of love in what is only a single part,—nor
in finding the so many and so various loves, united in the love of a
woman,—finding all uses in one instrument, as the savage has his sword,
sceptre and idol, all in one club-stick. Love is a very compound thing. I shall
give the intellectual part of my love to Men, the mighty dead, or illustrious
living; and determine to call a mere sensual instinct by as few fine names as
possible. What do I lose?

> (ii. 255–63)

---

[19] Eulalia is baffled by Chiappino's self-proclaimed inability to speak to her of his
love during all the years they have known each other. 'See how your words come from
you in a crowd!' she says (i. 149). But that is just the point: only *in a crowd* is
Chiappino master of a crowd of words.

Chiappino uses a metaphor of progress to account for his change of mind and heart: like a savage nation, he has become civilized, and is now 'better instructed'. His old passions of hatred and love now appear to him as primitive and unenlightened. The metaphor is double-edged, however, and the closing question has an uncomfortable answer. If, in Part I, Chiappino was a savage, he was also warrior, king, and worshipper. His transformation in Part II is a dissolution, a loss of identity or wholeness. Civilization is bad for him. Instead of his charged, passionate dialogue with Eulalia in Part I, where he is always on the offensive, he spends most of Part II being made fun of by Ogniben. The play's subtitle—'Part First, being what was called the Poetry of Chiappino's Life: and Part Second, its Prose'—graphically expresses what Chiappino has 'lost'. Poetry, like love, is 'a very compound thing'. In Part I, Chiappino's sexual frustration and jealousy of Luitolfo fuel his radical extremism in politics, and give him the edge over Eulalia. Why resolve compounds to simples as he himself disastrously attempts? We might be better off responding to Chiappino's mixed feelings, as Elizabeth Barrett did, with mixed feelings of our own: 'Chiappino is highly dramatic in that first part, & speaks so finely sometimes, that it is a wrench to one's sympathies to find him overthrown' (Kintner: 589).

It may be argued that the moral ground of hatred in both *Luria* and *A Soul's Tragedy* is unstable because it is also the ground of politics, where hypocrisy and self-deception are native elements. What then of 'pure' morality, the hatred of sin which might apply to the domestic passions? The first episode of *Pippa Passes* stands out here: it turns on a transformation of hatred from a wicked to a righteous emotion, and seems plainly to endorse the change. When the episode opens, Sebald and his lover Ottima have just murdered Ottima's old, rich, and disagreeable husband, Luca. Sebald is struggling with feelings of guilt and revulsion, which Ottima pretends to ignore. Sebald refuses to be distracted, morbidly dwelling on the murder and flinching at Ottima's euphemisms for it ('the deed', 'the event', 'our passion's fruit'). But if Ottima is nice about her terminology, she has the courage of her feelings: her love for Sebald is linked to her hatred for her husband, the murder is indeed their 'passion's fruit', and at length, stung by Sebald's behaviour, she confronts him with this truth:

Ottima. Love, to be wise, (one counsel pays another)
Should we have—months ago—when first we loved,
For instance that May morning we two stole
Under the green ascent of sycamores—
If we had come upon a thing like that
Suddenly—
   Sebald.   'A thing' . . there again—'a thing!'
   Ottima. Then, Venus' body, had we come upon
My husband Luca Gaddi's murdered corpse
Within there, at his couch-foot, covered close—
Would you have pored upon it? Why persist
In poring now upon it? For 'tis here—
As much as there in the deserted house—
You cannot rid your eyes of it: for me,
Now he is dead I hate him worse—I hate—
Dare you stay here? I would go back and hold
His two dead hands, and say, I hate you worse
Luca, than—
   Sebald. Off, off; take your hands off mine!

(i. 93–109)

Sex and death, love and hate are twinned in Ottima's mind: a classic
femme fatale, she swears by 'Venus' body' in one line, refers to
Luca's 'murdered corpse' in the next, and demonstrates how she
would hold the corpse's hands by grasping her lover's.[20] Her insistence on 'placing' the corpse at the scene of the earlier crime, that of
adultery, conflates the two; she darkens the pastoral, and comic,
associations of 'that May morning' and the 'green ascent of sycamores', and refuses to have her affair cast in the genre of fabliau, a
'Merchant's Tale' (Luca is a silk-merchant) in which Luca, she, and
Sebald would take on the roles of January, May, and Damian.[21]
Not only is Ottima's love for Sebald intimately connected to her

[20] I have argued in my edition of Rider Haggard's *She* (Oxford University Press
1991, p. 332) that the Ottima–Sebald scene may have influenced Haggard's portrayal
of 'She'; among other things Sebald calls Ottima 'my great white queen' (i. 213).
[21] This is how the affair seems to outsiders: to Pippa herself in the prologue (ll. 85–
95), and to the loitering 'Austrian Police' in the prose section of Part II, where the
corrupt domestic situation is interestingly linked to Luca's wealth and reactionary
politics: 'Old Luca Gaddi's [house], that owns the silk-mills here: he dozes by the
hour—wakes up, sighs deeply, says he should like to be Prince Metternich, and then
dozes again after having bidden young Sebald, the foreigner, set his wife to playing
draughts: never molest such a household, they mean well' (ll. 283–9).

hatred of Luca, it is connected also to her acceptance of both emotions as sinful and, consequently, deserving the hatred of God. Just as Ottima declared, of her husband, 'Now he is dead I hate him worse', so she tells Sebald 'I love you better now than ever', and, indeed, 'Best for the crime' (i. 149, 151). She draws Sebald into a duet of passionate memory in which death, guilt, and God's vengeance are interwoven with the very touches of the body:

> *Ottima.* Then our crowning night—
> *Sebald.* The July night?
> *Ottima.*   The day of it too, Sebald!
> When heaven's pillars seemed o'erbowed with heat,
> Its black-blue canopy seemed let descend
> Close on us both, to weigh down each to each,
> And smother up all life except our life.
> So lay we till the storm came.
>   *Sebald.*   How it came!
>   *Ottima.* Buried in woods we lay, you recollect;
> Swift ran the searching tempest overhead;
> And ever and anon some bright white shaft
> Burnt thro' the pine-tree roof—here burnt and there,
> As if God's messenger thro' the close wood screen
> Plunged and replunged his weapon at a venture,
> Feeling for guilty thee and me—then broke
> The thunder like a whole sea overhead—
>   *Sebald.* Yes.
>   *Ottima.*   While I stretched myself upon you, hands
> To hands, my mouth to your hot mouth, and shook
> All my locks loose, and covered you with them.

(i. 177–94)

Ottima makes the action of heaven seem terribly ambiguous here. The 'black-blue canopy' is sexually as well as morally oppressive, and God's messenger, plunging and replunging his weapon, has an erotic as well as vengeful force, answering to the eroticism of Ottima and Sebald that both fears and solicits its own punishment. As so often in Browning, language that calls up a sacred text may do so demonically: Ottima's fusion of herself with Sebald ('stretched myself upon you, hands | To hands, my mouth to your hot mouth') perversely remembers Elisha's resurrection of the child in 2 Kings 4: 34: 'And he went up, and lay upon the child, and put his mouth upon his mouth, and his eyes upon his eyes, and his hands upon his hands: and he stretched himself upon the child; and the flesh of the child waxed warm.'

Ottima's evocation of the 'crowning night' ends with her commanding Sebald: 'Crown me your queen, your spirit's arbitress, | Magnificent in sin. Say that!' (i. 211–12) Sebald is about to complete this somewhat melodramatic self-damning utterance when Pippa's song intervenes:

> The year's at the spring,
> And day's at the morn:
> Morning's at seven;
> The hill-side's dew-pearled:
> The lark's on the wing,
> The snail's on the thorn;
> God's in his heaven—
> All's right with the world!
>
> (i. 215–22)

These famous images of morning and spring, of lyrical freshness and earliness, are set against the overheated (literally as well as rhetorically: they meet in a greenhouse) sexuality of Ottima and Sebald, who have been up all night and who take a jaundiced view of daylight. Sebald, looking out at the beginning of the scene, had said: 'Morning? | It seems to me a night with a sun added: | Where's dew? where's freshness?' (ll. 28–30). Pippa's song answers him; and its closing lines trigger the *peripateia* of the episode:

> *Sebald.* Leave me!
> Go, get your clothes on—dress those shoulders.
>   *Ottima.*   Sebald?
>   *Sebald.* Wipe off that paint. I hate you!
>
> (i. 230–2)

The animus towards women's 'painting' evokes the Elizabethan and Jacobean drama on whose forms and themes Browning drew heavily for *Pippa Passes*. Ottima the hothouse plant is implicitly contrasted with Pippa the wildflower, a contrast which recalls a passage in *The Winter's Tale* where Perdita's rejection of cultivated flowers is linked to her not using make-up:

>   I'll not put
> The dibble in earth to set one slip of them;
> No more than were I painted I would wish

> This youth should say 'twere well, and only therefore
> Desire to breed by me.

(IV. iv. 99–103)

Sebald now sees Ottima as the antithesis of nature, of the lark and the snail (images of soaring and crawling bind low and high notes together in the divine harmony). Perhaps it would be truer to say that he had always seen her in this light, and that what changes is his own perception. Earlier he recalled how, before he knew Ottima, he used to pass her house and notice that it was always shut until noon: 'And wisely—you were plotting one thing there, | Nature another outside' (i. 18–19). Then Ottima's cultivated eroticism appealed to him; now she appears to him as that stock figure of Protestant male fantasy, the Scarlet Woman, half-naked and fully made-up.

It must be said that Sebald's conversion to righteous hatred is grating to the modern ear, and doesn't become less so as he goes on. His peroration is powerfully priggish and unpleasant:

> To think
> She would succeed in her absurd attempt
> And fascinate with sin! and show herself
> Superior—Guilt from its excess, superior
> To Innocence. That little peasant's voice
> Has righted all again. Though I be lost,
> I know which is the better, never fear,
> Of vice or virtue, purity or lust,
> Nature, or trick—I see what I have done
> Entirely now. Oh, I am proud to feel
> Such torments—let the world take credit that
> I, having done my deed, pay too its price!
> I hate, hate—curse you! God's in his heaven!

(i. 251–63)

Sebald's new knowledge, or new understanding, is expressed in terms of simple moral oppositions, arranged in an equally simple hierarchy:

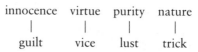

innocence	virtue	purity	nature
|	|	|	|
guilt	vice	lust	trick

This simplicity takes the place of Ottima's 'fascination' and 'excess'; Sebald is rejecting a Romantic (perhaps specifically Byronic) imbalance in the moral universe. Pippa's song has 'righted all' in a multiple sense of restoring order, balance, and moral priority (setting right, setting upright, setting to rights). Pippa herself is falsely incorporated into this order: Ottima had called her 'that little ragged girl' (l. 224), the word 'ragged' carrying associations of urban poverty, and told Sebald that she worked in the silk-mills; but to Sebald she must be a 'little peasant', a product of the landscape she describes, a pastoral and not a proletarian redeemer.

Alongside Sebald's paired moral terms goes another pairing, which relates to the moral economy of the episode: 'I, having done my deed, pay too its price'. Like Byron's Manfred, Sebald rejects an external machinery of retribution for his crime: he might say to the devil, as Manfred says: 'I bear within | A torture which could nothing gain from thine' (iii. iv. 127–8). Nevertheless, Sebald also insists that 'God's in his heaven': God authorizes and, as it were, guarantees Sebald's settlement of his debt. But what is perhaps most striking about this moral economy is its egotism, its exclusiveness. Sebald talks about himself (seven occurrences of 'I' in eight lines) and about Ottima in the third person: the only words he addresses *to* her are a rhetorical formality, the mark of his conversion: 'I hate, hate—curse you!' Ottima fully appreciates the significance of Sebald's turning away from her in speech: when it first happens she cries despairingly, 'Speak to me—not of me!' (l. 241). But just as her rhetorical sway over him had been founded on mutuality ('each to each ... my mouth to your hot mouth'), so his hatred of her expresses itself in an impersonal and objectifying grammar. This contrast persists to the end of the scene, in which Ottima shows herself still in love with Sebald, and in which her last words (after his death) are a good deal more humanly attractive than his:

> *Sebald.* My brain is drowned now—quite drowned: all I feel
> Is . . . is at swift-recurring intervals
> A hurrying-down within me, as of waters
> Loosened to smother up some ghastly pit—
> There they go—whirls from a black, fiery sea.
> *Ottima.* Not me—to him oh God be merciful!

> (i. 271–6)

Sebald is preoccupied with his moral rebirth here, with the breaking of the infernal 'waters' by which he is to be both punished and redeemed. Infernal, but also internal: 'A hurrying-down *within me*'. The climax of the episode from his point of view is an orgasm of self-absorption. Ottima, on the other hand, is still locked into relation-ship, still pleading, if not with her beloved, then at least on his behalf. His 'all I feel' draws a boundary around the self; her 'Not me' breaks through it.

The implication of all this is disturbing. Clearly the drama of moral transformation in each episode of *Pippa Passes* turns on Pippa's singing, and here we must recognize that it is Sebald, and not Ottima, who is affected. Indeed, Browning goes to some trouble to mark Ottima's carelessness and indifference to Pippa's song (i. 224–30). Yet Sebald, it seems, is precipitated by the song into a morally correct, but humanly repulsive, hatred; Ottima, who had figured as demon-temptress ('athirst for my whole soul and body', as Sebald puts it with characteristic understatement), turns out to love Sebald better than herself. Who is the true Christian, then? And what price the morally energizing power of hatred?

We can see this problem in other poems where there is no question of a 'conversion' to righteous hatred, rather an instinctive (and often violent) *repugnance* to evil. This theme makes its earliest appearance in 'Count Gismond' (first published in *Dramatic Lyrics*, 1842); other instances include Caponsacchi's championship of Pompilia in *The Ring and the Book*, and the Younger Man's tigerish killing of the Older Man at the climax of *The Inn Album*. By no coincidence these examples all centre on chivalric rescue and revenge by men on behalf of women. In dwelling on this phenomenon Browning manages both to depict an impeccable moral orthodoxy, and to complicate, if not actually to undermine it.

'Count Gismond' is set in the days of chivalry: a lady is falsely accused of unchastity; Gismond instinctively recognizes her inno-cence, challenges her accuser to single combat, and kills him. The lady, the speaker of the poem, presents Gismond as, in effect, divinely prompted:

> I felt quite sure that God had set
> Himself to Satan; who would spend
> A minute's mistrust on the end?

(ll. 70–2)

Gismond, as God's agent, is both infallible in his judgement (that the woman is indeed innocent) and invincible in his actions. The speaker gives the combat between him and Count Gauthier, the false accuser, the form of an allegorical encounter between truth and falsehood, with no moral or psychological complications. Needless to say, the genre of dramatic monologue does not tolerate this kind of simplicity. Not that Gismond's instinctive hatred of injustice and championing of the oppressed is directly questioned; but the ruthlessness of his physical action is associated in the speaker's imagery not with moral but with erotic energy, and its consequences not with vindication but with power. The speaker takes pleasure in Gismond's actions: 'I enjoyed | The heart of the joy', she says (ll. 79–80), a pleasure registered in sensuous physical detail:

> Did I not watch him while he let
>> His armourer just brace his greaves,
> Rivet his hauberk, on the fret
>> The while! His foot . . my memory leaves
> No least stamp out, nor how anon
> He pulled his ringing gauntlets on.
>
>> (ll. 85–90)

Impatient of foreplay, Gismond wants to go straight to penetration, and without any fancy moves, either:

> And e'en before the trumpet's sound
>> Was finished, there lay prone the Knight,
> Prone as his lie, upon the ground:
>> My Knight flew at him, used no sleight
> Of the sword, but open-breasted drove,
> Cleaving till out the truth he clove.
>
>> (ll. 91–6)

The speaker now sees Gauthier, whose 'lie' had violated her, in the posture of an erotic victim. 'Which done, he dragged him to my feet' (l. 97): the power relation is now completely reversed, the female spurns the defeated male at her feet, but only to restore (on behalf of the victor) the 'normal' pattern of courtship, the sequence of homage, demand, and surrender:

> Then Gismond, kneeling to me, asked
>> — What safe my heart holds . . .
>
>> .   .   .   .   .   .
>
>> Pass the rest
> Until I sank upon his breast.
>
>> (ll. 103–8)

How far, and how disturbingly, this sexual pattern is steeped in violence is suggested by the lines which immediately follow, in which the phallic nature of Gismond's 'sword' is as clear as in the combat scene:

> Over my head his arm he flung
>   Against the world; and scarce I felt
> His sword, that dripped by me and swung,
>   A little shifted in its belt . . .

(ll. 109–12)

It is this murderous eroticism which concludes the poem, in a chillingly 'casual' image that brings out the full implication of the speaker's earlier phrase, 'My Knight *flew at him*':

> Gismond here?
> And have you brought my tercel back?
> I just was telling Adela
> How many birds it struck since May.

Why the tercel, especially? Because it is the *male* of any kind of hawk.[22] The speaker's pleasure in killing finally reveals itself as gratuitous and excessive in relation to the moral framework of her story. Gismond's espousing of her cause looks less like the following of a divinely sanctioned moral instinct than the indulgence of a perverse erotic fantasy.

Is Browning suspicious of any assertion of a moral ground for hatred? The question raised by 'Count Gismond' reappears on the grand scale in *The Ring and the Book*, which I discuss in Chapter 10; but for the moment suppose we look at the problem from the other way round. That is, instead of considering hatred of sin in its righteous, biblical sense, we might think of hatred linked to moral vision in a more complex way. If the hatred felt by the speaker of 'Soliloquy of the Spanish Cloister', and by Lutwyche in the second episode of *Pippa Passes*, gives them access to a kind of creative power, might hatred also be a gateway to moral vision, irrespective of the 'righteousness' of its object?

A passage in 'Mr. Sludge, "the Medium"' suggests that it might. Sludge is exposing the dishonesty and hypocrisy of those who encour-

---

[22] For a parallel case involving the *female* of a species of hawk, see p. 194.

aged his career; and, after stigmatizing one 'hateful form of foolery'
after another, he concludes:

> These were my patrons: these, and the like of them
> Who, rising in my soul now, sicken it,—
> These I have injured! Gratitude to these?
> The gratitude, forsooth, of a prostitute
> To the greenhorn and the bully—friends of hers,
> From the wag that wants the queer jokes for his club,
> To the snuff-box decorator, honest man,
> Who just was at his wits' end where to find
> So genial a Pasiphae! All and each
> Pay, compliment, protect from the police:
> And how she hates them for their pains, like me!
>
> (ll. 780–90)

The ruthlessness of this analogy extends to its details—Pasiphae, for
example, is chosen as the snuff-box decorator's mythological subject
because her lover was a bestial monster, the Minotaur (Sludge's
interlocutor, remember, is himself called Horsefall, and Sludge later
refers to him as a 'brute-beast'). The poem takes us on a tour of the
all-encompassing social swindle in which Sludge's own cheating has
been fostered, not in order to excuse him but to demonstrate the
absurdity and self-contradiction inherent in society's moral categories. And where have we heard the phrase 'All and each' before? In
'My Last Duchess': it comes in the passage where the Duke recalls
his wife's gratitude for people's kindness to her: 'all and each |
Would draw from her alike the forward speech | Or blush, at least'
(ll. 29–31). So the medium-prostitute is a parody of the Duchess,
responding with hypocrisy and hatred instead of spontaneous pleasure to the 'pains' taken by his clients on his behalf, and which are
really a cover for the pains they inflict.

In his clear-sightedness about the social conditions of his existence,
Sludge is a very different kind of dramatic monologuist to Andrea
del Sarto: rather he is the successor to Bishop Blougram, another
man of religion whom his interlocutor believes to be a fraud. Sludge's
'apology', like Blougram's, is not self-pitying, but satirical, and
devoted to proving that his adversary is wrong to despise him. Both
Sludge and Blougram are presented as formidably clever and unscru-
pulous, and each, in his own way, takes advantage of his social
position to humiliate his interlocutor. Blougram's strength, his

'Status, *entourage*, worldly circumstance' (l. 26), enables him to condescend to Gigadibs; Sludge's resource is his weakness, which he uses to (in an un-spiritualist sense) turn the tables on Horsefall, to show him what his world looks like from the underside. The medium is compared to a prostitute, and also to that other familiar type of the Victorian outcast:

> Curse your superior, superintending sort,
> Who, since you hate smoke, send up boys that climb
> To cure your chimney, bid a 'medium' lie
> To sweep you truth down!

> (ll. 605–8)

Sludge's indignation, like Blougram's amused condescension, springs from an acute and (to his interlocutor) painful grasp of social realities, but neither man is any the 'better' for it. Indeed, Sludge's hatred of his patrons is 'righteous' precisely because he himself is unredeemed by it. Like Sebald, Sludge sees himself as having been seduced and ruined by a demonic tempter, in his case a collective social demon, but unlike Sebald he undergoes no conversion.[23] Sebald's hatred of Ottima is linked to his achievement of self-knowledge: 'I see what I have done | Entirely now'. But the very completeness of this self-knowledge blanks out his sense of anything outside it. By contrast, Sludge's hatred of Horsefall and the world which he represents is a product of his knowledge, not of self, but of others; it is a function of his power of observation. 'I like *knowing*,' Browning once remarked, 'and the power that comes of it.' The poet in 'How It Strikes a Contemporary' has this power in an innocent, because not literal form:

> He took such cognisance of men and things,
> If any beat a horse, you felt he saw;
> If any cursed a woman, he took note;
> Yet stared at nobody,—they stared at him,
> And found, less to their pleasure than surprise,
> He seemed to know them and expect as much.
> So, next time that a neighbour's tongue was loosed,
> It marked the shameful and notorious fact,

[23] In this respect, as in others, Sludge foreshadows Guido, in *The Ring and the Book*, another of Browning's great social critics, whose vision breeds, and is bred from, hatred, and who is the subject of my penultimate chapter.

> We had among us, not so much a spy,
> As a recording chief-inquisitor,
> The town's true master if the town but knew!
>
> (ll. 30–40)

In this poem the metaphor of the poet as 'recording chief-inquisitor' is just that—a metaphor—and the speaker carefully refrains from saying that the poet *did* know all these things: 'you felt he saw . . . He seemed to know them'. We understand his moral scrutiny of the town to be authorized by God, the 'king' to whom the poet writes his reports; the power that he exercises is not literal. When the same figure reappears in 'Mr. Sludge', however, it refers not to a metaphorical spy but to a literal one, a political informer on whose alert passivity Sludge models his technique for finding out things about people with which he will later amaze them in his seances. This man

> Was a hunchback cobbler, sat, stitched soles and sang,
> In some outlandish place, the city Rome,
> In a cellar by their Broadway, all day long;
> Never asked questions, stopped to listen or look,
> Nor lifted nose from lapstone; let the world
> Roll round his three-legged stool, and news run in
> The ears he hardly seemed to keep pricked up.
> Well, that man went on Sundays, touched his pay,
> And took his praise from government, you see;
> For something like two dollars every week,
> He'd engage tell you some one little thing
> Of some one man, which led to many more,
> (Because one truth leads right to the world's end)
> And make you that man's master—when he dined
> And on what dish, where walked to keep his health
> And to what street. His trade was, throwing thus
> His sense out, like an ant-eater's long tongue,
> Soft, innocent, warm, moist, impassible,
> And when 'twas crusted o'er with creatures—slick,
> Their juice enriched his palate.
>
> (ll. 524–43)

Like the 'hunchback cobbler', Sludge feels himself deformed and socially low, but able to exploit this very condition to 'enrich his palate'. The relish with which he deploys the animal image at the end, and the contempt it shows for his victims, mark the shift between this poem and 'How It Strikes a Contemporary'. The high moral purpose of the poet's observation gives way here to a malign surveillance, enabling a reactionary government to keep track of its dissidents (Browning of course had personal knowledge of such practices from his residence in Italy during a period of intense nationalist struggle). The poet in 'How It Strikes a Contemporary' has been (another metaphor) 'general-in-chief, | Thro' a whole campaign of the world's life and death' (ll. 104–5): his knowledge of the world is lofty, austere, disinterested, while Sludge's is sordid and practical. Sludge's 'campaign' has been one of Darwinian struggle and adaptation. And yet, again, it is this very refusal to dignify his trade which gives Sludge his authority and makes his hatred as clear-eyed to us as it is demeaning to him.

7

Aristophanes' Comic Weapon

Pat! He comes like the catastrophe of the old comedy; my cue is villainous melancholy.

(Shakespeare)[1]

I HAVE always thought that *Aristophanes' Apology*, which appeared in 1875, is one of the finest and most neglected of Browning's later poems. To the long-standing prejudice against Browning's work after *The Ring and the Book* (for its supposed garrulity, staleness, and didacticism) has been added, in the case of this particular poem, an off-putting reputation for recondite allusiveness.[2] From the moment the book appeared it was read as an exercise in Greek scholarship, and rumours circulated (to Browning's mingled amusement and exasperation) that the entire poem was nothing more than the 'transcript' of his conversations with Benjamin Jowett, the Master of Balliol (Hood: 171). Alfred Domett 'remarked . . . upon the large demands Browning makes in this book on his reader's knowledge, and said that I believed no one[,] even classical scholars, unless they were in the daily habit of reading Aristophanes, as tutors or schoolmasters, would be able to understand all the numerous allusions in it without referring over and over again to his Comedies; and that Browning thus wilfully restricted the number of his readers to comparatively few' (Horsman: 150). Certainly the number of readers qualified to read the poem according to Domett's criterion has diminished further from his day to ours! Browning's reply was

---

[1] *King Lear*, I. ii. 128–9.

[2] The poem 'suggests a masque staged by two muttering Greek professors in the airless corridors of a large library' and produces a 'stupefying effect of intricate, arid, allusive, and seemingly endless argumentation' (Irvine and Honan: 475–7). Even Clyde Ryals, who takes the poem's formal and thematic properties seriously, quotes Irvine and Honan's 'witty remark' about the Greek professors as one that most readers would endorse (Ryals: 117).

succinct: 'it could not be helped'. He did, indeed, write to F. J. Furnivall in 1882: 'As for *Aristophanes*—the allusions require a knowledge of the Scholia, besides acquaintance with the "Comicorum Graecorum Fragmenta," Athenaeus, Alciphron, and so forth, not forgotten', but he immediately, and somewhat mischievously, added: 'But I wrote in France, at an out of the way place, with none of these books' (Hood: 208).

Browning was proud of his classical learning, and displayed it to full advantage in *Aristophanes' Apology*; but even in 1875 there would have been little point in publishing a poem which *depended* on readers having the same degree of erudition.[3] I would add that the ostensible subject of the poem—a debate on the relative merits of Aristophanes and Euripides—was hardly a burning issue for the British public either then or now, and that if Browning really had set out to write the third longest of his poems (after *The Ring and the Book* and *Sordello*) on this topic it would deserve the treatment it has received. But he didn't, and it doesn't.

Since most readers even of a book about Browning will not have read the poem, I must say something about its context in his work and give some idea of its form and plot. The speaker of *Aristophanes' Apology*, all 5,705 lines of it (including Browning's translation of a complete play by Euripides, the *Herakles*[4]), is a Greek woman from Rhodes, Balaustion, the heroine of Browning's earlier poem *Balaustion's Adventure* (1871). In that poem, based on a passage in Plutarch's *Life of Nicias*, Balaustion recounted how the ship in which she was sailing from Rhodes to Athens was chased by pirates, and

---

[3] Adam Roberts concedes that there is 'no point in barren source-hunting', but argues that Browning's deployment of 'esoteric classical reference' 'allows him freedoms which a modern idiom would not'; he cites in particular Browning's use of Aristophanic obscenity and its connection with Aristophanes as a phallic artist (Roberts: 32–45). But Roberts's conclusion—that 'Browning was not looking for a wide audience ... because if the many had understood his full range of references there would have been considerable outrage'—over-states the case and, to use his own words, gives 'an unbalanced view of the work as a whole'.

[4] In both *Balaustion's Adventure* and *Aristophanes' Apology* Browning uses the system of Greek spelling which replaces conventional Anglicizations of Greek names with supposedly more accurate transliterations: hence, in this example, 'Herakles' for 'Heracles', and later 'Alkestis' for 'Alcestis'; other, more controversial, examples include 'Olumpos' for 'Olympus' and 'Klutaimnestra' for 'Clytemnestra'. Browning had adopted this system as early as 'Artemis Prologuizes' (*Dramatic Lyrics*, 1842) and defended it vigorously in the preface to his translation of Aeschylus' *Agamemnon* (1877). I have conformed to Browning's usage only in cases where my references to Greek names correspond to titles or passages of his poems which I quote in this book.

put into Syracuse harbour for refuge. The time was just after the defeat of the Athenian expedition against Sicily, towards the end of the Peloponnesian War. The Syracusans refused to allow the ship to enter the harbour, until Balaustion revealed her knowledge of the work of Euripides, for which, as Plutarch puts it, the Sicilians had 'a yearning fondness . . . they were forever learning by heart the little specimens and morsels of it which visitors brought them from time to time, and imparting them to one another with fond delight' (how Browning must have felt at reading that!). Balaustion promised to recite not just 'little specimens and morsels' but a whole play for them: the *Alkestis*, which was of particular interest to Syracuse, being concerned with the achievements of Herakles, who was held in great honour there.[5] The design of *Balaustion's Adventure* matches the rescue of Alkestis by Herakles with the rescue of Balaustion and her friends by the *Alkestis*, that is by the genius of Euripides.

The defeat of Athens by Sicily, it should be emphasized, was the occasion for Balaustion making the voyage in the first place. Revolted by the hurry of her fellow citizens in Rhodes to change sides and join the Spartan league, Balaustion sailed for Athens explicitly to affirm her loyalty to the values which Athenian civilization represented — including the 'tragic triad of immortal fames' of Aeschylus, Sophocles, and Euripides (ll. 32–9), but not including the comedies of Aristophanes. There was still hope, even after the defeat of the Sicilian expedition, that the war with Sparta might end in peace, if not outright victory. By the time of *Aristophanes' Apology*, however, the situation has changed. The later poem is set immediately after the final defeat of Athens by Sparta, and the demolition of the Long Walls connecting the city to the port of Piraeus, which had been built by Pericles and stood as the symbol of the city's supremacy.[6]

[5] The *Alkestis* is a tragedy with a happy ending. King Admetos of Thessaly was due to die, but Apollo persuaded the Fates to spare him if someone could be found to take his place. His wife Alkestis agreed to die in his place, but was rescued by Herakles. Browning returned to the myth in 'Apollo and the Fates', the prologue to his penultimate volume *Parleying with certain people of importance in their day* (1887). See also n. 8.

[6] The chronology of *Aristophanes' Apology* is deliberately unhistorical. Browning created a 'dramatic' time-scheme in which the death of Euripides coincides with the performance of a second (lost) version of Aristophanes' *Thesmophoriasuzae*; one year later his *Frogs* is swiftly followed by the fall of Athens. I have followed this time-scheme in my own references. Except in a few cases, I have also taken for granted Browning's many other anachronisms and adaptations of Greek history, mythology, and literature. Very few of these are attributable to ignorance or error; they mostly serve the poem's interpretative design.

As the poem opens, Balaustion and her husband Euthukles[7] are fleeing Athens and returning to Rhodes, not with a sense of disaster merely, but disillusion. For the final calamity which has befallen Athens is not, in Balaustion's eyes, that of some grand downfall, fit for the 'tragic triad', but a sordid and farcical collapse—an Aristophanic buffoonery. Nevertheless, by an effort of will Balaustion maintains that 'disinvolved | From the mere outside anguish and contempt, | Slowly a justice centred in a doom | Reveals itself' (ll. 67–8): that is, the fall of Athens is after all a fit subject for tragedy. To treat it as such, at any rate, will restore the element of the ideal so conspicuously lacking from the actual event. Accordingly, Balaustion proposes to Euthukles that they commemorate the fall of Athens 'on the stage of memory', themselves acting as the chorus, and that they do so not just once but 'oft again till life conclude | Lent for the lesson': for 'What else in life seems piteous any more | After such pity, or proves terrible | Beside such terror?' (ll. 171–6).

This Aristotelian purging of 'pity' and 'terror' is not, however, or not directly, the subject of the poem. As soon as she has proposed it, Balaustion swerves away:

> Beware precipitate approach! Rehearse
> Rather the prologue, well a year away,
> Than the main misery, a sunset old.
>
> (ll. 181–3)

The 'prologue' in fact displaces the 'main misery' and forms the bulk of the poem. It begins 'a year away' with the death of Euripides, in self-imposed exile in Macedon. On the same day that news of his death arrives in Athens, Aristophanes gains the prize for comedy with a second version of *Thesmophoriasouzae*, a lost play which Browning imagines to have contained as much satire of Euripides as the first, extant version, produced some years before. Ignoring this unseemly coincidence, Balaustion and Euthukles decide to pay homage to Euripides by reading aloud his *Herakles*, the manuscript of which Euripides had given to Balaustion before he left Athens.[8]

---

[7] With characteristic irony, Browning names the high-minded Balaustion's equally high-minded husband after a writer of Old (i.e. Aristophanic) Comedy, who survives only in the titles of two of his plays (see the entry on 'Euthycles' in the *Oxford Classical Dictionary*, 2nd edn.).

[8] The *Herakles* makes a fitting contrast to the *Alkestis* which was the focus of *Balaustion's Adventure* (see n. 5 above). In the later play Herakles again effects a

Just as they are about to begin their reading, Aristophanes and his entourage, who had been celebrating his victory, burst in. Aristophanes, who has just heard the news of Euripides' death, interrupts the mourning rites of Balaustion and Euthukles in a mood of drunken remorse and defiance. He confronts Balaustion and justifies himself for the numerous attacks on Euripides in his work (hence the dual sense of 'apology' in the title, which Browning had similarly used in 'Bishop Blougram's Apology' twenty years earlier). Aristophanes and Balaustion argue through the night about the nature and function of comedy in general, and the justice of Aristophanes' satire on Euripides in particular. As part of the debate, Balaustion resumes the reading of the *Herakles* which Aristophanes interrupted. At dawn Aristophanes leaves, promising playfully to make amends to Euripides with his next play. This turns out to be *The Frogs*, in which Euripides is even more outrageously pilloried.[9] In the same year, Athens is finally defeated by Sparta, which brings us up to the 'main misery' with which the poem opens, and which (in formal terms) is no more than an aftermath.

I want to make two general points about this complex structure. The first is the degree to which it is shaped by, and permeated with, dualities and oppositions—national, personal, ideological, literary. The war between Athens and Sparta is the setting for the whole poem; the conflict between Aristophanes and Euripides is articulated in a confrontation between Aristophanes himself and Balaustion, and takes the form of a literary debate as to the values, and value, of comedy and tragedy; Aristophanes represents a conservative social ethos, Euripides a progressive one; and so on. Each of these oppositions is the site of others. The war between Athens and Sparta, for example, involves the hatred of puritans for hedonists, provincial militarists for sophisticated city-dwellers; the opposition between

---

rescue, but this time there is a disastrous aftermath. After the success of his final labour, to bring the three-headed monster Cerberus up from Hades, Herakles returns to find his wife and children on the point of being murdered by King Lycus. He duly kills Lycus; but then, stung into madness by order of Hera, he turns on his own family and slaughters them. When he awakens from his madness he is plunged in despair, and is himself 'rescued' by Theseus, who leads him to Athens to purify him. Browning had used a phrase from the *Herakles* as the epigraph to *Prince Hohenstiel-Schwangau, Saviour of Society* (1871).

[9] *The Frogs* is also implicitly contrasted with the *Herakles*. In both plays there is a descent into the underworld: Bacchus brings back Aeschylus, Herakles Cerberus. Both 'resurrections' portend disaster: the fall of Athens, Herakles' slaughter of his family.

Aristophanes and Balaustion is connected to dichotomies of male and female, material and spiritual, profane and sacred, excess and restraint. The poem's form is also contested between speech and writing, and even between different kinds of quotation, which in turn reflect the opposition of 'wholeness' and 'fragmentation': Aristophanes' texts are alluded to in multiple, dispersed quotations, whereas Euripides has an entire play, called by Aristophanes 'one unfractured sheet' (l. 1564) and by Balaustion 'the perfect piece' (l. 3529).

If there is one opposition which governs all the others, it is that between love and hate. This opposition is one of the most persistent in Browning's work; it is also one of the most unstable. Accordingly, while each character, theme, and formal element has an opposite, each, too, is self-divided. It would certainly make things easier if we could think of the poem as a Homeric dispute over the body of a fallen hero (Euripides) between his ally (Balaustion) and his enemy (Aristophanes). Balaustion is trying to drag Euripides back to her lines for decent funeral rites to be performed; Aristophanes is trying to strip him of his armour and dishonour his corpse. In this epic reading, the characters of Balaustion and Aristophanes can be allegorized as 'love' and 'hate', with Euripides as their 'object'. Something of this view can be seen in Balaustion's beautiful valedictory words on Euripides' place of rest:

> He lies now in the little valley, laughed
> And moaned about by those mysterious streams,
> Boiling and freezing, like the love and hate
> Which helped or harmed him through his earthly course.
> They mix in Arethousa by his grave.
> The warm spring, traveller, dip thine arms into,
> Brighten thy brow with! Life detests black cold!

> (ll. 5673–9)

But even here an ambiguity persists: although it is certain that Balaustion enjoins us to abjure the 'black cold' of hatred, it is not certain that her 'warm spring' is equivalent to the 'boiling' stream (i.e. the stream of 'love'); it seems rather to mean the *mixture* of 'boiling' and 'freezing', 'love and hate'. 'Life's business', says the Pope in *The Ring and the Book*, is 'the terrible choice' between good and evil (x. 1237); but here the 'traveller' seems to be asked to choose 'life' as a mixed business—ironically in the name of a final, irreconcilable hatred: 'Life detests black cold'.

The second general point I want to make about the poem concerns
the violence of its language. I mean more by this than the invective
which Aristophanes and Balaustion make use of, though of course
this takes up a large part of the poem. I mean that the poem is in
love with the imagery of physical violence, that it obsessively renders
the war of ideas as a physical conflict, in which adversaries club,
batter, slash, cut, trample, flog, and kick each other. This recourse to
physical violence as a metaphor for intellectual or moral hatred is
part of a general habit of mind in Browning; in *Aristophanes'*
Apology it might be called a compulsion. 'Fighting' extends from the
disgusting to the sublime. 'Dog-face Eruxis, the small satirist', evidently a hit at Alfred Austin, is represented as 'fouling' Euripides by
pissing on him, though the 'manikin' can reach only as high as his
'flank' (ll. 1669–72). When Aristophanes wants to make the point
that he attacked his enemies while they were still alive, he says that
he 'flogged while skin could purple and flesh start' (l. 1654). Like
Pope in *The Dunciad* he spatters his opponents with shit—regretting
only that, in the process, they become 'Immortally immerded'
(l. 1655). Balaustion, for her part, expresses the prophetic righteousness of Euripides' art in an image of him as a murderous divinity,
whose hatred of sin she approvingly describes as untainted by human
weakness or fellow-feeling:

> not flagellating foe
> With simple rose and lily, gibe and jeer,
> Sly wink of boon-companion o'er his bowze
> Who, while he blames the liquor, smacks the lip,
> Blames, doubtless, but leers condonation too,—
> No, the balled fist broke brow like thunderbolt,
> Battered till brain flew!

> (ll. 1715–21)

What lies behind such images and, so to speak, guarantees their
authenticity? When Aristophanes proposes to 'Cut, thrust, hack, hew
at heap-on-heaped | Abomination' (ll. 2324–5), he is 'remembering'
Guido in *The Ring and the Book*, abolishing Violante's 'detested life'
(v. 1664). There the murder was literal, and the violence which
pervades the language of the poem as much as it does that of
Aristophanes' Apology has always some connection with the physical
action at its centre. In *Aristophanes' Apology* it is the war between
Athens and Sparta, or more accurately the outcome of the war, the

downfall of Athens, which lends its countenance to the war of words between Aristophanes and Balaustion. And the reason is that their quarrel turns out to be *literally* connected to the outcome of the war. It is a two-way circuit: physical and rhetorical violence are an effect of each other's cause. Two varieties of moral hatred are on offer, those of tragedy and comedy, Euripides and Aristophanes. They each claim to 'save the city' by purifying it of vice and civic corruption. Athens, in embracing Aristophanes and rejecting Euripides, is making a rhetorical or emblematic choice with literal consequences, namely defeat by Sparta.

So much for the intellectual framework; but the relish with which the imagery of physical violence is deployed by both Balaustion and Aristophanes remains to be accounted for, particularly in the case of the former. And here we return to Browning's understanding of the darkness, or doubleness, which troubles our moral terms and makes dialectical oppositions so hard to clarify and sustain. It may well be that a wrong choice between the positions taken up by Balaustion and Aristophanes leads Athens, in its tragic blindness and folly, to disaster; but it might also be *the nature of the choice itself* which is responsible for the outcome. That is, there might be something in the 'right' path, that of Euripides, as represented by Balaustion, which is as much to blame for the tragedy as its opposite.

Two hatreds confront each other in the poem, one of them (that of Balaustion for Aristophanes) disguised as something else. In order to understand the doubleness, you might even say the treachery of this confrontation, we need to take summary account of three specific parallels in classical literature. The first, frequently remarked on, is with Plato's *Symposium*, which has a similar narrative structure, and which is set shortly after the victory of a dramatist; there is a drunken interruption; Aristophanes is a leading character; the work can be read as a defence of Socrates (another target of Aristophanes' satire); it concludes with a scene glimpsed by the sleepy Aristodemus at the end of the dinner party in which Socrates is arguing with the tragic dramatist Agathon and Aristophanes that a writer of tragedy should be able to compose comedy, and vice versa, a point directly taken up in Browning's poem. The second parallel is with Euripides' *Alkestis*. In that play, the arrival of Herakles in the house of Admetos, on an occasion of mourning, and his subsequent ribald behaviour, anticipate the irruption of Aristophanes into the grief-stricken household of Balaustion and Euthukles. Finally there is a parallel with Aristophanes' own play *The Frogs*, also set after the death of Euripides, and also involving a contest between two poets. In *The Frogs* Bacchus descends to the underworld to bring back a poet to 'save the city'. The contest is between Euripides and Aeschylus, and Aeschylus wins. In *Aristophanes' Apology* the contest between Euripides and Aristophanes, representing the forces of political progress and reaction, has similar implications for 'saving the city'.[10]

The first two parallels, with the *Symposium* and the *Alkestis*, correspond to the two sides of a division in Browning's Aristophanes. The drunken interruption in the *Symposium* is made by Alcibiades, who, at the time the dinner party is supposed to occur, has yet to launch the disastrous Athenian expedition against Sicily. His brilliant wit, irreverence, and erotic power would have been displayed, for Plato's readers, against this dark unspoken background. Aristophanes triumphs in similar ignorance of the impending downfall of Athens; and Balaustion comes close to identifying his art with the moral degeneracy which precipitates that downfall. The case of the *Alkestis* is different, however. There the interrupter is the hero Herakles, whose drunkenness and comic energy are glossed over in *Balaustion's Adventure* as life-affirming, part of 'The irresistible sound wholesome heart | O' the hero' (ll. 1055–6). In that poem Herakles was identified with Euripides; but in *Aristophanes' Apology* the image of him as a comic, earthy folk-hero is close to that of Aristophanes himself.

Aristophanes, then, is like Alcibiades in presaging the ruin of the city he purports to lead, and like Herakles in being its semi-divine rescuer; and this doubleness extends to his championship of comedy as a means of social regeneration, of 'saving the city'. Here the third parallel, with *The Frogs*, comes in. When he hears Balaustion read the final lines of the *Herakles*, which Browning translates as 'The greatest of all our friends of yore | We have lost for evermore!' (ll. 5076–8), Aristophanes immediately understands that Balaustion

---

[10] Most critics of the poem have assumed that the decision goes in favour of Euripides (reversing Aristophanes' verdict in *The Frogs*) but there is no clear evidence of this in the poem once the positions of Balaustion and Browning are seen to be distinct. In 1881 Browning wrote to Swinburne: 'Indeed, I am no enemy of that Aristophanes, all on fire with invention,—and such music! I am confident that Euripides bore his fun and parodying good humoredly enough . . . but a friend of Euripides,—above all, a woman friend,—feels no such need of magnanimity: when I had done with her, I had all but done with anything like enmity to him—the reservation being simply due to the circumstance that Euripides was not triumphantly happy like Sophocles' (Hood: 193).

intends him to think of Euripides himself as the 'best friend' of Athens. But he does not accept the identification: he claims it for himself and the genre he practises. Declaring his intention to write *The Frogs*, he tells Balaustion and Euthukles to decide the question after his anticipated triumph:

> Say whether light Muse, Rosy-finger-tips,
> Or 'best-friend's' Heavy-hand, Melpomené,
> Touched lyre to purpose, played Amphion's part,
> And built Athenai to the skies once more!
>
> (ll. 5311–14)

Amphion was the son of Zeus who built the walls of Thebes with the music of his lyre. For Balaustion the image falls pat to purpose (a little too pat, in fact), since it is realized in exactly the opposite way to that which Aristophanes intends: when the Spartans demolish the Long Walls a year later, they add insult to injury by doing so to the music of the flute-girls Aristophanes was so fond of employing, and who, to Balaustion, symbolize the obscenity and moral corruption of his work.

The political opposition between Aristophanes and Euripides is inseparable from the aesthetic one. Aristophanes is an aristocratic reactionary, suspicious of anything which smacks of modernity, 'progress', or the 'rationalist' challenge to the old order in morals, politics, and religion. (The relevance of this to Browning's contemporary audience is clear: the sceptical attitude of the Sophists to the Olympic pantheon, for example, echoed by Euripides in his plays, and attacked by Aristophanes, would instantly remind Victorian readers of the twin assault on Christian fundamentalism from evolutionary theory and the 'Higher Criticism' of the Bible.) The sum of Aristophanes' creed is 'Hold by the usual!' (l. 2435), and like many conservatives he looks back to a golden age of social harmony, a 'whole Republic' in both senses, where hierarchy and differentiation (of gender, of function) produce organic unity (as in the familiar metaphor of the body politic).[11]

---

[11] Compare, for example, Guido's version of utopia at the end of his first monologue in *The Ring and the Book*: 'Rome rife with honest women and strong men, | Manners reformed, old habits back once more, | Customs that recognize the standard worth,— | The wholesome household rule in force again' (v. 2039–42). Not much has changed on the conservative agenda. Guido himself doesn't believe in this idealized past, but he calculates that it will appeal to his judges.

I represent the whole Republic,—gods,
Heroes, priests, legislators, poets,—prone,
And pummelled into insignificance
If will in him were matched with power of stroke.
For see what he has changed or hoped to change!
How few years since, when he began the fight,
Did there beat life indeed Athenai through!
Plenty and peace, then! Hellas thundersmote
The Persian. He himself had birth, you say,
That morn salvation broke at Salamis,
And heroes still walked earth. Themistokles—
Surely his mere back-stretch of hand could still
Find, not so lost in dark, Odusseus?—he
Holding as surely on to Herakles,—
Who touched Zeus, link and link, the unruptured chain!
Were poets absent? Aischulos might hail—
With Pindaros, Theognis,—whom for sire?
Homeros' self, departed yesterday!
While Hellas, saved and sung to, then and thus,—
Ah, people,—ah, lost antique liberty!
We lived, ourselves, undoubted lords of earth:
Wherever olives flourish, corn yields crop
To constitute our title—ours such land!
Outside of oil and breadstuff—barbarism!
What need of conquest? Let barbarians starve!
Devote our whole strength to our sole defence,
Content with peerless native products, home,
Beauty profuse in earth's mere sights and sounds,
Such men, such women, and such gods their guard!

(ll. 1966–94)

'Surely' in l. 1977 is briefly tentative; but Aristophanes resolutely quells the doubt with the second 'surely' in l. 1979. His vision of hierarchy, and of the patriarchal 'chain' ascending from the present to a divine originating Father, does not allow for more than a moment's hesitation, wills itself to become 'undoubted' and exclamatory. It is also a vision of plenitude, of self-containment: the rhetoric would strike a chord with American isolationism, in its double assertion that the Greeks are 'lords of earth' but decline 'conquest', their 'whole strength' turned inward towards the protection and consumption of 'peerless native products'.

The condition of this ideal 'antique' state, like that of all paradises, is that it has been 'lost'. But Aristophanes' opposition to Euripides cannot afford to base itself exclusively on this pathos. As his opening qualification makes clear, he needs to leave the door open for a reassertion of conservative values in the here-and-now. Moreover, Aristophanes wants to establish a continuity between the paradisal past and the threatened present in terms of 'earth's mere sights and sounds'. Besides being the unsettling agent of change in the old order of things, he characterizes Euripides as life-denying, abstract, philosophizing, prudish, in contrast to his own robust earthiness:

> 'Unworld the world' frowns he, my opposite.
> I cry 'Life!' 'Death,' he groans, 'our better Life!'
> Despise what is—the good and graspable,
> Prefer the out of sight and in at mind,
> To village-joy, the well-side violet-patch,
> The jolly club-feast when our field's in soak,
> Roast thrushes, haresoup, peasoup, deep washed down
> With Peparethian; the prompt paying off
> That black-eyed brown-skinned country-flavoured wench
> We caught among our brushwood foraging:
> On these look fig-juice, curdle up life's cream,
> And fall to magnifying misery!
>
> (ll. 1947–58)

The thumping alliteration and compound-worded coarseness of these images are not accidental: they express Aristophanes' masculine contempt for what he sees as the refinement (the thinness, the effeminacy) of Euripides' art. The image of the landowner 'paying off' a trespassing 'wench' reflects Aristophanes' view of Euripides as disturbing the 'natural' order both in sexual and social terms by his sympathetic representation of women and slaves on the stage. Aristophanes makes it clear in other passages that he sees the appetite for religious faith in the same terms as the appetite for food and sex: a basic, healthy human instinct, which Euripides attempts to complicate, question, and pervert.

Euripides' position is identified with tragedy, that of Aristophanes with comedy. Tragedy, according to Aristophanes, is *high*-minded, and therefore *narrow*-minded: it can only deal with experience in a mode of idealism and abstraction.[12] Comedy is of the earth, earthy. Aristophanes ('following' Aristotle's *Poetics*) traces the origins of

[12] See especially the image of the 'kottabos' game, ll. 5095 ff. This view contradicts another of Aristophanes' grudges against Euripides, that he lowered the dignity of

comedy to 'recurrence of festivity | Occasioned by black mother-
earth's good will | To children, as they took her vintage-gifts'
(ll. 1787–9). As part of these harvest festivals, people found that 'wine
unlocked the stiffest lip, and loosed | The tongue late dry and
reticent of joke', and thus 'Renewed man's privilege, grown obsolete
| Of telling truth nor dreading punishment' (ll. 1791–2, 1796–7). At
first, a band of drunken truth-tellers would simply tour around the
countryside on a cart, disguised in animal skins and with wine-lees
daubed on their faces, and shout, 'Neighbour, you are fool,
you—knave, | You,—hard to serve, you,—stingy to reward!'
(ll. 1800–1). Then, 'by degrees, a happier burst of thought, | The
notion came—not simply this to say, | But this to do' (ll. 1804–6), in
other words to act themselves the neighbours at whom they were
pointing the finger. Aristophanes claims to have inherited this 'engine
proper for rough chastisement' (l. 1826), to have extended its scope
and improved its operation, but not to have altered its nature.
Instead of satirizing the 'coarse fool and the clownish knave'
(l. 1834), his target is 'malpractice that affects the State' (l. 1840).
Aristophanes advances the traditional defence of satire, that it attacks
types, not individuals:

> I pursued my warfare till each wound
> Went through the mere man, reached the principle
> Worth purging from Athenai. Lamachos?
> No, I attacked war's representative.
> Kleon? No, flattery of the populace;
> Sokrates? No, but that pernicious seed
> Of sophists whereby hopeful youth is taught
> To jabber argument, chop logic, pore
> On sun and moon, and worship Whirligig.

> (ll. 1861–9)

Still, his comedy remains faithful to its origins: the comic poet is the
spokesman of the community, his satire an instrument of social
correction, and the community's values are those of the harvest
festival at which the performance takes place.

Moreover, Aristophanes links the *rhetoric* of his comedy with
its phallic and Dionysiac origins. 'Telling truth' in this scheme is
not some elevated or ideal process such as takes place in the

---

tragedy by making it realistic and colloquial (l. 2109). It is one of many such contradictions.

super-refined moral universe of Euripides (whatever brain-bashing metaphors Balaustion finds for it) but a debunking, a bringing down to earth. The coarseness of comedy, its obscenity and profanity, its mockery of everything 'high' and dignified, is an essential feature of its original attachment to 'black mother-earth's good will', what Mikhail Bakhtin, in *Rabelais and His World*, calls 'the material-bodily principle'. Rebuked by Balaustion for the rabid (and, she claims, self-defeating) excess of his satire, Aristophanes defends his method by arguing that 'polished Tragedy' is unfitted as an instrument of social criticism, since it aims at the 'vulgar':

> As well expect, should Pheidias carve Zeus' self
> And set him up, some half a mile away,
> His frown would frighten sparrows from your field!
> Eagles may recognize their lord, belike,
> But as for vulgar sparrows,—change the god,
> And plant some big Priapos with a pole!
> I wield the Comic weapon rather—hate!
> Hate! honest, earnest, and directest hate—
> Warfare wherein I close with enemy,
> Call him one name and fifty epithets,
> Remind you his great-grandfather sold bran,
> Describe the new exomion, sleeveless coat
> He knocked me down last night and robbed me of,
> Protest he voted for a tax on air!
> And all this hate—if I write Comedy—
> Finds[13] tolerance, most like—applause, perhaps
> True veneration; for I praise the god
> Present in person of his minister,
> And pay—the wilder my extravagance—
> The more appropriate worship to the Power
> Adulterous, night-roaming and the rest:
> Otherwise,—that originative force
> Of nature, impulse stirring death to life
> Which, underlying law, seems lawlessness,
> Yet is the outbreak which, ere order be,
> Must thrill creation through, warm stocks and stones,
> Phales Iacchos.
>
> (ll. 2336–62)

---

[13] In l. 2351 I adopt the revised reading from the *Poetical Works* of 1888–9; the first edition has 'With tolerance', which is grammatically defective. In the manuscript ll. 2350–1 originally read: 'Do all this—now that you write Comedy— | With tolerance [etc.]'. Browning forgot to alter l. 2351 after revising the preceding line.

'Phales Iacchos' is a personification of the phallus;[14] there is a song in honour of Phales in Aristophanes' *Acharnians* where he is celebrated as a 'companion of Bacchus, | fellow-reveller, night-rover, | adulterer and pederast' ('the rest' which Browning tactfully suppresses). He is therefore equivalent to the 'big Priapos with a pole': comedy is both a preserver of social order and an 'originative force | Of nature'. But in his 'veneration' of the phallus Aristophanes is paying tribute to a power as destructive as it is life-giving. In adopting comedy as the vehicle for articulating the conservative principles in which he believes, Aristophanes invokes the 'Power' that most threatens these principles. Drunkenness (the keynote of his first appearance in Balaustion's house, and which he associates with the origin of comedy as a social institution) can madden as well as inspire; phallic energy both generates and preys upon the society that worships it.

The image of a necessary 'outbreak' of phallic 'lawlessness', with comic or lighthearted overtones, had been with Browning for a long time. Forty-five years previously, in a passage of *Sordello* describing the evolution of civil society, he had used it to characterize the age of Charlemagne as a rough, but inevitable, first stage in the formation of 'order'; and here, too, a phallic image makes its appearance:

> That loose eternal unrest—who devised
> An apparition i' the midst? the rout
> Who checked, the breathless ring who formed about
> That sudden flower? Get round at any risk
> The gold-rough pointel, silver-blazing disk
> O' the lily! Swords across it! Reign thy reign
> And serve thy frolic service, Charlemagne!
> —The very child of over-joyousness,
> Unfeeling thence, strong therefore: Strength by stress
> Of Strength comes of a forehead confident,
> Two widened eyes expecting heart's content,
> A calm as out of just-quelled noise, nor swerves
> The ample cheek for doubt, in gracious curves

---

[14] Adam Roberts says that critics have been confused over 'Phales Iacchos' and have wrongly assumed there to be a god called 'Iacchos', whereas 'Iacchos' is in fact a cry of celebration. But there *was* a deity called 'Iacchus', as Roberts himself states, and Browning does seem to have intended an allusion here to 'Phales Iacchos' as the compound name of the god: the proof is in the mention of Phales and Iacchos as *separate* names for the phallic principle at l. 562.

> Abutting on the upthrust nether lip—
> He wills, how should he doubt then?
>
> (v. 118–32)

Charlemagne brings primitive order to chaos, the 'loose eternal unrest' of the Dark Ages. To do so he must be confident, thrusting, unselfconsciously phallic, an embodiment of 'will'. He must also be *fun*: he himself is a 'very child', and the process Browning describes, of forming a 'breathless ring' around the 'sudden flower', is like a children's game, full of 'frolic'. The epithet might raise some historians' eyebrows, but Browning's portrait of Charlemagne belongs to a historical and ideological dialectic in which power is associated with 'over-joyousness', a spilling over of sexual energy which clearly anticipates Aristophanes' 'impulse stirring death to life'. The 'sudden flower', with its 'gold-rough pointel' and 'silver-blazing disk', alludes overtly to the fleur-de-lys, the emblem of French royalty, but its phallic connotations are suggested by lines in 'Popularity': 'the centre-spike of gold | Which burns deep in the blue-bell's womb' (ll. 46–7). Charlemagne's physical characteristics look forward to those of Aristophanes, as Balaustion describes him on his first appearance, 'all his head one brow', whose

> nostrils wide
> Waited their incense; while the pursed mouth's pout
> Aggressive, while the beak supreme above,
> While the head, face, nay, pillared throat thrown back,
> Beard whitening under like a vinous foam,
> These made a glory, of such insolence—
> I thought,—such domineering deity
> Hephaistos might have carved to cut the brine
> For his gay brother's prow, imbrue that path
> Which, purpling, recognized the conqueror.
>
> (ll. 604–13)[15]

Comparing the two passages shows up a significant difference, though. The portrait of Charlemagne is both critical and whole-hearted: it presents its subject with an enthusiasm moderated and controlled by the narrator's intellectual (and syntactical) grasp. By contrast there is something unbalanced and suspect about Balaus-

---

[15] The 'domineering deity' must be Poseidon, since the sea purples in his wake; Browning erroneously refers to him as the 'brother' of Hephaistos, who was the son of Poseidon's brother Zeus.

tion's rhetoric. She makes Aristophanes into a carved figurehead of
Poseidon, distancing herself from his sexuality while paying homage
to it. Already, before the image of him as a sea-god has taken shape,
it is foreshadowed in the nostrils waiting for 'incense' (compare
Charlemagne's more human eyes 'expecting heart's content'). Aristophanes' divinity licenses Balaustion's fulsome worship of his 'aggres-
sive' and 'domineering' masculinity. It intellectualizes him, and Balaustion enjoys the *idea* of power, likes to play with imagery of conquest
and triumph (imagery which has a long association with male
sexuality). The blush of the sea which 'recognized the conqueror'
alludes to female submission (and possibly to the breaking of the
hymen), but it does so in a figure of speech. We are a long way from
the 'prompt paying off | That black-eyed brown-skinned country-
flavoured wench | We caught among our brushwood foraging' which
is Aristophanes' idea of the same thing.

The truth is that Balaustion hates Aristophanes, hates the phallus,
and that her 'recognition' of Aristophanes' conquering sexuality is
the prelude to her unmasking and unmaking of it. She wants comedy
to be everything that Aristophanes rejects: decorous, fair-minded,
uplifting: 'Suave summer-lightning lambency that plays ... Then
vanishes with unvindictive smile' (ll. 779–81). Against Aristophanes'
homage to the 'Power | Adulterous, night-roaming and the rest' we
might set Balaustion's feminist revision of the fable of Andromeda
and the sea-monster, in which the 'intolerable mystery and fear' of
phallic comedy, threatening violence and violation, is tamed by its
prey and turns into its opposite:

> Once, in my Rhodes, a portent of the wave
> Appalled our coast: for many a darkened day,
> Intolerable mystery and fear.
> Who snatched a furtive glance through crannied peak,
> Could but report of snake-scale, lizard-limb,—
> So swam what, making whirlpools as it went,
> Madded the brine with wrath or monstrous sport.
> ''Tis Tuphon, loose, unmanacled from mount,'
> Declared the priests, 'no way appeasable
> Unless perchance by virgin-sacrifice!'
> Thus grew the terror and o'erhung the doom—
> Until one eve a certain female-child
> Strayed in safe ignorance to seacoast edge,
> And there sate down and sang to please herself.
> When all at once, large-looming from his wave,

> Out leaned, chin hand-propped, pensive on the ledge,
> A sea-worn face, sad as mortality,
> Divine with yearning after fellowship.
> He rose but breast-high.

> (ll. 803–22)

Remembering the way in which the Andromeda myth is used else-where in Browning to suggest a threatening sexuality, we can appreci-ate the degree of distortion to which Balaustion subjects it here, summed up in that last, telling phrase 'He rose but breast-high'.[16] The god's 'monstrous sport' (a good description of Aristophanes' comedy) is stilled into a 'large-looming' presence, 'pensive on the ledge', a watcher and listener rather than an actor. Instead of devouring his 'virgin-sacrifice', he is attracted to a 'female-child' pleasing herself. (The hyphen in 'female-child' means something. When the phrase is first introduced, by Aristophanes at l. 774, and picked up by Balaustion at l. 802, it is without a hyphen, and means simply 'little girl'. 'Female-child', as a compound, means something more: it equates the two terms, matching femaleness with sexual innocence. In this context the use of the word 'strayed' in l. 815 is also significant: the 'female-child' is *un*like Milton's Eve in being able to 'stray in safe ignorance' and remain not just unfallen, but untempted.) Potency may be suggested, but is admired for its suppres-sion, not its display, which has connotations of voyeurism ('a furtive glance through crannied peak') and demonic power ('snake-scale, lizard-limb'). Like a female Lear, Balaustion's view of men is godlike down to the waist: 'Beneath is all the fiends'; | There's hell, there's darkness, there is the sulphurous pit' (IV. vi. 126–7). 'Making whirl-pools' is a fishy business.

Balaustion's repulsion at the sexual frankness of Aristophanes' plays springs from her sense of the grossness of the material body itself, which she identifies with bestiality, corruption, and dirt. She never really accounts for this feeling, but all her speeches are instinct with it, as Aristophanes recognizes. Flowing from this hatred of the body is a denial that it can have anything to do with artistic value. Balaustion's greatest outrage is reserved for plays where just this

---

[16] In 'England in Italy' (l. 206) Browning uses 'breast-high' with the opposite implication (i.e. an affirmation of the erotic, not a denial, since the subject is female) to describe one of the isles of the siren; he ignored Elizabeth Barrett's suggestion, made 'for rhythm' when the poem was in manuscript, that 'breast' should be changed to 'bosom'.

claim is made. She recalls Athenian 'friends' urging her, as a timid country mouse, to broaden her mind by going to see a comedy 'where truth calls spade a spade' (l. 413), and reacting like Mary Whitehouse to *Last Tango in Paris*. The play was the *Lysistrata*, in which the women of all the warring Greek states compel their menfolk to make peace by going on sexual strike. 'Waves, said to wash pollution from the world,' cries Balaustion, 'Take that plague-memory, cure that pustule caught | As, past escape, I sat and saw the piece' (ll. 415–17). She contrasts the play with Euripides' *Hippolytus*, with its 'chaste' heroine (or anti-heroine) Phaedra,

> Whom, because chaste, the wicked goddess chained
> To that same serpent of unchastity
> She loathed most, and who, coiled so, died distraught
> Rather than make submission, loose one limb
> Love-wards, at lambency of honeyed tongue,
> Or torture of the scales which scraped her snow . . .
>
> (ll. 419–24)

Balaustion's reading of the *Hippolytus*, which is idiosyncratic to say the least,[17] dramatizes her own loathing of the 'serpent of unchastity', and her fear of becoming what she beholds: 'coiled so' pictures Phaedra as both entangled in the coils of a snake, and coiled up like one herself. Balaustion's terror of beng touched, whether in pleasure or pain, is palpable here.

The connection between her physical nausea at what she calls Aristophanes' 'stomach-turning stew' (l. 3343) and 'hog's-lard' (l. 3416), and the disaster for which she blames him, is suggested by the appeal to the waves to wash her clean of the pollution. If we go back to the very beginning of the poem, we find Balaustion and Euthukles escaping by the purifying medium of water from an Athens which has been conquered in a sexual as well as military sense, which has been raped and which, worst of all, has acquiesced in her own desecration. It is a calamity not of annihilation, but defilement: 'Death's entry, Hades' outrage' as she calls it (l. 9). In contrast to this brutal penetration, Balaustion imagines an ideal, ecstatic ravishment, in which sexuality would have been purged in the least physical of the elements, the one closest to pure spirit:

---

[17] Compare the account of the play in 'Artemis Prologizes', in which the goddess accuses Phaedra of killing herself out of injured pride and of wickedly slandering Hippolytus in her dying letter to Theseus.

> Fire should have flung a passion of embrace
> About thee till, resplendently inarmed,
> (Temple by temple folded to his breast,
> All thy white wonder fainting out in ash)
> Some vaporous sigh of soul had lightly 'scaped,
> And so the Immortals bade Athenai back!
>
> (ll. 10–15)

This vision of fire making love to the city, of the 'vaporous sigh of soul' as its orgasmic death, is a consciously idealized fantasy: in reality, as Balaustion goes on to make clear, the fall of Athens was a sexual fall, truly a 'catastrophe of the old comedy'. In her account of events in the days following the Spartans' entry into the city, she contrasts two episodes which she loads with symbolic import. The first begins with the Spartan commander, Lysander, realizing the full extent of 'the prostration of his enemy . . . Past hope of hatred even' (ll. 5483–5), so that 'corpse-like lay | Powerless Athenai, late predominant | Lady of Hellas,—Sparté's slave-prize now!' (ll. 5490–2). It dawns on 'the half-helot captain and his crew' (l. 5471) that they can have their wicked way with the aristocratic 'Lady' without fear of the consequences; they decree the destruction of Athens:

> Leave not one stone upon another, raze
> Athenai to the rock! Let hill and plain
> Become a waste, a grassy pasture-ground
> Where sheep may wander, grazing goats depend
> From shapeless crags once columns! so at last
> Shall peace inhabit there, and peace enough.
>
> (ll. 5528–33)

If only Balaustion could see that Lysander's hatred of Athens is 'another way of love'! For is not this 'grassy pasture-ground' the landscape of 'Love Among the Ruins'? The death of a great civilization is contemplated there with ironic equanimity, and Eros as well as peace inhabits the scene. But the lovers in the earlier poem (whose reckless bliss brings them closer to Aristophanes than to Balaustion) become would-be violators in the later one. What stops them is the intervention of Balaustion's husband, who stands up in the assembly and sings a fragment of a chorus from Euripides' *Electra*:

> Ay, facing fury of revenge, and lust
> Of hate, and malice moaning to appease

> Hunger on prey presumptuous, prostrate now—
> Full in the hideous faces—last resource,
> He flung that choric flower, my Euthukles!

(ll. 5548–52)[18]

For Balaustion the fact that the play is the *Electra* is a gift, because in it Electra is represented as having been married by force to a local farmer, as a means of degrading her; but the pious man refrains from touching her. In Balaustion's confused reading, Athens figures as Electra, Sparta as both Clytemnestra who has dishonoured her and the peasant who spares her. The 'lust | Of hate' is defeated, and the connection between lust and hate is made explicit:

> The assembled foe,
> Heaving and swaying with strange friendliness,
> Cried 'Reverence Elektra!'—cried 'Abstain
> Like that chaste Herdsman, nor dare violate
> The sanctity of such reverse! Let stand
> Athenai!'

(ll. 5578–83)

But Balaustion cannot—indeed, does not wish to—sustain the image of Athens as Electra, a tragic heroine 'lost by fault | Of her own kindred' (ll. 5565–6). This image acts as an interlude, almost a nostalgic one; it is soon replaced by Balaustion's disgusted and indignant representation of Athens as lost by her own fault. Her second episode, accordingly, is associated with the comedy of Aristophanes, not the tragedy of Euripides. The Spartans, after grudgingly sparing Athens, decide to press ahead with the plan to tear down the Long Walls, the symbol of Athenian pride and power. Lysander speaks:

> 'Athenai's self be saved then, thank the Lyre!
> If Tragedy withdraws her presence—quick,
> If Comedy replace her,—what more just?
> Let Comedy do service, frisk away,
> Dance off stage these indomitable stones,
> Long Walls, Peiraian bulwarks!

(ll. 5619–24)

So the arch from beginning to end of the poem is completed, and

---

[18] This is not Browning's invention; it is based on an anecdote in Plutarch's *Life of Lysander*, where the action is attributed to an unnamed man from Phocis.

Balaustion returns to the image of Athens' degradation with which she began, that of 'the city's lyric troop, | Chantress and psaltress, flute-girl, dancing-girl' (ll. 97–8), whose erotic gyrations are in sexual time with the hammer-blows of the Spartans tearing down the Long Walls. Against these obscene and blasphemous rhythms she has set, throughout the poem, the grave, exalted plainness of her own verse-speaking; and the poem concludes with her cry of triumph:

> 'He lives!' hark,—waves say, winds sing out the same,
> And yonder dares the citied ridge of Rhodes
> Its headlong plunge from sky to sea, disparts
> North bay from south,—each guarded calm, that guest
> May enter gladly, blow what wind there will,—
> Boiled round with breakers, to no other cry!
> All in one choros,—what the master-word
> They take up?—hark! 'There are no gods, no gods!'
> Glory to God—who saves Euripides!'

Balaustion began the poem by imploring the wind and the waves to carry her from Athens; now that they have accomplished this, they become the mouthpiece of her final, totalizing interpretation of the journey. Athens has chosen Aristophanes and fallen; Balaustion at least has borne witness to 'God, who saves Euripides!'. The present tense of 'saves' takes Euripides out of time, while Aristophanes is left behind in the doomed city; Balaustion's flight, too, carries her beyond the sphere of corruption into an apocalyptic ending, with the extraordinary sight of Rhodes as both plunging and rock-rigid, daring a Phaeton- or Icarus-like fall 'from sky to sea' yet remaining a 'citied ridge', a form of the New Jerusalem, where a 'guest | May enter gladly, blow what wind there will'. She is safe now; Aristophanes' voice cannot penetrate the 'guarded calm' to which she has attained, and she hears only the 'master-word' which she herself projects as the sound of wind and wave. She assumes in this moment the full burden of the Romantic sublime, without taking into account Aristophanes' devastating assault, not on her fitness to bear it, but on its fitness to be borne at all.

8

Hatred's Double Face

Following Anaximander he [Heraclitus] conceived the universe as a ceaseless conflict of opposites regulated by an unchanging law, but he found in this law the proper object of understanding; it is the Logos which spans but could not exist without the cosmic process: 'people do not understand how what is at variance accords . . . with itself, an agreement in tension as with bow and lyre' . . . This Logos Heraclitus equated with transcendent wisdom and the elemental fire.

(*Oxford Classical Dictionary*, 2nd edn., 1970)

Without Contraries is no progression. Attraction and Repulsion, Reason and Energy, Love and Hate, are necessary to Human existence.

(Blake)[1]

the hateful siege
Of contraries . . .

(Milton)[2]

BROWNING'S dualism has often been remarked upon. He is a writer obsessed as much as Blake (or Yeats, or Lawrence) with contraries, with binary opposites; and, like these writers, he sees such contraries as essential to human identity and behaviour, constitutive of each individual, of the relations between individuals, and of all the forms of social life. Contraries work through historical time (in the political struggle between progress and reaction, for example) and through personal time (in the moral conflicts that shape a life). It is not too much to say that Browning's poetry works, is driven by oppositions, at every level of structure, theme, and style. Sometimes these oppositions are enshrined in the titles of paired poems ('Meeting

[1] *The Marriage of Heaven and Hell*, pl. 3.
[2] *Paradise Lost*, ix. 121–2.

at Night/Parting at Morning', 'Love in a Life/Life in a Love', 'One
Way of Love/Another Way of Love', 'Before/After', etc.),[3] sometimes
in the subtitles of individual works or volumes: *A Soul's Tragedy*
('Part First, being what was called the Poetry of Chiappino's Life:
and Part Second, its Prose'), *Red Cotton Night-Cap Country* ('Turf
and Towers'), and *Asolando* ('Fancies and Facts'). But more important than these formal gestures is the sense in which every Browning
poem is oppositional in nature: both he and the characters he creates
are seized with the passion of conflict and argument, whether with
others or themselves. And these arguments come down to fundamental divisions, to radical and irreconcilable opposites: male and female,
good and evil, soul and body; or at any rate to divisions that *seem*
fundamental, to opposites that *start out* as fixed and unalterable, for
the same poem which begins by taking them for granted may end up
by calling them into question.

The opposition between love and hate, as I pointed out in the
previous chapter, is among the most basic of all in Browning's work.
Its importance can be measured by the frequency with which the two
terms, or their cognates, are paired in single or adjoining lines. In the
concordance I count at a glance over a hundred such pairings: take
as an example the following, all from *The Ring and the Book*:

> Thus, two ways, does she love her love to the end,
> And hate her hate,—death, hell is no such price
> To pay for these,—lovers and haters hold.
>
> (iv. 1473–5)

> Too nakedly you hate
> Me whom you looked as if you loved once . . .
>
> (v. 790–1)

> I am not ignorant,—know what I say,
> Declaring this is sought for hate, not love.
>
> (vii. 805–6)

> 'Your husband dashes you against the stones;
> This man would place each fragment in a shrine:
> You hate him, love your husband!'
>
> I returned,

---

[3] See Karlin 1981 for a discussion of Browning's paired poems.

'It is not true I love my husband, — no,
Nor hate this man.

(vii. 1160–5)[4]

My babe nor was, nor is, nor yet shall be
Count Guido Franceschini's child at all —
Only his mother's, born of love not hate!

(vii. 1762–4)

Give me my wife: how should I use my wife,
Love her or hate her?

(xi. 961–2)

What I call God's hand, — you, perhaps, — this chance
Of the true instinct of an old good man
Who happens to hate darkness and love light, —

(xii. 592–4)

All these examples have one thing in common: they assume an absolute and stable opposition between the two terms 'love' and 'hate', whatever *kind* of feeling or state these terms describe (in the first example sexual passion, in the second parental love, in the fifth spiritual symbolism, in the last moral allegiance). Duality is produced, of course, by division: the final example overtly alludes to the primary division of creation itself:

And God said, Let there be light: and there was light. And God saw the light, that it was good: and God divided the light from the darkness. And God called the light Day, and the darkness he called Night.   (Genesis 1: 3–5)

From this primary division all others flow: physical, metaphysical, moral. One of Browning's most extraordinary late poems, 'Pan and Luna' (published in *Dramatic Idyls, Second Series*, 1880), itself a meditation on the duality of male and female, opens with a version of Genesis, in which the utter darkness of an Arcadian night abolishes the distinction between earth and sky ('the pines, | Mountains and vallies mingling made one mass | Of black with void black heaven', ll. 4–6), a distinction which is then restored, re-created by 'The naked Moon, full-orbed antagonist | Of night and dark' (ll. 20–1).

Such oppositions are productive — in the examples from *The Ring and the Book* productive of meaning, since without distinction the

---

[4] The first edition of *The Ring and the Book* (unusually for 19th-cent. verse) has line numbers, which I follow, and which count incomplete lines as wholes; hence 'I returned' counts here as l. 1163.

characters could not express ideas or emotions; productive of behaviour, too, since they lead to moral and other choices.[5] Oppositions play a dynamic and progressive role, as Bishop Blougram insists:

> No, when the fight begins within himself,
> A man's worth something. God stoops o'er his head,
> Satan looks up between his feet—both tug—
> He's left, himself, in the middle: the soul wakes
> And grows. Prolong that battle through his life!
> Never leave growing till the life to come!
>
> (ll. 693–8)

But the principle of division is not in itself a neutral one. It is light that God creates and finds good, not darkness; his division is also a judgement (as is the parable of the sheep and the goats, for that matter). In Blougram's tableau, after all, God is on top and Satan underneath (though with characteristic ambiguity God is stooping and Satan looking up). Christian dualism sets out to combat the Gnostic or Manichaean heresy that the principles of light and dark, good and evil are separate and equal forces, and of equal value in creation. Christian eschatology posits a struggle between opposites, but also, as Blougram acknowledges by alluding to 'the life to come', an apocalyptic end to the struggle, in which God triumphs over Satan, Heaven over Hell, the saved over the damned.

Even where the model is not explicitly Christian, it follows the same pattern: Juan, in *Fifine at the Fair*, imagines a progress of the soul towards ultimate truth whose prime requirement is that 'soul look up, not down, not hate but love, | As truth successively takes shape' (ll. 2172–3). In Carlyle's *Sartor Resartus* the 'Everlasting No' gives way to the 'Everlasting Yes': the dualistic division of the cosmos is ultimately progressive, as it operates both externally (in the political and social world) and within each individual. Moreover, Carlyle follows traditional Christian polemics (first formulated by Augustine, who drew on the work of Plotinus and other Neoplatonic sources) in his insistence that the negative side is all the time, however unwittingly and unwillingly, doing the work of the positive. When Teufelsdröckh is in the toils of negativity and doubt, 'perhaps

---

[5] In 'Pan and Luna' sexuality is produced by the division of light from dark, but in an odd, indirect, and disturbing way: the absolute contrast between the moon's brightness and the surrounding dark is figured as the moon's consciousness of nakedness, which impels her to take refuge in a cloud; the cloud turns out to be a disguise assumed by Pan.

at no era of his life was he more decisively the Servant of Goodness, the Servant of God' (chapter 7). Perhaps the fullest (if not the most straightforward) development of this idea in Browning comes in *Fifine at the Fair*, in Juan's vision of the carnival of souls: progressing from his initial impression of repulsive and apparently unredeemable evil, Juan comes to see that the vices of mankind are necessary and, indeed, praiseworthy:

> Are we not here to learn the good of peace through strife,
> Of love through hate, and reach knowledge by ignorance?
> Why, those are helps thereto, which late we eyed askance,
> And nicknamed unaware!

> (ll. 1768–71)

Following Augustinian logic, not only can the necessity of evil be demonstrated, but its very existence (as a substantive force in its own right) is called into question, since its operation is governed by divine providence, as part of an all-encompassing divine plan. In *Paradise Lost*, accordingly, when Satan raises himself from the burning lake he has only the illusion of heroic autonomy: in reality 'the will | And high permission of all-ruling heaven | Left him at large to his own dark designs' (i. 211–13), heaven's own design being to show 'How all his malice served but to bring forth | Infinite goodness' (ll. 216–17). It is this providential design of making hatred itself generate love which Adam perceives as his crowning consolation at the end of the poem:

> O goodness infinite, goodness immense!
> That all this good of evil shall produce,
> And evil turn to good; more wonderful
> Than that by which creation first brought forth
> Light out of darkness!

> (xii. 469–73)

According to this principle, one term of any pair is always subordinate to the other: light/dark, heat/cold, love/hate, each forms part of a vertical structure, a hierarchy of purpose and value. Good and evil co-operate, but only to produce good; equivalence of effort does not imply a balance in the outcome.

Browning's dualism is not, however, as orthodox or as optimistic as Milton's. Take, for example, its application to the political struggle between progressive and reactionary forces. Browning inherited from both Shelley and the tradition of radical Dissent a deep reverence for Milton's republicanism; but could anything be less Miltonic than Ogniben's emollient statement of the case in *A Soul's Tragedy*?

> you begin to perceive that, when all's done and said, both great parties in the state, the advocators of change in the present system of things, and the opponents of it, patriot and anti-patriot, are found working together for the common good, and that in the midst of their efforts for and against its progress, the world somehow or other still advances—to which result they contribute in equal proportions, those who spent their life in pushing it onward as those who gave theirs to the business of pulling it back—now, if you found the world stand still between the opposite forces, and were glad, I should conceive you—but it steadily advances, you rejoice to see! (ii. 408–21)

What's wrong with this jovial view of things? Just what its tone suggests: that it is a burlesque, which the clever and manipulative papal legate is recommending to the political turncoat Chiappino as a means of justifying his betrayal of the popular revolution he has recently led, all the while intending to unmask him and restore the status quo. Ogniben offers Chiappino the argument that, since 'both great parties in the state' contribute equally to 'the common good', it doesn't matter which side he supports. Chiappino falls into the trap: he begins to slide into the comfortable position that good and evil not only co-operate with each other, but that in the course of their struggle they come to resemble each other, to turn into each other: 'the bitterest adversaries get to discover certain points of similarity between each other, common sympathies—do they not?' (ll. 433–5) Whereupon Ogniben pulls the rug from under him with sardonic relish:

> Ay, had the young David but sate first to dine on his cheeses with the Philistine, he had soon discovered an abundance of such common sympathies . . . but, for the sake of one broad antipathy that had existed from the beginning, David slung the stone, cut off the giant's head, made a spoil of it, and after ate his cheeses with the better appetite for all I can learn. My friend, as you, with a quickened eyesight, go on discovering much good on the worse side, remember that the same process should proportionably magnify and demonstrate to you the much more good on the better side . . . (ll. 436–50)[6]

---

[6] The 'cheeses' are those which David brought from his father Jesse as a present to the captain of the troop in which his older brothers were serving: see 1 Sam. 17.

So Ogniben would, after all, preserve the distinction between the two terms of every opposition, and if Chiappino had the wit to see it he would realize where the argument was leading. To support reform is honourable, and to support reaction is honourable; but to support both (or neither) is dishonourable, because it abolishes the moral distinction between them. The integrity of Chiappino's position is destroyed, and Ogniben will proceed with conscious irony to restore the 'present system of things'—not because he believes that reaction is superior to reform, but because Chiappino is a spurious reformer, a David who sits down to eat his cheeses with Goliath rather than holding to 'one broad antipathy that had existed from the beginning'.

Ogniben would agree with Blake that the reconciling of opposites is a treacherous ideal. In *The Marriage of Heaven and Hell*, Blake praises Christ for rejecting such a reconciliation. Referring to the division of humanity between the 'prolific' and the 'devouring', he writes:

> These two classes of men are always upon earth, & they should be enemies; whoever tries to reconcile them seeks to destroy existence.
> Religion is an endeavour to reconcile the two.
> Note. Jesus Christ did not wish to unite but to seperate them, as in the Parable of sheep and goats! & he says I came not to send Peace but a Sword.
>
> (plates 16–17)[7]

Where Ogniben would differ from Blake is in Blake's refusal to acknowledge hierarchy as well as difference. Blake cites the parable of the sheep and the goats without acknowledging that it relates to an eschatological division between the saved and the damned. Ogniben would argue that the Gnostic division of the world between equal, contending forces leads inevitably to the very reconciling which Blake purports to shun. Each is the mirror image of the other; each might as well be the other.

Sordello discovers (with, for a poet, an appropriate rhetorical flourish of parallelism and chiasmus) that the warring factions of the Guelfs and the Ghibellins are fundamentally identical, each degraded by self-interest and violence: 'men ranged with men, | And deed with deed, blaze, blood, with blood and blaze' (iv. 908–9). Or, in plainer language:

---

[7] The spelling of 'seperate' is authorial. The parable of the sheep and the goats is in Matt. 25: 31–46; 'I came not to send peace, but a sword' is in Matt. 10: 34.

> Two parties take the world up, and allow
> No third, yet have one principle, subsist
> By the same method; whoso shall enlist
> With either, ranks with man's inveterate foes.
>
> (ll. 914–17)

Sordello tries to replace one dualism with another: instead of an illusory battle between two parties, one oppressive and the other liberal, there is a real battle between the two equally oppressive parties on the one hand, and the cause of mankind on the other. But this ideal dualism turns out to be itself illusory and impractical: setting up the cause of mankind outside existing conditions is either utopian foolishness or cowardly quietism, but in either case self-defeating. In the end, Sordello has to choose the less evil of the two existing parties, to convert equivalence (Guelf = Ghibellin) into hierarchy (Guelf > Ghibellin). He has to confer differing value where none apparently exists, or, more accurately, to perceive such value in a larger historical context. The Guelfs are part of the progressive movement of history, and must therefore be supported, even though their local behaviour is indistinguishable from that of their opponents. Moreover—like a supporter of Communism in the 1930s—Sordello confronts the unpalatable fact that the god of Humanity is worshipped with human sacrifice. For the sake of the future he must 'hate what Now [he] loved, | Love what [he] hated' (vi. 211–12). These human sympathies are in themselves aspects of a dualism, so that one opposition (between what is humanly lovable and hateful) has got tangled up with another (between what is politically good and bad).

Browning is both disturbed and exhilarated by the facility with which contraries can turn into each other, adopt each other's mask, employ each other's rhetoric. Seeking to express his unbounded admiration for Elizabeth Barrett's poetry, he wrote to her of a 'friend' who wanted to express his unbounded *dis*like of the efforts of 'a sonnet-writing somebody', and who was forced to coin 'a generous mintage of words to meet the sudden run on his epithets', from the simple 'bad, worse, worst' to 'worser, worserer, worserest . . . worster, worsterer, worsterest' and so on. At the end he commented: 'What an illustration of the law by which opposite ideas suggest opposite, and contrary images come together!' (Kintner: 11). Browning offers his homage to Elizabeth Barrett's 'affluent language' (as he called it in his first letter to her) by his own 'generous mintage of words', by sporting in the element of language for her delight and his own. The action of the 'law' is benign: love expresses itself by means of its contrary, with an added ingenuity, a spice of playfulness, as Aristophanes argues in *Aristophanes' Apology*:

> For come, concede me truth's in thing not word,
> Meaning not manner! Love smiles 'rogue' and 'wretch'
> When 'sweet' and 'dear' seem vapid; Hate adopts
> Love's 'sweet' and 'dear,' when 'rogue' and 'wretch' fall flat;
> Love, Hate—are truths, then, each in sense not sound.
>
> (ll. 2498–501)

But this attempt to divorce rhetoric from substance, to allow mobility in language without threatening the 'truths' that underlie it, can't be sustained either philosophically or practically. Meaning constantly threatens to collapse into manner: love represented by hate may be indistinguishable from hate itself (this is the argument Balaustion uses against Aristophanes himself).[8] In *Pippa Passes* the evil Lutwyche tells his enemy (or is it his beloved?) Jules that love and hate are 'the warders | Each of the other's borders' (ii. 168–9), and it is clear that in this relationship the very stability of the terms 'love' and 'hate' is in question.[9]

In *The Ring and the Book*, Pompilia is threatened in Guido's house at Arezzo by just such a dissolving of categories, when Guido's brother (with Guido's connivance) tries to seduce her with 'love' which is 'worse than hate' (ii. 1291–2), a phrase which Pompilia herself repeats in her monologue, but modifies in her anxiety to separate name and thing: 'worse than husband's hate, I had to bear | The love,—soliciting to shame called love,— | Of his brother' (vii. 843–5). In such an atmosphere she pleads with her parents (in the letter which the sympathetic, but cowardly, friar agrees to write on her behalf but never sends):

---

[8] Browning may well have recalled Coleridge's lines at the end of *Christabel*, in which a father's love for his child is so intense 'that he at last | Must needs express his love's excess | With words of unmeant bitterness. | Perhaps 'tis pretty to force together | Thoughts so all unlike each other; | To mutter and mock a broken charm, | To dally with wrong that does no harm' (ll. 663–9). De Quincey quotes and comments on this passage in his 1839 essay on Wordsworth, agreeing that 'love in excess' is 'capable of prompting such appellations as that of "wretch" to the beloved objects' (p. 163).

[9] For a detailed discussion of this scene in *Pippa Passes*, see pp. 85–93.

Even suppose you altered,—there's your hate,
To ask for: hate of you two dearest ones
I shall find liker love than love found here,
If husbands love their wives. Take me away
And hate me as you do the gnats and fleas,
Even the scorpions!

(vii. 1295–1300)

Pompilia's reflections extend back to her real mother, the prostitute who sold her to Violante Comparini: and here, too, she sees the conventional definitions cracking at the foundations:

The rather do I understand her now,—
From my experience of what hate calls love,—
Much love might be in what their love called hate.

(vii. 875–7)

Pompilia is striving to preserve the quality itself from the label which denominates it, since in her experience the labels have got mixed up. To Caponsacchi, no punishment for Guido seems more fitting than a nightmarish fusion of love and hate: in his fantasy of Guido's damnation he imagines him, 'at the doleful end' of hell, encountering and getting entangled with his soul-mate Judas Iscariot:

The two are at one now! Let them love their love
That bites and claws like hate, or hate their hate
That mops and mows and makes as it were love!

(vi. 1938–40)[10]

The desire which underlies Caponsacchi's vision is for love and hate to be kept distinct, since an exchange of qualities threatens both their identity and the hierarchy of value in which they should be fixed. Caponsacchi cannot, in the nature of things, acknowledge that Guido's hatred is in any way *like* love, except as a perversion, a travesty. Even less can he acknowledge that such hatred might have an equal value in the moral universe, that it might be as truthful as love, that it might bear witness with the same integrity to a divine principle, a divine creativity (though Pompilia herself recognizes that hate is 'the truth' of Guido (vii. 1727)). He would agree with Browning's tiresome sage Ferishtah, who adjures his 'foolishest' student in 'A Pillar at Sebzevar' to 'love the loveable':

[10] For a detailed discussion of this passage, see pp. 220–2.

'And what may be unloveable?'
                    'Why, hate!
If out of sand comes sand and nought but sand,
Affect not to be quaffing at mirage,
Nor nickname pain as pleasure.'

(ll. 116–19)

Again and again in Browning's writing this strenuous effort to maintain a division between absolutes proves unavailing. Ferishtah's injunction to love the lovable and hate the hateful is simplistic rather than simple. It cannot be obeyed, first because the energy which animates love and hate seems to come from the same source and to pour itself indifferently in either channel, and second because the opposition between the two terms is always on the point of collapse.

In 'A Forgiveness', the speaker wonders whether his wife might have been ready to admit her adultery because she was 'hungry for my hate . . . Eager to end an irksome lie, and taste | Our tingling true relation, hate embraced | By hate one naked moment' (ll. 62–5). This 'one naked moment' is no different in kind from the 'moment, one and infinite' of the lovers in 'By the Fire-Side'. It turns out, as the speaker of 'A Forgiveness' later realizes, that this was not what his wife had in mind at all: but he speaks truer than he knows, because hatred is indeed, in this instance, the mouthpiece of love. His wife declares:

I love him as I hate you. Kill me! Strike
At one blow both infinitudes alike
Out of existence—hate and love! Whence love?
That's safe inside my heart, nor will remove
For any searching of your steel, I think.
Whence hate? The secret lay on lip, at brink
Of speech, in one fierce tremble to escape,
At every form wherein your love took shape,
At each new provocation of your kiss.

(ll. 79–87)

The 'secret' couldn't be plainer, you would think: it reveals itself as an instinctive physical repulsion, similar to that which Pompilia, unlike the woman here, was never able to hide from Guido:

Deceive you for a second, if you may,
In presence of the child that so loves age,

> Whose neck writhes, cords itself your kiss,
> Whose hand you wring stark, rigid with despair!

(xi. 1017–20)

But later on in 'A Forgiveness' the speaker's wife tells him that her outburst of sexual hatred had been a lie: that she had loved him all along, but had been jealous of his neglect of her. The 'love' she speaks of was indeed safe in her heart, but it was love for her husband, not her lover; the hatred she expressed was the inverse image of her desire for him. When the speaker hears this, he says:

>   your words retrieve
> Importantly the past. No hate assumed
> The mask of love at any time! There gloomed
> A moment when love took hate's semblance, urged
> By causes you declare; but love's self purged
> Away a fancied wrong I did both loves
> —Yours and my own: by no hate's help, it proves,
> Purgation was attempted.

(ll. 354–61)

What matters to the speaker is the 'retrieval' of the past, the knowledge that his wife had concealed not her hatred of him but her love—that it was love masked as hate, and not hate masked as love, which motivated her actions. The hierarchy of love over hate reasserts itself, and allows the woman, in turn, to 'rise | High by how many a grade!' (ll. 361–2) in the speaker's estimation: his former contempt for her gives way to hatred, and hatred (after he has killed her) to love.[11]

But though the speaker may be relieved that his wife, like Bishop Blougram, had 'said true things but called them by wrong names', the reader may wonder whether it might not be put the other way round. The rhetoric of hatred in the poem—that of the speaker as well as his wife's—is more powerful and more convincing than the love of which it is supposed to be merely the disguise, and which we have to take on trust. The 'tingling true relation, hate embraced | By hate' has a stamp of Browningesque reality which the speaker's own hatefulness does nothing to diminish.

It is hard to keep separate the opposed terms of love and hate, to

---

[11] I am not concerned here with the dramatic or psychological probability of this story, or indeed with its narrator's chilling and repugnant character, but with the specific terms of his response. For more on the poem see pp. 203–8.

maintain them as 'pure' qualities in a hierarchy of value. At the very end of his visionary, deathbed speech, Paracelsus attempts to restore this hierarchy, to reinterpret his own bitter experience in terms of a Miltonic salvaging of good from evil, love from hate. But he cannot end there: he goes on in an attempt to resolve the duality itself, not by envisaging the eventual triumph of love over hate, but by finding a third term, a reconciling and 'temperate' state. He tells Festus that he learned from 'love's undoing', the tragedy of the poet Aprile's failure, 'the worth of love in man's estate, | And what proportion love should hold with power' (v. 841–3). Love, the desire for power, must always exceed the power actually available; the engine of human evolution is driven by *lack*, as human beings attempt to bridge (or leap) the gap between, to use Browning's own favourite terms, 'fancy' and 'fact', what can be imagined and what can be done. In Aprile's case, the gap had been too great: he failed, and perished, because love became an absolute for him; his desire to be a consummate artist overwhelmed his ability to be any sort of artist at all.

But Paracelsus does not fully understand the lesson of Aprile's fate. He is warned in time to engage with the world, to share some of his discoveries with mankind, and not to wait, like Aprile, for an ultimate revelation which will never come; but he preserves his vision of this ultimate revelation separate and intact, and despises those who cannot see beyond the immediate 'facts' to the consummate 'fancy':

> And thus, when men received with stupid wonder
> My first revealings—would have worshipp'd me—
> And I despised and loathed their proffered praise;
> When, with awaken'd eyes, they took revenge
> For past credulity in casting shame
> On my real knowledge—and I hated them—
> It was not strange I saw no good in man
>
> .   .   .   .   .   .
>
> In my own heart love had not been made wise
> To trace love's faint beginnings in mankind—
> To know even hate is but a mask of love's;
> To see a good in evil, and a hope
> In ill-success.
>
> .   .   .   .   .   .
>
> All this I knew not, and I fail'd; let men
> Regard me, and the poet dead long ago

Who lov'd too rashly; and shape forth a third,
And better temper'd spirit, warn'd by both;
As from the over-radiant star too mad
To drink the light-springs, beamless thence itself—
And the dark orb which borders the abyss,
Ingulf'd in icy night, might have its course
A temperate and equidistant world . . .

(v. 849–80)

Paracelsus starts by suggesting that he ought to have overcome his hatred of mankind (for their ignorance and malice towards him) by analogy with his own internal development. Just as he has been forced to acknowledge that perfection can only be attained by imperfect advances, so mankind's response to *him* was an imperfect, but not negative phenomenon: their hatred of him is a mask of love, in that their disappointment at his 'ill-success' measures the 'hope' they had of him. Seen in its right context, his rejection by mankind was not just inevitable, but cherishable.

Yet Paracelsus's vision does not culminate in this transformation of hate into love, or rather the subordination of hate into a means of love. What happens instead is that Paracelsus shifts his ground: he envisages a reconciling of opposites, and the production of a 'better temper'd spirit'. Although the opposition between Aprile and Paracelsus has been posed throughout the poem as that of 'Love' and 'Knowledge', Paracelsus's language here implies that it would be equally true to call it the opposition of love and hate, figured by a traditional imagery of heat and cold, light and dark, fire and ice, star and abyss.[12] Paracelsus's pursuit of knowledge has led him to hate and be hated, to the brink of 'the abyss, | Ingulf'd in icy night' (remember that in Dante's Inferno, it gets colder the lower down you go: and these are degrees of lovelessness, of distance from the divine 'love which moves the sun and the other stars'); Aprile's 'love', by contrast, acted like the gravitational pull of a black hole, absorbing creative energy into the ecstatic self, but giving nothing back. The notion of a 'temperate and equidistant world' between these two extremes is a way of evading an otherwise ineluctable dualism: for

[12] This imagery may be found in, for example, the poetry of courtly love, especially that of Petrarch and his imitators. Its origin is in Neoplatonic cosmology, which divided the elements and their qualities into the attractive (air, light, fire, warmth, lightness) and the repulsive (earth, dark, water, cold, heaviness).

clearly the first solution, making hatred serve the purposes of love, is not tenable. Nor is the third term a transcendent and over-ruling force, such as that which operates in Wyatt's poem 'To cause accord':

> To cause accord or to agree
> Two contraries in one degree,
> And in one point, as seemeth me,
> To all man's wit it cannot be:
> It is impossible.
>
> .   .   .   .   .   .
>
> Yet Love, that all things doth subdue,
> Whose power there may no life eschew,
> Hath wrought in me that I may rue
> These miracles to be so true
> That are impossible.

Wyatt's 'Love' holds the opposition of contraries in a paradoxical suspension, so that the lover can both burn and freeze, live and die, but it does this by rhetorical *force majeure*. The 'better temper'd spirit' envisaged by Paracelsus is produced by an 'accord' of contraries some time in the future. And there lies the problem. It turns out, here and elsewhere in Browning, that the fusion of opposites is always being deferred to a future beyond the reach of the warring parties themselves. In his essay on Shelley, for example, the union of 'objective' and 'subjective' poetry is said to be theoretically possible, but also never to have occurred in practice:

there [is no] reason why these two modes of poetic faculty may not issue hereafter from the same poet in successive perfect works, examples of which ... we have hitherto possessed in distinct individuals only. A mere running-in of one faculty upon the other is, of course, the ordinary circumstance. Far more rarely it happens that either is found so decidedly prominent and superior, as to be pronounced comparatively pure: while of the perfect shield, with the gold and the silver side set up for all comers to challenge, there has as yet been no instance.[13]

Browning looks forward to two kinds of union between the contrary 'modes of poetic faculty', either their being jointly possessed by a

[13] The essay was published in 1852 as the preface to a volume of Shelley's letters, which was withdrawn soon after publication when the letters were discovered to be forgeries; it is reprinted in Pettigrew and Collins: 1001–13. The passage quoted is on p. 1003.

single artist, who can produce purely objective or purely subjective
works, or to their fusion in a single work, the 'perfect shield'. What
he rejects is a false reconciliation, the 'mere running-in of one faculty
upon the other', *con*fusion rather than fusion. But in any case it
hasn't happened yet: it is a utopian fiction, similar to the one
proposed by Balaustion in *Aristophanes' Apology*, and half-ironically
accepted by her antagonist, of a poet who could reconcile the modes
of comedy and tragedy:

> Had you, I dream . . .
>
> .   .   .   .   .
>
> Made Comedy and Tragedy combine,
> Prove some Both-yet-neither, all one bard,
> Euripides with Aristophanes
> Coöperant! this, reproducing Now
> As that gave Then existence: Life to-day,
> This, as that other—Life dead long ago!
> The mob decrees such feat no crown, perchance,
> But—why call crowning the reward of quest?
> Tell him, my other poet,—where thou walk'st
> Some rarer world than e'er Ilissos washed!
>
> But dream goes idly in the air. To earth!
>
> (ll. 3430–45)

Aristophanes agrees with Balaustion as to the desirability of this
'Both-yet-neither', who can incorporate both the contemporary realism of comedy and the mythic truth of tragedy—and agrees with her
as to its fancifulness:

> as to your imaginary Third
> Who,—stationed (by mechanics past my guess)
> So as to take in every side at once,
> And not successively,—may reconcile
> The High and Low in tragicomic verse,—
> He shall be hailed superior to us both
> When born—in the Tin-islands! Meantime, here
> In bright Athenai, I contest the claim . . .
>
> (ll. 5134–41)[14]

Both Aristophanes and Balaustion deliberately bring themselves back

[14] The 'Cassiterides' or 'Tin-islands' was the name given to Cornwall and the Scilly
Islands in classical times, and here signifies (to the poem's readers) the whole of
Britain. The 'other poet' or 'imaginary Third' therefore 'really' arrived in time: he is

'to earth', to the here and now of 'bright Athenai', from the 'dream' of a reconciliation between contraries. We might say that the fulfilment of this dream, like Andrea del Sarto's heaven, is necessarily and beneficially out of reach: that the strife of contraries works towards a resolution which is perpetually deferred, and which thus guarantees continued progress — assuming, as Bishop Blougram does, such strife to be progressive in the first place. This idea depends, however, on each side of the opposition keeping its integrity, refusing, so to speak, to be influenced by the future. Aristophanes refuses to *try* to be 'the imaginary Third': 'Half-doing his work, leaving mine untouched, | That were the failure!' (ll. 5155–6).

It seems, then, that the very value of the 'temperate and equidistant world' foreseen by Paracelsus depends on the preservation of the radical opposition it is meant to resolve. Ten years after *Paracelsus*, Browning returned to the metaphor of fire and ice, once in a letter to Elizabeth Barrett (20 May 1845) and once in his play *Luria* (1846); and each time he did so in terms of *un*reconciled opposites. In *Luria*, Luria and his antagonist Braccio are emblems of love and hate: and Braccio claims that each has its function in the service of Florence to which both he and Luria are dedicated:

> Florence took up, turned all one way the soul
> Of Luria with its fires, and here he stands!
> She takes me out of all the world as him,
> Fixing my coldness till like ice it stays
> The fire! So, Braccio, Luria, which is best?
>
> (iii. 222–6)[15]

Notice that Braccio specifically does not say that there is a 'temperate and equidistant' ground between himself and Luria, but that their conflict is governed by a Heraclitan 'Logos', a transcendent term, 'Florence'. In his letter to Elizabeth Barrett, Browning moves the conflict of ice and fire inside the psyche, so that identity itself becomes the transcendent term:

To be grand in a simile, for every poor speck of a Vesuvius or a Stromboli in my microcosm there are huge layers of ice and pits of black cold water — and

Shakespeare, of whose 'mechanics' neither Balaustion nor Aristophanes can conceive. To them Shakespeare is a mythical projection; but it should be noted that, to Browning, Shakespeare was himself the type of the 'objective' poet, the supreme representative of one side of an opposition.

[15] For a more detailed discussion of hatred in *Luria*, see pp. 128–31.

I make the most of my two or three fire-eyes, because I know by experience, alas, how these tend to extinction—and the ice grows & grows—still this last is true part of me, most characteristic part, *best* part perhaps, and I disown nothing—. (Kintner: 74)

Volcanoes are 'fire-eyes' because they resemble the Cyclops, the one-eyed artificers who, in classical mythology, labour in the forge of Vulcan, the god of fire, traditionally located beneath mount Aetna. The image generates as much light as heat, since the eye is the organ of perception (both physical and intellectual); together, light and fire make up an image of creativity, of sexual and artistic potency: we might say, an image of love. Against these 'fire-eyes' are set the 'huge layers of ice and pits of black cold water' which represent inhibition, impotence, hatred, and death. Moving the metaphorical ground from mythology to science, Browning then alludes to the theory that the earth was formed by processes of eruption and cooling, first advanced in James Hutton's *Theory of the Earth* (1795). He does so to emphasize that the forces of attraction and repulsion are equally 'natural', equally 'true' and 'characteristic' of his 'microcosm'; this microcosmic self is like 'Florence' in the passage from *Luria*, the 'Logos' which governs a strife of opposites. As Bishop Blougram puts it, man is 'left, himself, in the middle' of the struggle between God and Satan. The commas single out 'himself' like a spotlight: the self is the star of the show. Browning's letter gives the self an equally central role; but whereas Blougram, as I pointed out earlier, implicitly subscribes to the idea that God is also the director of the play, Browning's scientific metaphor implies the opposite: that, by a natural process, the divine fire 'tends to extinction' while 'the ice grows and grows'.[16] The self is bleakly neutral, certainly not allied to a transcendent and over-ruling value.

But Browning was unwilling to abandon the quest for such a value, for a 'Logos' which would govern the oppositions of human nature without collapsing them into each other. Yet this result perversely arises before the quester at every turn, as the Dark Tower arises before Childe Roland. At the end of his life, Sordello receives a final revelation, a 'closing-truth' which both sums up his experience and allows him to transcend it:

---

[16] Since Browning goes on to speculate that the 'ice' might in fact be the 'best part' of his nature, it could be argued that Providence has rescued itself by an exchange of qualities between the two contraries; but this seems a desperate recourse to paradox.

> he cast
> Himself quite thro' mere secondary states
> Of his soul's essence, little loves and hates,
> Into the mid vague yearnings overlaid
> By these; as who should pierce hill, plain, grove, glade,
> And so into the very nucleus probe
> That first determined there exist a Globe:
> And as that's easiest half the globe dissolved,
> So seemed Sordello's closing-truth evolved
> In his flesh-half's break-up—the sudden swell
> Of his expanding soul showed Ill and Well,
> Sorrow and Joy, Beauty and Ugliness,
> Virtue and Vice, the Larger and the Less,
> All qualities, in fine, recorded here,
> Might be but Modes of Time and this one Sphere,
> Urgent on these but not of force to bind
> As Time—Eternity, as Matter—Mind,
> If Mind, Eternity shall choose assert
> Their attributes within a Life . . .

> (vi. 456–74)[17]

All life's qualities are relative, defined only in relation to the conditions of human existence and identity, time, and matter; these conditions are 'urgent on' our life, that is they dictate its course, but are not 'of force to bind' what happens beyond their reach. The binary categories of human understanding collapse under the stress of an action which Browning represents as both radical, reaching to the 'very nucleus' of the world and the self, and transcendent, the self breaking through existing boundaries to a new kind of knowledge.

Sordello now sees his 'little loves and hates' as 'mere secondary states | Of his soul's essence', since that soul partakes (as do all human souls) of the absolute, the condition in which contraries are reconciled and the very principle of division is abolished. What he achieves is not absolute knowledge itself, but the projection of his self *into* 'vague yearnings', a state of desire whose object is the 'very nucleus' of life. What will this nucleus consist of? And what would happen to the self if it actually reached it? The 'probe/globe' rhyme

[17] 'Mid' in l. 459 means 'midst of'; 'with' is understood after 'easiest' in l. 463, the sense being: 'And as this process [of probing into the nucleus] is easiest when the surface has been stripped away . . .'. The achievement of transcendental understanding is linked in both religious and philosophical tradition to the mind or soul freeing itself from the body.

takes us back to Book II of the poem, and to the platitudes of Naddo, Sordello's critic and hanger-on:

> Would you have your songs endure?
> Build on the human heart!—Why to be sure
> Yours is one sort of heart—but I mean theirs,
> Ours, every one's, the healthy heart one cares
> To build on! Central peace, mother of strength,
> That's father of . . . nay, go yourself that length,
> Ask those calm-hearted doers what they do
> When they have got their calm! Nay, is it true
> Fire rankles at the heart of every globe?
> Perhaps! But these are matters one may probe
> Too deeply for poetic purposes:
> Rather select a theory that . . . yes
> Laugh! what does that prove? . . . stations you midway
> And saves some little o'er-refining.

(ii. 798–810)[18]

Sordello is laughing at Naddo for offering a timid, compromised 'theory' of art, which rests in turn on a view of the self as stable and 'calm-hearted'. Naddo's language ('Central peace, mother of strength, | That's father of . . .') may be clear as mud, but his argument is coherent enough: it can be found better expressed in Pope, not to mention Horace. His disagreement with Sordello can also be seen as a disagreement within Romanticism: Sordello defends Byronic individualism ('one sort of heart') against Naddo's espousal of Wordsworthian common humanity ('theirs, ours, every one's'). And true to his Byronic programme, Sordello sees not stability, but imbalance at the heart of the creative self. The word 'rankles' is especially sharp here: it is associated with an inward action of physical corruption or mental suffering, has no positive connotations that I can find in any dictionary,[19] and uncompromisingly expresses Sordello's belief that creative power is born of dissatisfaction and pain. Like the speaker of 'Two in the Campagna', he turns from 'Silence and passion, joy and peace' to ask the key question: 'Where does the fault lie? What

---

[18] In l. 802, the sentence should be completed by something like 'the artist's works'; this is implied by what follows: 'nay, find out for yourself how full of energy are the works of those who are inwardly calm'. The passage is one of several prototypical dramatic monologues in *Sordello*, where the presence or utterance of an interlocutor (in this case Sordello himself) is inferred from what the speaker says.

[19] Dr Johnson is typically unequivocal: 'To fester; to breed corruption; to be inflamed in body or mind'.

the core | Of the wound, since wound must be?' (ll. 23, 39–40). To be stationed 'midway' is indeed to be saved the trouble of *ore refining*, of getting at what lies 'at the heart of every globe'. Alchemists (Browning's Paracelsus among them) believed that gold and other precious metals were deposits of fire:

> The centre-fire heaves underneath the earth,
> And the earth changes like a human face;
> The molten ore bursts up among the rocks—
> Winds into the stone's heart—outbranches bright
> In hidden mines—
>
> (v. 638–42)

Might we say, then, that what Sordello is probing for at the end of his life is such a 'centre-fire', a hidden, volcanic source of energy and creation? Perhaps; but if the desire to reach this 'nucleus' is a desire for the intensest kind of life, it is also 'evolved' by, and directed towards, death.

The nearness of plenitude to nothingness is a philosophical commonplace, and a commonplace in Browning's poetry. 'What's come to perfection perishes', he writes in 'Old Pictures in Florence' (l. 130); and in the idyllic landscape of 'Love Among the Ruins', with its 'plenty and perfection ... of grass', the bliss of sexual union is figured as annihilation:

> When I do come, she will speak not, she will stand,
>   Either hand
> On my shoulder, give her eyes the first embrace
>   Of my face,
> Ere we rush, ere we extinguish sight and speech
>   Each on each.
>
> (ll. 67–72)

The extinction of sight and speech means the extinction of personality, of selfhood, of the capacity to discern and express *difference*. The closing of the eyes and stopping of the voice by a kiss reappear in the last lines of 'Now' (published in *Asolando*, 1889): 'When ecstasy's utmost we clutch at the core | While cheeks burn, arms open, eyes shut and lips meet!' Here, moreover, the suppression of the lovers' personal identities in their 'moment eternal' of sexual bliss is figured by the grammatical suppression of the personal pronouns. Such a state of rapture, of the loss of self, is also a feature

of the consummation of hatred in Browning's poems. In his first
monologue in *The Ring and the Book*, Guido tells of his reaction
when Violante Comparini opened the door of the villa:

> She the mock-mother, she that made the match
> And married me to perdition, spring and source
> O' the fire inside me that boiled up from heart
> To brain and hailed the Fury gave it birth, —
> Violante Comparini, she it was,
> With the old grin amid the wrinkles yet,
> Opened . . .
>
> .   .   .   .   .   .
>
> Then was I rapt away by the impulse, one
> Immeasurable everlasting wave of a need
> To abolish that detested life.
>
> (v. 1651–63)

Guido's description of Violante as 'spring and source | O' the fire
inside me' suggests that in abolishing her he is abolishing the principle
of his own existence, the fire that rankles at the heart of his globe of
self.

Hatred, like love, can precipitate the loss of self as well as the
realization, the achievement of selfhood. In Part I of *Pippa Passes*,
the murderer Sebald is drowned and reborn in the 'black, fiery sea'
of his hatred (of Ottima, his accomplice, and of himself). Which is
the 'true outcome', salvation or damnation? The poem doesn't tell.
Similarly, at the end of his second monologue in *The Ring and the
Book*, Guido defiantly refuses to 'unhate [his] hates': 'I use up my
last strength to strike once more . . .' (xi. 2399). Is he used up, or
fulfilled? Perhaps the narrator, Browning, who follows hard on
Guido's heels with the final book of the poem, can tell us:

> Here were the end, had anything an end:
> Thus, lit and launched, up and up roared and soared
> A rocket, till the key o' the vault was reached,
> And wide heaven held, a breathless minute-space,
> In brilliant usurpature . . .
>
> .   .   .   .   .   .
>
> now decline must be.
>
> (xii. 1–8)

The phrase 'wide heaven' is Miltonic, and alerts us to the parallel
between Guido and Satan, with his soaring ambition and 'immortal

hate' (*Paradise Lost*, i. 107). But the difference is that, for a 'breathless minute-space', Guido's 'usurpature' of heaven succeeds. In 'Two in the Campagna' the speaker has a similar upward-moving triumph, followed by a similar 'decline':

> I yearn upward—touch you close,
> Then stand away. I kiss your cheek,
> Catch your soul's warmth,—I pluck the rose,
> And love it more than tongue can speak—
> Then the good minute goes.
>
> (ll. 46–50)

Just as Guido's 'usurpature' of heaven associates him with Satan, so the speaker's love associates him with divine rapture, with Dante's vision of the divine rose at the climax of the *Paradiso*. Dante, too, is able to grasp the full splendour of his vision only in a flash of perception, instantly followed by failure:

> la mia mente fu percossa
> da un fulgore, in che sua voglia venne.
> All' alta fantasia qui mancò possa;
>   ma già volgeva il mio disiro e il *velle*,
>   sì come rota ch' egualmente è mossa,
> l'amor che move il sole e l'altre stelle.
>
> (xxxiii. 140–5)[20]

It is the last qualifying *but* which is missing in 'Two in the Campagna': in Dante 'desire and will' are at one with divine love, even though consciousness fails to contain or express its fullness. Even Wordsworth's sublime diminishment of Dante, at the end of 'A slumber did my spirit seal', where death and loss accomplish the work of love, and the great wheel of heaven is reduced to the inanimate movement of the earth ('No motion has she now, no force . . . Rolled round in earth's diurnal course')—even this is unavailable to Browning. The speaker of 'Two in the Campagna' answers the speaker of 'Love Among the Ruins' by refusing the rush to a death-like embrace, by 'standing away' from the kiss which seals up utterance; and he answers Sordello by refusing to 'cast | Himself

---

[20] 'My mind was smitten by a flash wherein its will came to it. To the high fantasy here power failed; but already my desire and will were rolled—even as a wheel that moveth equally—by the Love that moves the sun and the other stars' (trans. Wicksteed, Temple Classics edn.).

quite thro' mere secondary states | Of his soul's essence', asserting instead the separation of the will from its object, the obstinate aloneness of the perceiving self and the grandeur of its negation: 'Only I discern— | Infinite passion, and the pain | Of finite hearts that yearn' (ll. 68–70). The lover's tragedy—or the hater's—is the writer's opportunity.

9

Twist her neck!

Odi et amo: quare id faciam, fortasse requiris.

(Catullus)[1]

COUNT GUIDO FRANCESCHINI is reflecting (in court) on his
marriage to the young girl he murdered:

> Pompilia was no pigeon, Venus' pet,
> That shuffled from between her pressing paps
> To sit on my rough shoulder,—but a hawk,
> I bought at a hawk's price and carried home
> To do hawk's service—at the Rotunda, say,
> Where, six o' the callow nestlings in a row,
> You pick and choose and pay the price for such.
> I have paid my pound, await my penny's worth,
> So, hoodwink, starve and properly train my bird,
> And, should she prove a haggard,—twist her neck!
>
> (v. 701–10)

Animal imagery is typical of Guido's two monologues in *The Ring
and the Book*—he has a beastly turn of mind and phrase—and so is
the image of marriage as an economic transaction. The image of
woman as hawk, however, is not new in Browning's poetry. It first
appears in a precursor-poem of *The Ring and the Book*, 'The Flight
of the Duchess' (*Dramatic Romances and Lyrics*, 1845). There the
narrator, an old huntsman, tells of the unhappy marriage of the
young, beautiful, life-affirming Duchess (visibly a prototype of Pompilia) to the dry, empty-headed, self-obsessed Duke. After relating how
the Duke mistreated his wife, the narrator then comments sardoni-
cally on his demand that she should take an interest in his pastimes:

> Now, my friend, if you had so little religion
> As to catch a hawk, some falcon-lanner,
> And thrust her broad wings like a banner

---

[1] 'I hate and I love: why I do you may well ask' (*Carmina* lxxxv).

> Into a coop for a vulgar pigeon;
> And if day by day, and week by week,
> You cut her claws, and sealed her eyes,
> And clipped her wings, and tied her beak,
> Would it cause you any great surprise
> If when you decided to give her an airing
> You found she needed a little preparing?
> —I say, should you be such a curmudgeon,
> If she clung to her perch, as to take it in dudgeon?
>
> (ll. 268–79)

Browning's vocabulary is famously eccentric, but why 'falcon-*lanner*'? This is *Falco lanarius*, a Mediterranean species, one of the largest of the true falcons (hence 'broad wings'). More to the point, only the female is used in falconry. The choice here is exactly equivalent to that of the tercel in 'Count Gismond'. Gismond was 'flown' at the lady's enemies in that poem and tore the guts out of one of them, 'Cleaving till out the truth he clove'. It is instructive to look back a few lines and see what pastime the Duchess was declining to take part in. The Duke is infatuated with medievalism (the poem satirizes this fad, at its height in the 1840s, the decade of Young England and the Eglinton tournament) and wants to go deer hunting in antiquarian fashion. He asks if the Duchess should have 'some share in the business' (l. 255; the ghost of an economic metaphor haunts this phrase, too):

> And, after much laying of heads together,
> Somebody's cap got a notable feather
> By the announcement with proper unction
> That he had discovered the lady's function;
> Since ancient authors held this tenet,
> 'When horns wind a mort and the deer is at siege,
> Let the dame of the Castle prick forth on her jennet,
> And with water to wash the hands of her liege
> In a clean ewer with a fair toweling
> Let her preside at the disemboweling.'
>
> (ll. 258–67)

The Duchess is the victim of an etymological joke here: the retainer who discovers 'the lady's function' gets a feather in his cap because that was originally the reward of a successful huntsman.[2] No wonder

---

[2] According to Brewer, 'In Scotland and Wales it is still customary for the sportsman

the Duchess isn't keen, you may think; but the narrator's point seems
rather to be that she might have presided with good grace if she
hadn't been cooped up like a vulgar pigeon, but treated as a proper
lanner; earlier in the poem he regretted the cooping up of the old
Duke, the present Duke's father, at an effeminate princely court
where he had to wear velvet and silk, was 'Petticoated like a herald',
and was denied the activities (of riding and hunting) that corre-
sponded to his manliness:

> Oh for a noble falcon-lanner
> To flap each broad wing like a banner,
> And turn in the wind, and dance like flame!
>
> (ll. 80–2)

That, by implication, is what the Duchess should have been doing;
then she would have been content to be the Duke's hawk. The
female's erotic and violent dance is admirable if its performance
serves its owner, and if that owner is himself vested with the
attributes of masculine mastery. Instead, she is asked to 'preside' at a
ceremony which represents a horrific compound of her husband's
impotence and cruelty, and which gives her an image of her own
powerlessness. Browning wrote to Elizabeth Barrett not long after
the poem's publication that his nightmares 'have invariably been of
one sort—I stand by (powerless to interpose by a word even) and
see the infliction of tyranny on the unresisting—man or beast
(generally the last)—and I wake just in time not to die: let no one try
this kind of experiment on me or mine!' (Kintner: 399). By the end of
that sentence it is unclear whether the 'experiment' refers to watching
or suffering, which indeed have become merged. Still, what about
turning in the wind and dancing like flame? My *Oxford Illustrated
Encyclopedia* says of falcons: 'With remarkable speed and agility
they outfly other birds and strike them in flight, following them
down to kill on the ground. Their spectacular hunting methods form
the basis of the art of falconry.' I hear a note of admiration and
approval here, a trope of pleasure carrying over from 'remarkable' to
'spectacular' so that a quality worthy of *remark* becomes the subject
of a *spectacle* and then, in turn, the basis of an *art*. The narrator of
'The *Flight* of the Duchess' clearly has such an art in mind: the Duke

who kills the first woodcock to pluck out a feather and stick it in his cap' (*Dictionary
of Phrase and Fable*, 1894 edn.).

has only himself to blame if his wife *flies* in the sense of escaping from his perverted sexuality rather than in the sense of giving him 'spectacular' pleasure.

Guido's terms, though drawn from the technical vocabulary of falconry, are vulnerable to other figurative meanings ('hoodwinked'), or to their being taken literally ('starved') and therefore suggesting cruelty rather than 'proper training'. I would also argue that the narrator-huntsman's insistence that the Duchess is not a 'vulgar pigeon' places a clear comparative value on her beside which Guido's hawk/pigeon contrast looks confused and unstable. What kind of female sexuality is Guido looking for? A 'pigeon' can be a young girl, a prostitute, a coward, an informer, and (with no further pun intended) a gull; Guido's contrast between Pompilia as purchasable hawk and a 'pigeon, Venus' pet, | That shuffled from between her pressing paps' also draws on the classical association of Venus with the dove and recalls the extraordinary graphic image in *Sordello* in which 'mother Venus' kiss-creased nipples pant | Back into pristine pulpiness' (v. 44–5). Guido both desires this kind of erotic relation and fears it. If Pompilia is barred, rhetorically, from the sexual nature represented by 'Venus' pressing paps', she is open to the charge of being a 'haggard'. A nice confluence of senses here: the word originally applied to an untamed adult female hawk, whence it easily transferred to the sexual behaviour of women. Hero says of Beatrice in *Much Ado About Nothing*, 'I know her spirits are as coy and wild | As haggards of the rock'; in *The Taming of the Shrew* Petruchio proposes to starve Kate in terms which probably directly influenced the language given by Browning to Guido:

> My falcon now is sharp and passing empty,
> And till she stoop she must not be full-gorg'd,
> For then she never looks upon her lure.
> Another way I have to man my haggard,
> To make her come, and know her keeper's call,
> That is, to watch her, as we watch these kites
> That bate and beat, and will not be obedient.

(IV. i. 174–80)

A 'haggard' also came to be used in the late seventeenth century as a synonym for 'hag' or 'witch', probably, as *OED* suggests, by adding the suffix 'ard' to 'hag' by false analogy with words such as 'dotard' and 'laggard'. The adjective 'haggard' is commonly applied to ageing women (*OED* cites Carlyle: 'She is getting haggard beyond the power of rouge'), and, as Jane Mills points out, could imply both unchastity (Othello of Desdemona: 'If I do prove her haggard, | Though that her jesses were my dear heart-strings, | I'd whistle her off and let her down the wind | To prey at fortune', III. iii. 264–7) and reluctance to yield to wooing (Mills: 113–14).[3] Guido's metaphor has plenty of misogynist bite. But that doesn't make it any less confused, because, to go back to the falconry aspect, a 'haggard' is an *adult* bird and Guido says quite clearly that Pompilia is a 'callow nestling' (which is accurate, of course). If you buy a callow nestling the one thing she *can't* turn out to be is a haggard. It may be (at one level this is certainly the case) that Guido's defence requires Pompilia to have been, when he acquired her, both malleable child and grown-up witch, so that her betrayal of him can be seen as both unexpected and only-to-be-expected. But the more disturbing explanation is not that Pompilia 'proves'—turns out to be—a haggard, but that Guido turns her into one, 'properly trains' her for that role, because what he really wants is to twist her neck.

He wouldn't be the first in Browning's poetry, and isn't the most famous. But before I come to Porphyria's lover I want to say a little more about the Duke in 'The Flight of the Duchess', and about two other aristocrats—one a precursor of Guido's, the other a successor—who also kill their wives.

Sexual hatred in 'The Flight of the Duchess' is linked to a classic neurosis, that of an absent father and a dominating mother. After the old Duke's death, says the narrator, 'the sick tall yellow Duchess | Was left with the infant in her clutches' (ll. 89–90); the Duke is brought up in Paris, and comes back to his Ruritanian home 'the pertest ape | That ever affronted human shape' (ll. 99–100). The father-lack which causes his deformity is projected as a false ancestor-worship, 'aping' the 'Heroic Time' of his forefathers:

> So, all the old Dukes had been, without knowing it,
> This Duke would fain know he was, without being it;
> 'Twas not for the joy's self, but the joy of his showing it,
> Nor for the pride's self, but the pride of our seeing it.

---

[3] Mills surprisingly makes no mention of 'pigeon' in her entry on 'bird'-words; it would seem a classic example of an endearment which has potential or actual pejorative connotations.

He revived all usages thoroughly worn-out,
The souls of them fumed-forth, the hearts of them torn-out . . .

(ll. 112–17)

The satire of the Duke's phoney primitivism has a Carlylean as well
as Freudian accent here, in its scorn for modern self-consciousness
('knowing' rather than 'being'), for the artificial reconstruction of the
past (today the Duke would undoubtedly turn his estate into a
historical theme park), and especially for the substitution of specular
pleasure for 'the joy's self'. The Duke's revival of old customs is
vampiric, and anticipates his interest in watching his wife 'preside at the
disemboweling'. He is also associated with images of sexual repression
and confinement, and here his mother makes her presence overtly felt:
when the young Duchess comes from the convent to marry him,

The Duke stepped rather aside than forward,
And welcomed her with his grandest smile;
And, mind you, his mother all the while
Chilled in the rear, like a wind to Nor'ward;
And up, like a weary yawn, with its pullies
Went, in a shriek, the rusty portcullis . . .

(ll. 158–63)

Not much hope for sexual fulfilment is offered here, and none is
forthcoming. (These images of imprisonment, cold, and cruel senility
are repeated and elaborated in *The Ring and the Book* in descriptions
of Pompilia's arrival at Guido's family home in Arezzo.) The narrator
goes as far as he can (in 1845) in hinting at the Duchess's sexual
energy—

She was active, stirring, all fire—
Could not rest, could not tire—
To a stone she had given life!

(ll. 174–6)

—and at the Duke's worse than stony response:

the Duke's plan admitted a wife, at most,
To meet his eye, with the other trophies,
Now outside the Hall, now in it,
To sit thus, stand thus, see and be seen,
At the proper place in the proper minute,
And die away the life between . . .

(ll. 186–91)

Again the emphasis on *seeing*, added to which there is the sense of
the Duchess as an object on which 'life' is conferred only when it
'meets the eye' of its master and reflects his self-image—hence the
use of 'trophies' with its connotations of conquest and hunting.

The Duke's obsession with authentic medieval rituals and especially costumes (another very Carlylean touch, that) points to his
sexual emptiness; it may be thought of as the reverse of the speaker's
formalism in 'Soliloquy of the Spanish Cloister', which covers over
the demonic energy of his inner life. The Duke has literally nothing
to hide, except the wound inflicted on him by his mother, the nature
of which is suggested by her reaction to the Duchess's eventual
escape: 'How she turned as a shark to snap the spare-rib | Clean off,
sailors say, from a pearl-diving Carib' (ll. 791–2). But as Brother
Lawrence and the Duchess share an unaffected spontaneous enjoyment of life, so the monk and the Duke have in common a hatred for
that enjoyment and a desire to spoil or denigrate it. The Duke,
indeed, goes one step further (a step which Guido will follow and
improve upon) in that, by a very human paradox, he hates his wife
both for being what she is and for not being it. He crushes her spirit
and then perceives her lack of spirit as dumb insolence:

> So the little Lady grew silent and thin,
>   Paling and ever paling,
> As the way is with a hid chagrin;
>   And the Duke perceived that she was ailing,
> And said in his heart, ''Tis done to spite me,
> But I shall find in my power to right me!'
>
> (ll. 208–13)

What makes the difference in 'The Flight of the Duchess' is that,
since the Duke is a burlesque figure and the poem a romantic
comedy, his 'power' is limited and, in the end, easily circumvented.
This is true in social as well as personal terms, since the Duke's
failure to live up to his wife is linked to his failure to live up to his
position. In this sense the opening of the poem, with its description
of the 'great wild country' which forms the Duke's domain (ll. 6–31)
gives a deceptive image of his authority. It is a virtuoso piece of
landscape painting, leading the eye from a vantage point on 'our
castle's top' past rich agricultural land, vineyards, pasture, 'open-
chase', mountains, a 'vast red drear burnt-up plain . . . Whence iron's
dug, and copper's dealt' (an industrial landscape anticipating the

plain in 'Childe Roland') all the way to the 'salt sand hoar of the
great sea-shore'. 'And the whole is our Duke's country!' exclaims the
narrator; but the Duke is not modelled on the scale of what he owns.
He is, so to speak, an *imp*otentate. The disproportion between the
size and resources of the country and the physical and spiritual
debility of its nominal possessor was a common feature of contemporary radical criticism of the aristocracy, and we can see such a
critique in the narrator's scornful account of the Duke's retreat into
the past and into dependence on his mother. Since the Duke isn't up
to the Duchess, can't cope either sexually or socially with her
dynamic and progressive spirit, his apparently unwitting part in her
escape (he lets in the old gypsy who persuades the Duchess to leave)
is founded on an unstated complicity. As the narrator remarks, 'The
Duchess was gone and the Duke was glad of it, | And the old one
was in the young one's stead' (ll. 819–20). It's a happy ending all
round (except for the narrator, who is left behind to tell the story
like the lame boy at the end of 'The Pied Piper of Hamelin'), and it's
the only point in the poem when the word 'glad', which is otherwise
associated with the Duchess's love of life, is applied to the Duke.

If the form of 'The Flight of the Duchess' limits the Duke's ability
to harm his wife, this is partly because he is an inadequate aristocrat,
who 'knows' what he is rather than simply 'being' it. He descends
bathetically from the Duke in 'My Last Duchess' (*Dramatic Lyrics*,
1842) who represents the genuine article in murderous aristocratic
ego. A historical degeneration, and again a very Carlylean one, is in
operation here, from Renaissance authenticity to modern unreality
and hollowness. The contrast between them can be seen in the way
an image of unbending integrity descends from the sublime to the
ridiculous. In 'My Last Duchess' the Duke rejects the paltry expedient
of rebuking his wife for what he perceives to be her misconduct with
the famous words: 'E'en then would be some stooping, and I chuse |
Never to stoop' (ll. 42–3). This choice sums up an aspect of aristocratic *hauteur* which commands respect because of its very extremity,
because it is the quintessence of itself. In 'The Flight of the Duchess'
the Duke also chooses not to stoop, but he is made to look an ass in
the process. Too cowardly to rebuke his wife himself, he leaves the
task to his mother; and when she ends her harangue he stalks out of
the room, 'making (he hoped) a face | Like Emperor Nero or Sultan
Saladin . . . From door to staircase—oh, such a solemn | Unbending
of the vertebral column!' (ll. 326–31). The act of will by which the

Duke of Ferrara chooses to be himself becomes, for the later Duke, a feeble act, a performance vitiated by self-conscious anxiety to appear the thing he is not.

Nevertheless, it seems that the Duke of Ferrara hates his wife for the same reason as the Duke in 'The Flight of the Duchess', because of the 'life and gladness | That *over*-filled her' (ll. 137–8, my italics). This element of excess is very important: in 'My Last Duchess' the Duchess has 'A heart . . . too soon made glad, | Too easily impressed' (ll. 22–3), and even in his mimicry of the painter, Frà Pandolf's, professional courtesy the Duke can't resist the gratuitous, the exuberant note: 'perhaps | Frà Pandolf chanced to say "Her mantle laps | Over my Lady's wrist too much" ' (ll. 15–17). Brother Lawrence, too, drains his 'watered orange-pulp' at one gulp, looks forward to 'feasting' on a slice of melon, hopes his flowers will bear 'double' blossoms. In *Pippa Passes* the sun rises because it cannot be contained: 'the whole sunrise, not to be supprest, | Rose-reddened, and its seething breast | Flickered in bounds, grew gold, then overflowed the world' (Introduction, ll. 10–12). In *The Inn Album* a young girl, who resembles Pippa in her innocent gladness, babbles to herself in 'a voice that sounds like song', prompted by a 'stir of heart | That unsubduably must bubble forth' (ll. 3049–52). The blood rises to the Duchess's face in a 'spot of joy' which, as the Duke obscurely but acutely grasps, is a mark of self-delight rather than self-regard.

But if 'My Last Duchess' remains a more powerful and interesting poem than 'The Flight of the Duchess', it is partly because the Duke's hatred of his wife is not exactly comparable in the two poems. In 'The Flight of the Duchess' the Duke hates his wife because he fails to desire her, shrinks from the pleasure she offers. The Duke in 'My Last Duchess' is a much more complex figure because his hatred of his wife is *itself a mode of desire*. It is precisely because he is a true aristocrat that the conflict between his desire for the Duchess and his self-image is so sharp, and why the outcome can be seen as tragic on his side as well as on hers.

Here is his catalogue of the occasions on which the Duchess took her promiscuous pleasure:

> she liked whate'er
> She looked on, and her looks went everywhere.
> Sir, 'twas all one! My favor at her breast,
> The dropping of the daylight in the West,

> The bough of cherries some officious fool
> Broke in the orchard for her, the white mule
> She rode with round the terrace—all and each
> Would draw from her alike the forward speech,
> Or blush, at least. She thanked men,—good; but thanked
> Somehow . . I know not how . . as if she ranked
> My gift of a nine hundred years old name
> With anybody's gift.
>
> (ll. 23–34)

Some of these images can be given a sexual colouring, and there is certainly a sexual connotation in 'forward' and 'blush', but even ignoring this the lines would still carry the burden of the Duke's sexual feeling. His resentment is linked, as in 'The Flight of the Duchess', with the Duchess's transgression of an aristocratic role, with the indiscriminate—you might say the democratic, the *levelling*—nature of her gratified 'looks'. But there is a suggestion in the use of the word 'gift' which is quite foreign to the Duke in 'The Flight of the Duchess', and, indeed, quite foreign to the Duke of Ferrara as he appears at the end of the poem, when he resumes discussion with the envoy about his second marriage:

> The Count your Master's known munificence
> Is ample warrant that no just pretence
> Of mine for dowry will be disallowed;
> Though his fair daughter's self, as I avowed
> At starting, is my object.
>
> (ll. 49–53)

The Duke's language signals the diplomatic hypocrisy of negotiation, and readers are no doubt meant to understand that he *is* at least as interested in the 'dowry' as the 'self' which, as has often been remarked, he makes into an 'object' to be owned. Certainly the transaction which ends the poem looks forward to Guido's blunt statement that he bargained with his *name* for Pompilia's wealth;[4] but no such bargain is implied in the case of the Duke's first marriage. What rankles with the Duke is that the Duchess doesn't prize his *gift* more highly than that of other people. He is recording, however obliquely, that he, like everyone else (like every other man,

---

[4] He is especially insistent on the point in his first monologue: 'Did I not pay my name and style, my hope, | And trust, my all?' (v. 711–12).

we had better say perhaps), was touched with desire for the Duchess, wanted both to please her and to be 'thanked', to offer her a seductive 'gift'. The Duke is *like* Frà Pandolf with his compliments, or the 'officious fool' who breaks a bough of cherries for her, not distinguished from them except by the possession of a 'nine hundred years old name' which gives the Duchess no more or less pleasure than 'the dropping of the daylight in the West'.

Hatred in 'My Last Duchess', then, is intimately tied to, and is indeed a product of, a sexual desire which cannot tolerate the very quality in its object which elicited the desire in the first place. The Duke would not have wanted to 'give' his name to the Duchess or (in an equivalent metonymic gesture) place his 'favor at her breast' had she not been the kind of person whose indiscriminate erotic joy would also cause him to murder her. Murder is the logical outcome of the dilemma, or rather murder is a logical means of achieving (by the possession and recurrent, obsessive display of the painting) the outcome which the Duchess denied to him in life. In life 'her *looks* went everywhere'; in art she is painted '*Looking as if* she were alive', but with her look closed off except at the Duke's discretion.

'My Last Duchess' and 'The Flight of the Duchess' remain joined at this point: that what cannot be tolerated is the scandal of a female sexuality which 'laps over' the categories set up to contain it. The ideal of female sexuality which the huntsman-narrator of 'The Flight of the Duchess' articulates in the metaphor of the falcon turning in the wind and dancing like flame is grounded in an assumption that down there, on the ground, is the falconer for whom the dance is performed. This position is taken to extremes in *The Ring and the Book*, where Guido's flawed maleness, like that of the Duke in 'The Flight of the Duchess', gives his fear and hatred of his wife an extra intensity. But in the last of Browning's poems about aristocratic wife-killers, hatred of the female is a pathological product not of anxiety but of self-regard. If the Duke of 'My Last Duchess' has a direct descendant in Browning's poetry, it is the Spanish nobleman (of exalted but unspecified rank) who speaks 'A Forgiveness'; but the line swerves, with irremediable perverseness, through the debased anti-hero of *The Ring and the Book*.

The story of 'A Forgiveness' (published in *Pacchiarotto . . . with other Poems*, 1876) is one of the oddest in Browning's later work, a mixture of the conventional, the grotesque, and the subtle. Like *The*

Inn Album, published the year before, it is influenced by the contemporary 'sensation' novel, with its lurid sexual melodrama, but also displays a Jamesian refinement of motivation.[5] A Spanish grandee, with an important (but again unspecified) political position, kneels at the 'confession-grate' in a monastery, telling the monk the story of his marriage. He idolized his wife until he returned home early one day and caught her with her lover. The man escaped, and the wife declared her hatred for her husband. However, he did not kill her then, in order to save the appearance of his marriage which was necessary for his work. For three years they remained together, preserving the public image of the marriage but shunning one another in private. But at the end of three years the wife requested an interview with her husband. She revealed to him that she had always loved him, but had been jealous of his work and had engaged in the affair in order to draw attention to her neglected state. She also revealed that she was dying of the anguish which 'the truth concealed' was causing her. He responded by explaining to her that he had spared her out of contempt as well as convenience; now, however, she has become worthy of his hatred. He makes her sign a humiliating confession in her own blood, drawn with a dagger which turns out to be poisoned. By her consenting death her crime against him is truly expiated, and in turn his hatred is re-transformed into the love he first felt for her. The poem ends (somewhat too neatly) with the speaker stabbing the monk through the grate, since he is in fact the wife's former lover.

Browning liked this poem: when Edmund Gosse asked him to choose four medium-length poems as fairly representing his work, he chose 'A Forgiveness' in the 'narrative' category.[6] But it doesn't hang together; its interest lies elsewhere than in the psychological realism of the plot or the conduct of the action (which, especially in the final part, is absurdly and garishly theatrical). In some of its aspects the

---

[5] The comparison with James is made by Langbaum with reference to this poem and 'Porphyria's Lover': 'it is generally true that extraordinary motives in Browning come not from disordered subconscious urges but, as in Henry James, from the highest moral and intellectual refinement' (Langbaum: 88). I am not sure, however, that Langbaum's categorical distinction is helpful here. It seems to me more typical of Browning that 'the highest moral and intellectual refinement' should be the *product* of 'disordered subconscious urges'.

[6] See Hood: 235. The others were 'Saul' or 'Abt Vogler' in the 'lyrical' category, 'Caliban upon Setebos' in the 'dramatic', and 'Clive' in the 'Idyllic (in the Greek sense)'.

poem is laughably banal, as in the husband-coming-home-early scene which Fra Lippo Lippi (another adulterous monk) had long ago made fun of:

> I shuffle sideways with my blushing face
> Under the cover of a hundred wings
> Thrown like a spread of kirtles when you're gay
> And play hot cockles, all the doors being shut,
> Till, wholly unexpected, in there pops
> The hothead husband!

(ll. 378–83)

The wife's revelation that her affair sprang from resentment at her husband spending too much time at the office is also out of proportion with the poem's grandiose emotional flourishes. A visit to the marriage guidance counsellor would seem more appropriate. This disproportion leads with bathetic logic to Clyde Ryals's reading of the poem in terms of the woman's failure to understand her husband's judicious balance between home and work: 'The speaker of "A Forgiveness" had been glad to have love and duty combined . . . But the wife became jealous of her husband's attention to his work and pretended to love another so as to provoke her husband to forgo the claims of duty. The result is the unhappiness of both and eventually her death' (Ryals: 136). *So it's all the little woman's fault!* Surely this sacrifices more of the poem than it saves.

I propose a different reading, one which takes the poem's thinness and implausibility as an indication that Browning invested his imaginative energy in other aspects of its design. The poem returns to the sexual triangle of *The Ring and the Book*: aristocratic husband, wife, priest-lover. The speaker is like a rehabilitation of the odious Guido; he is like Guido's day-dream of himself. Wealthy, powerful, commanding, desirable, free of the imputation of sordid motives, he has a wife who hurts him out of mistaken malice but then crawls back to him begging to be punished, and a sneaking coward of a rival whom he gets to murder at the end. Throughout the poem his self-conceit is as untouched as that of the Duke in 'My Last Duchess', but unlike him he has no unwilling erotic tribute to pay to his wife. Narrative power is self-serving, and the speaker makes full use of it. The retrospective form of the poem allows him to incorporate *his* humiliation at the discovery that he is a cuckold into a larger narrative, that of *her* humiliation and his grotesque 'forgiveness' of her.

Another narrative device, that of digression, gives this perfected or self-vindicated Guido some of his darkest enjoyments. When his wife confesses to him that she had loved him all along, instead of replying directly he engages in a lengthy description of his collection of oriental daggers:

> I think there never was such—how express?—
> Horror coquetting with voluptuousness,
> As in those arms of Eastern workmanship.
> Yataghan, kandjar, things that rend and rip,
> Gash rough, slash smooth, help hate so many ways,
> Yet ever keep a beauty that betrays
> Love still at work with the artificer
> Throughout his quaint devising. Why prefer,
> Except for love's sake, that a blade should writhe
> And bicker like a flame?—now play the scythe
> As if some broad neck tempted,—now contract
> And needle off into a fineness lacked
> For just that puncture which the heart demands?
>
> (ll. 247–59)

He then goes on to describe one such weapon in loving detail:

> No asp
> Is diapered more delicate round throat
> Than this below the handle! These denote
> —These mazy lines meandering, to end
> Only in flesh they open—what intend
> They else but water-purlings—pale contrast
> With the life-crimson where they blend at last?
>
> (ll. 264–70)

What is this digression for? To record (with however slender relevance) that a friend had recently bequeathed Browning himself such a collection (DeVane: 409)? That is only a little less likely than the idea that it somehow 'fits' the speaker's character (Spanish, decadent nobleman, connoisseur, etc.). It might, but it would not have the same precise link with the action of the poem as the similar passage in 'The Laboratory' in which the *ancien régime* speaker fantasizes about the decorative disguises available to the poisoner: 'To carry pure death in an earring, a casket, | A signet, a fan-mount, a filagree-basket!' (ll. 19–20). Nor is it quite the same as the passage from *The Ring and the Book* which it more obviously 'quotes', the description of the weapon with which Guido murdered Pompilia and the Comparini:

> how the dagger laid there at the feet,
> Caused the peculiar cuts; I mind its make,
> Triangular i' the blade, a Genoese,
> Armed with those little hook-teeth on the edge
> To open in the flesh nor shut again . . .

> (ii. 145–9)

The speaker's assumed detachment intends to disguise his relish here: it belongs to that (currently popular) genre of writing about crime, whether real or fictional, which licences you to enjoy the pleasures of cruelty by masking them in impersonal 'technical' detail. But though the speaker of 'A Forgiveness' may well be savouring such pleasure, he is also, and perhaps more importantly, savouring the pleasure of *delay*. After all, he is telling the whole story to the man he intends to kill at the end of it.[7] He resembles Ogniben, in *A Soul's Tragedy*, in his enjoyment of a secret knowledge which he will spring on his victim at the critical moment. But Ogniben does not have the speaker's murderous coquetry. The bulk of the poem is foreplay to the assassination that consummates it. And within the poem the speaker's digression defers the consummation of his murder of his wife, which is also (as we shall see in the case of Porphyria's lover) a recovery, a resumption of his earlier power over her.

The collection of daggers is housed in his study, a place which is of special significance to the speaker, because it metaphorically denotes his inner and hidden 'self'. It is a 'secret domicile' (l. 199), secluded from the public apartments and reached by a devious and winding route: the 'damp | Blind disused serpentining ways' and 'stairs tunneled through the stone' recall the 'maze of corridors contrived for sin, | Dusk winding-stairs, dim galleries' which lead to the 'inmost chambers' of the castle of Goito, and especially to the 'maple-panelled room' where Sordello's mother, unbeknownst to him, lies buried in the carved stone font (i. 390 ff.). In 'A Forgiveness' the 'lone | Chamber sepulchred for my very own | Out of the palace-quarry' (ll. 180–2) is also a place of death, presided over not by the mother, however, but by 'my father's gift, the arquebuss' which hangs on the wall (l. 201). It has served the speaker successively in boyhood as his 'fortress, stronghold from annoy, | Proof-positive of

[7] Probably with the very dagger he describes: he says to the monk (who can't see through the grate, of course): 'Nay, behold! | Fancy my favorite—which I seem to grasp | While I describe the luxury' (ll. 262–4).

ownership' (ll. 183–4), in youth as the repository of 'precious relics of vain hopes, vain fears' (l. 186), and finally in manhood as his retreat from his public self, his 'closet of entrenchment to withstand | Invasion of the foe on every hand' (ll. 188–9). The speaker's masculinity is bound up with this sense of threat, of having to guard constantly against a hostile force which will desecrate the treasures of his inner life and call into question his 'ownership' of himself. The degree of protection suggests the degree of vulnerability. It is in this room that the wife makes her 'confession' to the speaker, and in which he 'absolves' her by death—the death which he will go on to inflict as a 'penitent' on the monk who is confessing *him*. He deliberately occupies every position of power in the poem, because the scale of his threatened displacement is so enormous. What the speaker restores to himself, through his murder of both wife and lover, is his very sense of himself, so that at the end of the poem the words he says at the beginning—'Power and place | I had as still I have' (ll. 7–8)—should be affirmed beyond further question.

'Proof-positive of ownership', therefore, is what the speaker desires; it comes to him in the form of his wife's testimony that she *always* loved him and *still* loves him; it is this testimony that he makes her write in her own blood, pricking herself with the poisoned dagger. In the words of an earlier murderer: 'That moment she was mine'. Porphyria's lover repeats it, marvelling to himself: 'That moment she was mine,—mine, fair, | Perfectly pure and good' (ll. 36–7). He, too, re-enters a lost paradise of possession which turns out to be a place of death.

Because of its association with 'Johannes Agricola', especially in the form of their temporary pairing under the collective title 'Madhouse Cells', 'Porphyria' has invited critical consideration as a poem 'about' madness.[8] But to put it in this way may imply that the specific form—that of sexual violence—taken by the speaker's madness in the poem is less important than the representation of madness as such. The poem's two individual titles may differ as to whether the focus should be on Porphyria or on her lover, but they agree that Porphyria has something to do with it. She is his subject, and should be ours.

---

[8] For the publication history see Woolford and Karlin: i. 328. 'Porphyria' was later renamed 'Porphyria's Lover', and 'Johannes Agricola' became 'Johannes Agricola in Meditation'. The best discussion of 'Porphyria' as a poem about madness is by Michael Mason, in Armstrong: 254–66.

The poem may be represented structurally as follows: an introduction (ll. 1–5) setting the scene and the speaker's state of mind; Porphyria's entry, actions (lighting the fire, removing her wet clothes, etc.), and words (ll. 6–21); the speaker's negative reflection on her character (ll. 21–5); his more positive judgement of her (ll. 26–30); his realization that she 'worships' him (ll. 31–5); the murder and its immediate aftermath (ll. 36–57); the speaker's concluding comment, which shifts from the past tense to the present and lengthens the time-scale (ll. 58–60).

I take pains over this structural outline because its importance is rarely acknowledged in criticism of the poem. In particular, it suggests that the turning-point in the poem is not an external event or action but an interpretation of Porphyria's actions, and that this interpretation leads to a reversal of the power relation between Porphyria and her lover. This interpretation (which, like that of the speaker of 'A Forgiveness' of his wife's conduct, 'retrieves | Importantly the past') is the outcome of a struggle in the speaker's mind between two judgements of Porphyria: one that she is weak and selfish, the other that she is strong and devoted. These judgements, in turn, relate to Porphyria's social class, to her being the speaker's social superior.[9] He lives in a 'cottage' in the grounds of her estate (it has elm-trees and a lake); her dress and physical attributes are socially marked, as every contemporary reader would have recognized: cloak and shawl, delicate gloves (they have been 'soiled' by the bad weather and are also 'soiled' by association with her wealth), hat, bound-up hair, 'smooth white shoulder bare' (i.e. a *décolleté* dress); she comes from a 'gay feast' to his cottage with its 'cheerless grate'. When the speaker describes how the 'sullen wind . . . tore the elm-tops down for spite | And did its best to vex the lake' (ll. 2–4), the violence which he projects onto the natural world carries a social as well as sexual charge; so does his depiction of Porphyria's actions when she enters the cottage:

> I listened, with heart fit to break,
> When glided in Porphyria: straight
> She shut the cold out and the storm,
> And kneeled and made the cheerless grate

[9] W. D. Shaw points out that 'the strangler's scheme for prolonging sexual submission . . . inverts the social reverence which an inferior owes to a member of a higher social order' (Shaw: 75). But I cannot agree with Shaw that the design of the poem is 'deliberately shallow in the moral dimension', a 'one-act thriller'.

Blaze up, and all the cottage warm;
Which done, she rose, and from her form
Withdrew the dripping cloak and shawl,
　　And laid her soiled gloves by; untied
Her hat and let the damp hair fall,
　　And, last, she sate down by my side
And called me. When no voice replied,
She put my arm about her waist,
　　And made her smooth white shoulder bare,
And all her yellow hair displaced,
　　And, stooping, made my cheek lie there
And spread o'er all her yellow hair,
Murmuring how she loved me—she
　　Too weak, for all her heart's endeavour,
To set its struggling passion free
　　From pride, and vainer ties dissever,
And give herself to me for ever.

(ll. 5–25)

Even if Browning didn't know that a 'porphyre' was an archaic term
for a species of snake, Porphyria's 'gliding in' would be enough,
taken with her long yellow hair, to establish her serpentine qualities;
as in Andrea del Sarto's description of Lucrezia's 'serpentining
beauty, rounds on rounds', the implication is that she is desirable but
can't be trusted. Her actions amount, in the speaker's eyes, to a
seduction, a power play. Porphyria *makes* things happen: '*made* the
cheerless grate | Blaze up . . . *made* her smooth white shoulder bare
. . . *made* my cheek lie there'. Her undressing is sensuous but not
yielding; even her 'kneeling' and 'stooping' are the preludes to acts of
compulsion. Porphyria has power to bind and to loose, both to 'shut
the cold out and the storm' and 'let the damp hair fall'. A tiny detail
registers how she threatens to overcome him, the change of meaning
of the word 'all' in the repeated phrase 'all her yellow hair', where it
means first (l. 18) that she pushes away all her hair and then (l. 20)
that she spreads her hair like a net across all of his face.

Had Porphyria read Browning's *Pauline* she might have thought
twice about the effect on the speaker of her erotic, nurturing, and
entrapping gestures. They come associated in the opening lines of
that poem with a threat of the release of violent 'fancies':

Pauline, mine own, bend o'er me—thy soft breast
Shall pant to mine—bend o'er me—thy sweet eyes,

> And loosened hair, and breathing lips, and arms
> Drawing me to thee—these build up a screen
> To shut me in with thee, and from all fear,
> So that I might unlock the sleepless brood
> Of fancies from my soul, their lurking place,
> Nor doubt that each would pass, ne'er to return
> To one so watched, so loved, and so secured.
>
> (ll. 1–9)

I wouldn't feel reassured by the speaker's lack of doubt here, even if it weren't immediately contradicted in the next lines, which worry that 'whoso sucks a poisoned wound | Envenoms his own veins' (ll. 11–12). I might notice how the word 'loved' is handcuffed between 'watched' and 'secured' in l. 9, and wonder what resentment might flow from that, and whether being shut in with someone in order for him to unlock his sleepless brood of fancies is altogether a healthy idea. Any anxiety I felt would not diminish when later on I found my sexuality cited as a stimulus to murder:

> How the blood lies upon her cheek, all spread
> As thinned by kisses; only in her lips
> It wells and pulses like a living thing,
> And her neck looks like marble misted o'er
> With love-breath, a dear thing to kiss and love,
> Standing beneath me—looking out to me
> As I might kill her and be loved for it.
>
> (ll. 896–902)[10]

These lines bring us close to 'Porphyria', as several editors and critics have noticed; moreover the physical relationship has altered from that of the opening lines of the poem, so that the woman is now 'beneath' her lover, in a position where his dominance, whether expressed as kissing or killing, is invited by her erotic passivity.

In *Pauline* this image of a woman seduced by the idea of death forms part of the protagonist's 'sleepless brood | Of fancies', and partakes of the instability, rapid shifts, and incoherence of his mental

---

[10] In the revised version of the poem published in the *Poetical Works* of 1888–9, Browning changed the last three lines to read: 'With love-breath,—a Pauline from heights above, | Stooping beneath me, looking up—one look | As I might kill her and be loved the more'. The 'heights above' are almost certainly intended to be spiritual, and to replace what Browning probably saw as the 'Cockney-school' vulgarity and frankness of the original, but together with 'stooping' the revision brings the passage even closer to 'Porphyria', whose heroine pays dearly for her descent from social 'heights'.

processes, where every movement of thought may be contradicted
and disowned—as, indeed, is this one in the very next lines: 'All
these words are wild and weak, | Believe them not, Pauline' (ll. 904–
5). In 'Porphyria' the image is 'for real' (in terms of its dramatic
consequences) and the speaker is in control of the sequence of events.
He may be mad, but he hasn't lost his mind. But he does not take the
same route as the protagonist of *Pauline* to get to the point where he
sees in Porphyria's eyes the look which tells him that he may 'kill her
and be loved for it'. Murder is not a consummation of eroticism but
the outcome of an argument by which the speaker reverses Porphyria's mastery. His response to her behaviour makes a semantic bridge
between her willingness to minister to him (to warm him, to undress
for him, to express her love for him in words and gestures), in all of
which he sees the mark of her superiority to him, and her *un*willingness to undo that superiority itself, to descend from the social
situation which enables her to condescend to him. She unties her hat
but not the 'vainer social ties' (those of her wealth, possibly even her
marriage). Against the actions of freeing and loosening which express
Porphyria's sexual and social power the speaker sets the action of
freeing and loosening he wants her to take: 'To set its [i.e. her heart's]
struggling passion free | From pride . . . And give herself to me for
ever.'

'Passion' in the female connotes such a self-surrender. In 'The
Flight of the Duchess' the old gypsy woman offers the Duchess this
prospect of self-fulfilment: but it is crucially not the *only* prospect,
but part of a dualism.[11] The Duchess may find sexual fulfilment
either as the dominant or the submissive partner, 'as climbing-plant
or propping-tree':

> Shall some one deck thee, over and down,
> Up and about, with blossoms and leaves?
> Fix his heart's fruit for thy garland crown,
> Cling with his soul as the gourd-vine cleaves,
> Die on thy boughs and disappear
> While not a leaf of thine is sere?
> Or is the other fate in store,
> And art thou fitted to adore,
> To give thy wondrous self away,

[11] The gypsy contends that a true and equal *union* between male and female is
impossible, and that there must be a stronger and weaker partner in each relationship;
for Browning's re-examination of this idea in 'By the Fire-Side', see Ch. 11.

And take a stronger nature's sway?

(ll. 636-45)

In 'Porphyria' the first of these alternatives is invoked and rejected; only the second is allowed. In 'The Flight of the Duchess' it is a question of discovering what one's nature is 'fitted' for. There may be something inherently disturbing in the images of surrender, of dying and disappearing, of taking a stronger nature's sway, but it is not a disturbance that contradicts or undoes the whole of the gypsy's ecstatic incantation.[12] But in 'Porphyria' the alternatives are seen in terms of a power-struggle: sexual violence *fixes* the relation between Porphyria and her lover as 'climbing-plant' and 'propping-tree' respectively. The speaker's powerful refusal to let Porphyria be the 'propping-tree' is expressed by his conscious reversal of their literal, physical positions on the couch where they are sitting: before the murder she makes his head rest on her shoulder, but afterwards

> I propped her head up as before,
> Only, this time my shoulder bore
> Her head—which droops upon it still . . .

(ll. 49-51)

The word 'droops' is especially chilling in this context because it is *empty of volition*. It insists that Porphyria's 'utmost will' is to have no power left to will either in physical or metaphysical terms. We are far from the erotic fantasy in 'A Toccata of Galuppi's' of 'the breast's superb abundance where a man might base his head' (l. 15).

Porphyria's lover differs from his precursor in *Pauline* in another way. In *Pauline* there is the sense of an equivalence between killing and intercourse. It would not be surprising if the narrator had stabbing in mind. Knives are commonly used to terrify rape victims; Titian's picture of the rape of Lucrece shows the figure of Tarquin with raised dagger and knee thrust between Lucrece's legs in order to force them open. The two kinds of penetration are fused in one of the principal 'literary' sources for 'Porphyria', extracts from a fictional 'madman's diary' in *Blackwood's Magazine*: 'Do you think there was no pleasure in murdering her? I grasped her by that radiant, that golden hair, I bared those snow-white breasts,—I dragged her sweet body towards me, and, as God is my witness, I

---

[12] Palma, in *Sordello*, is an example of someone who takes 'a stronger nature's sway': she ends up in the heaven of Venus in Dante's *Paradiso* 'because the light of this star overcame me'.

stabbed, and stabbed her with this dagger, forty times.'[13] God is a witness in 'Porphyria', too—a silent one, as the speaker famously remarks in the last line of the poem—but what he sees is not this blatant sexual 'stabbing' but an insanely logical act of redress. Porphyria's lover does not murder her because he feels the act of murder to be the equivalent of sexual intercourse, but in order to achieve the desired balance of power in his relationship with her. If the *Blackwood's* passage has a direct descendant in Browning's work, it is rather Tertium Quid's description, in *The Ring and the Book*, of Guido's murder of Pompilia:

> And last, Pompilia rushes here and there
> Like a dove among lightnings in her brake,
> Falls also: Guido's, this last husband's-act.
> He lifts her by the long dishevelled hair,
> Holds her away at arms' length with one hand,
> While the other tries if life come from the mouth—
> Looks out his whole heart's hate on the shut eyes,
> Draws a deep satisfied breath, 'So—dead at last!'
>
> (iv. 1382–9)

The image of Pompilia as a 'dove' (which rebuts Guido's contention that she was 'no pigeon, Venus' pet'), the allusion to Guido's 'husband's-act' and his 'deep satisfied breath', make clear that, in Tertium Quid's view at any rate, the murder is equivalent to a sexual consummation. But Porphyria's lover strangles her not (or not simply) because strangling is a displacement of erotic desire but because strangling takes its place in the poem's *rhetorical* scheme of binding and loosing, closing and opening:

> all her hair
> In one long yellow string I wound
> Three times her little throat around
> And strangled her. No pain felt she—
> I am quite sure she felt no pain.
> As a shut bud that holds a bee
> I warily oped her lids—again
> Laughed the blue eyes without a stain.
> And I untightened next the tress
> About her neck—her cheek once more
> Blushed bright beneath my burning kiss . . .
>
> (ll. 38–48)

---

[13] For further details on this source see Woolford and Karlin: i. 328.

The physiological detail here is significantly half-accurate. (I don't count the speaker's idea that being strangled is, on the whole, a rather jolly experience.) A strangled person's eyes initially protrude, then close when the supply of blood to the brain is cut off and death occurs; but simultaneously their face, initially suffused with blood, becomes pale and would *not* re-redden when the pressure was released, because there would be no circulatory motion left.[14] Porphyria's eyes would indeed be shut, but her face would not 'blush bright' beneath her lover's kiss, no matter how 'burning'. The speaker's saying that it did is a rhetorical assertion of his power over her: 'life' is literally conferred on her by *his* action. Consciousness itself is represented by the blush (*combining* modesty and sexual consent), since blushing is intrinsically a mark of the inner life.[15] And like the image of the eyes as buds it refers to a *release* of feeling which follows his untightening of the tress. What is released is Porphyria's *passion,* the 'struggling passion' which wanted to be 'set free' from 'pride' and 'vainer ties'. What then of the speaker's 'wariness' in opening Porphyria's eyes? Elsewhere in Browning's poetry the bee in the bud is an image of intense erotic suggestiveness.[16] But not here, in its first appearance. What the speaker hopes to find inside the 'shut bud', when he opens it, is nothing, the absence of a 'stain'. It is not sexual intercourse that he desires, but the control of Porphyria's sexuality and the abolition, or reversal, of its power.

Robert Langbaum is not right, I think, to say that the speaker 'strangles Porphyria with her own hair, as a culminating expression of his love' (Langbaum: 88). On the contrary, his use of Porphyria's own hair points to a hatred of the sexual nature which it signifies. Masses of hair, whether golden or dark, radiate female sensuality in Browning as in many other male writers. The whole of Titian's painting of Mary Magdalene, he declared, 'must have once been golden in its degree to justify that heap of hair in her hands' (Kintner: 7). In 'The Statue and the Bust', 'Hair in heaps lay heavily | Over a pale brow spirit-pure' (ll. 19–20). 'Dear dead women, with such hair, too—what's become of all the gold | Used to hang and

---

[14] I am grateful to the late Dr John Henderson CBE for this information.

[15] According to Darwin, the 'essential element' in all the mental states which induce blushing is 'self-attention' (p. 345).

[16] See *Pippa Passes* i. 160–5, 'Popularity' 46–50, and especially 'Women and Roses' 28–32: 'Deep as drops from a statue's plinth | The bee sucked in by the hyacinth, | So will I bury me while burning, | Quench like him at a plunge my yearning, | Eyes in your eyes, lips on your lips!'

brush their bosoms?' sighs the speaker at the end of 'A Toccata of Galuppi's' (ll. 44–5). Letting down such hair is a sexual invitation; nothing more connotes the obsessive, auto-erotic sexuality of the girl in 'Gold Hair' than her keeping her hair *bound* up as a hiding-place for her hoard of gold coins. But to Porphyria's gesture in letting down her yellow hair the speaker responds by tying it up again. He intends to release it on *his* terms. Many years after the publication of the poem, a friend of Browning's recorded in her diary that during an excursion with him in Scotland a young girl called Agnes Carnegie 'let down her golden hair to please Browning as we sat by the waterfall—he said poets ought to be indulged by such sights' (Surtees: 17). If Porphyria were looking to indulge her lover in this way she was badly mistaken.

10

Guido's Strange Colours

We feel the full force of the spirit of hatred . . . As we read, we
throw aside the trammels of civilisation, the flimsy veil of
humanity. 'Off, you lendings!' The wild beast resumes its sway
within us, we feel like hunting-animals, and as the hound starts
in his sleep and rushes on the chase in fancy, the heart rouses
itself in its native lair, and utters a wild cry of joy, at being
restored once more to freedom and lawless, unrestrained impulses.

(Hazlitt)[1]

IN February 1845, in one of his earliest letters to Elizabeth Barrett,
Browning gave a thumbnail sketch of the plot and main characters of
the play he was about to begin writing, *Luria*:

Luria is a Moor, of Othello's country, and devotes himself to something
he thinks Florence, and the old fortune follows—all in my brain, yet, but
the bright weather helps and I will soon loosen my Bɪaccio and Puccio—
(a pale discontented man)—and Tiburzio (the Pisan, good true fellow,
this one), and Domizia the Lady .. loosen all these on dear foolish (ravish-
ing must his folly be)—golden-hearted Luria, all these with their worldly-
wisdom, and Tuscan shrewd ways,—and, for me, the misfortune is, I
sympathise just as much with these as with him,—so there can come no
good of keeping this wild company any longer ... I shall stoop of a
sudden under and out of this dancing ring of men & women hand in
hand. (Kintner: 26)

But he chose never to stoop; the 'dancing ring of men & women'
circled around him till the end, in *Men and Women* itself, of course,
but also, as the title suggests, in *The Ring and the Book*. In that
poem, moreover, Browning recognized the value of the 'wild

[1] 'On the Pleasure of Hating', *The Plain Speaker: Opinions on Books, Men and
Things* (1826) in Hazlitt: xii. 129. The quotation is from *King Lear*, when Lear
encounters Edgar disguised as Poor Tom (III. iv. 107).

company' he kept: that it was his fortune, not misfortune, to 'sympathise just as much' with the evil as the good.

As the tone of his letter indicates, Browning felt uneasy at his inability, as he saw it, to be single-minded. And there is indeed a contradiction in *Luria* between plurality of sympathy and unity of design. The play's action is that of a trial, in the legal, religious, and (al)chemical senses: Luria is 'acquitted' of treason, and his heart is 'proved' by external and internal testing to be pure gold. His 'folly' is that of innocence: he is a holy fool subjected to the ordeal of other people's cynicism and hatred. At all times he is the central figure, however: the whole mechanism of the drama is geared to displaying his golden heart. He is one of Browning's Andromeda-figures, exposed to the malice of the monster, and there is no *question* of his 'virginity'. What room does this leave for Browning's other sympathies to operate? The trouble with the play is that these sympathies make the monster (principally represented by Braccio) more complex and interesting than the victim, but without altering the moral framework. Braccio is a divided and ambivalent figure, but his divisions and ambivalence make no difference to his external function in the play as the agent of Luria's downfall. He might as well be purely wicked, a factor in the play's moral sum; his not being so is, so to speak, a distraction from the wearying spectacle of Luria working it out.

Like *Luria*, *The Ring and the Book* can be read as a story in which good and evil influences (including 'worldly-wisdom, and Tuscan shrewd ways') are 'loosed' on a central, 'golden-hearted' figure. It was so read by Julia Wedgwood, to whom Browning sent the poem soon after its publication. Taking it for granted that Pompilia was the moral focus of the work, she wrote:

Here ... you have one pure, delicate, soft bit of pearly colouring; but the effect is marred, to my mind, by the black being carried up to its very edge, while its area is needlessly restricted. ... We need the atmosphere of meanness and cruelty to exhibit fully the luminous soul that centres the picture. But surely, surely we have more of this than that small white figure can bear. One's memory seems filled by the despicable husband, the vulgar parents, the brutal cutthroats, the pathetic child is jostled into a corner. I long for more space for her. ... There is, what seems to me an absolute superfluity of detail in the hideous portraits, whatever may be bestowed elsewhere. (Curle: 153–4)

Long before she saw the poem, Wedgwood had expressed to Browning her suspicion of what lay behind this 'superfluity', her distrust of his artistic motivation. In 1864, when her emotional involvement with Browning was growing, she worried that he might be among those 'who hold that one may fetch fire from Heaven or Hell so that one's torch burns brightly. No, I know you don't exactly say that, but the artist mind demands intensity above every thing else, and there are some things you can't set square with that Gospel. I could be intense enough, if I might hate and scorn' (Curle: 48–9). Wedgwood's criticism of *The Ring and the Book* therefore rests on the premiss that Browning's artistic impulse (the desire for 'intensity above everything else') had overwhelmed his moral design ('to exhibit fully the luminous soul that centres the picture'). In his reply Browning accepts the criticism, but rejects its application to *The Ring and the Book*:

In this case, I think you do correctly indicate a fault of my nature—not perhaps a fault in this particular work, artistically regarded: I believe I do unduly like the study of morbid cases of the soul,—and I will try and get over that taste in future works; because, even if I still think that mine was the proper way to treat this particular subject,—the objection still holds, 'Why prefer this sort of subject?'—as my conscience lets me know I do. . . . I was struck with the enormous wickedness and weakness of the main composition of the piece, and with the incidental evolution of good thereby—good to the priest, to the poor girl, to the old Pope . . . and, I would fain hope, to who reads and applies my reasoning to his own experience, which is not likely to fail him. The curious depth below depth of depravity here—in this chance lump taken as a sample of the soil— might well have warned another from spreading it out,—but I thought that, since I could do it, and even liked to do it, my affair it was rather than another's. (Curle: 158–9)

Browning's promise to Julia Wedgwood went the way of his earlier one to Elizabeth Barrett: he never did get over his 'taste for the study of morbid cases of the soul'.[2] Nor is the note of apology and self-deprecation quite convincing in the face of Browning's pointed rebuttal of Wedgwood's argument. He picks up her pictorial metaphor and changes its emphasis. Instead of a single, central figure he speaks of 'the main composition of the piece'. We should recall that

---

[2] *Balaustion's Adventure* (1871), which immediately followed *The Ring and the Book*, may be seen in part as an attempt to satisfy Julia Wedgwood's demands, but other works of the 1870s (*Fifine at the Fair*, *Red Cotton Night-Cap Country*, *The Inn Album*) revert emphatically to type.

Browning's original, preferred title for the poem was *The Frances-chini*, a group portrait. The goodness which for Wedgwood is the 'luminous' centre of the design becomes an 'incidental evolution' of 'enormous wickedness and weakness'. Pompilia is only one, and not even the first-named (not named at all, in fact—'the poor girl') of those to whom 'good' comes. What *strikes* Browning is 'wickedness', what he savours as *curious* is the 'depth below depth of depravity'. Unlike Fra Lippo Lippi, Browning is not confined, and will not confine himself, to painting 'saints and saints | And saints again' (ll. 48–9). His avowed interest in 'morbid cases of the soul' implies that, if anyone is at the centre of the 'composition', it is Guido.

If we go back to the analogy with *Luria*, we would expect to find Pompilia 'tried' by the various characters who are 'loosed' on her, emerging pure and vindicated from her ordeal. She is and does, but that does not make her, like Luria, the 'luminous' centre of the picture. The processes of trial, test, and ordeal apply in *The Ring and the Book* in multiple forms. Pompilia's is not the only ordeal on offer. After all, the Old Yellow Book, the documentary source of the poem, consisted mainly of pleadings in Guido's criminal trial (in the course of which he was physically tortured). Even leaving aside the many subsidiary trials, ordeals, tests, and probations to which the poem alludes (those of Pompilia's putative parents the Comparini, of Caponsacchi, of the Pope), we might reduce the design of the poem to that of two, interlocking ordeals, those undergone by Pompilia and Guido. As much is 'loosed' on him as on her. Both are 'proved' to be what they are by the trials they undergo; indeed, each proves to be 'golden-hearted', taking gold to symbolize, as it does so often in Browning, evil as well as good, corruption as well as purity, deception as well as truth.[3]

The most powerful expression of hatred in the poem is that of Caponsacchi for Guido. Caponsacchi indulges in a reverie of revenge, in which Guido is not formally punished, but left alone, shunned by the community: he will be found, Caponsacchi muses,

> Not to die so much as slide out of life,
> Pushed by the general horror and common hate
> Low, lower,—left o' the very ledge of things,
> I seem to see him catch convulsively
> One by one at all honest forms of life,

[3] See Barbara Melchiori's discussion of 'bright' and 'dark' gold in Browning's work, Melchiori: 40–89.

At reason, order, decency and use—
To cramp him and get foothold by at least;
And still they disengage them from his clutch.
'What, you are he, then, had Pompilia once
And so forwent her? Take not up with us!'
And thus I see him slowly and surely edged
Off all the table-land whence life upsprings
Aspiring to be immortality,
As the snake, hatched on hill-top by mischance,
Despite his wriggling, slips, slides, slidders down
Hill-side, lies low and prostrate on the smooth
Level of the outer place, lapsed in the vale:
So I lose Guido in the loneliness,
Silence and dusk, till at the doleful end,
At the horizontal line, creation's verge,
From what just is to absolute nothingness—
Lo, what is this he meets, strains onward still?
What other man deep further in the fate,
Who, turning at the prize of a footfall
To flatter him and promise fellowship,
Discovers in the act a frightful face—
Judas, made monstrous by much solitude!
The two are at one now! Let them love their love
That bites and claws like hate, or hate their hate
That mops and mows and makes as it were love!
There, let them each tear each in devil's-fun,
Or fondle this the other while malice aches—
Both teach, both learn detestability!
Kiss him the kiss, Iscariot! Pay that back,
That smatch o' the slaver blistering on your lip—
By the better trick, the insult he spared Christ—
Lure him the lure o' the letters, Aretine!
Lick him o'er slimy-smooth with jelly-filth
O' the verse-and-prose pollution in love's guise!
The cockatrice is with the basilisk!
There let them grapple, denizens o' the dark,
Foes or friends, but indissolubly bound,
In their one spot out of the ken of God
Or care of man, for ever and ever more!

(vi. 1911–54)[4]

---

[4] The 'lure o' the letters' refers to love-letters between Caponsacchi and Pompilia which Guido is alleged to have forged in order to tempt each of them into an affair, so as to obtain a ground of divorce.

Caponsacchi's lurid, violent, and nauseating day-dream may well be influenced by the culminating horror of Dante's *Inferno*: at the lowest point of hell, Dante encounters Judas Iscariot and two fellow-traitors, Brutus and Cassius, the murderers of Caesar. (They are each being chewed in one of the triple-headed Satan's mouths.) But this is also a quintessentially Victorian, and post-Darwinian, vision, one of devolution, of regression from the high to the low. Guido descends not just a moral scale but a quasi-scientific one, and meets Judas not at the bottom of a pit but at a 'horizontal line' dividing creation from 'absolute nothingness'. This is why Caponsacchi elides the actual moment of Guido's physical death: he is representing a different transformation, by which Guido 'slips, slides, slidders down' from humanity into a lower form. And then another metamorphosis occurs, from science to myth: Guido's marriage to the 'monstrous' figure of Judas converts both into fables of hate-in-love or love-in-hate: 'The cockatrice is with the basilisk!' All of Caponsacchi's unspeakable physical passion for Pompilia comes out in the disgust, the grossness, with which he imagines the coupling of the 'denizens o' the dark', 'indissolubly bound' as he and Pompilia are eternally separated. For the spectacle of Guido's fate is in some sense a nightmarish version of Caponsacchi's own. At the end of the poem he indulges a fantasy of what life might have held had he not been a priest and had been able to marry Pompilia: from this fantasy he awakes to 'the old solitary nothingness'. Caponsacchi, too, ends up on 'creation's verge'.

Caponsacchi purports to represent the 'general horror and common hate' which, he says, will drive Guido from 'all honest forms of life'. But it is these very forms to which Guido makes his appeal, and on the whole they support him. The Pope, at the end of his monologue, hears the voices of 'reason, order, decency and use' commanding him to let Guido off, and anticipating general rejoicing if he obeys. His condemnation of Guido goes *against* the grain, and deals a justice which exceeds the norms of society, a transcendent justice: in this sense it is the Pope, and not Caponsacchi, who is Pompilia's true rescuer, the godlike saviour who comes 'in thunder from the stars' to rescue Andromeda. Like his love for Pompilia, Caponsacchi's hatred of Guido is not authoritative, public, and impersonal, but contingent and personal. His damnation of Guido is neither literally nor figuratively the last word.

To see Guido as an emblem of hatred is to see him from the

outside. Caponsacchi has no real interest in Guido: like Gabriel in *Paradise Lost*, confronting Satan, he sees only the stereotype of a devil. (It is we, the readers, who are privy to Satan's anguished and humanizing soliloquies.) Caponsacchi's first sight of Guido is of a child's bogeyman, 'lurking there i' the black o' the box' at the theatre (vi. 414), and Guido never loses for him this quality of theatrical villainy. Caponsacchi is so preoccupied with his own frustrated life that it never occurs to him that Guido, too, might have a human history. Pompilia never makes this mistake; she *wonders* about Guido, how he could behave as he did, but she never demonizes him, except in oblique images such as her childhood memory of a sculpture in the Church of San Lorenzo:

> I used to wonder, when I stood scarce high
> As the bed here, what the marble lion meant,
> With half his body rushing from the wall,
> Eating the figure of a prostrate man—
> (To the right, it is, of entry by the door)
> An ominous sign to one baptized like me,
> Married, and to be buried there, I hope.

(vii. 21–7)

It is easy enough to connect this passage with the image of the devil who 'as a roaring lion, walketh about, seeking whom he may devour' (1 Peter 5: 8), but it is not Pompilia who makes this connection, or not explicitly. That there is something demonic about Guido, and something bestial too, is not at issue: what matters is whether such imagery is used as metaphor or allegory, as a way of describing the man, or of transforming him from a man into a figure of speech.

   In one sense, of course, Browning recognizes the compulsion to allegorize as a creative necessity, without which narrative itself would have no meaning. In Book I of the poem he tells how, standing on the terrace of Casa Guidi on the day he found the Old Yellow Book, he imaginatively *grasped* the story, realized its meaning to himself: this is, so to speak, the first *reading* of the poem, without which it could never have been written. And the tone of this reading is highly coloured, emotional, and compulsively figurative. All the characters, not just Guido, figure in a masque of good and evil, costumed accordingly: Pompilia wears white, Caponsacchi appears 'in a glory of armour like Saint George', the Pope is 'a great guardian

of the fold', and so on. Guido, his associates, and even his residence
at Arezzo, are entirely covered over in this figurative embroidery.
The Comparini (mistaking one sort of nobility for another) think
Guido a 'star' from a 'sphere of purer life than theirs' (ll. 535–6),
whereas he is in fact a 'fog o' the fen, | Gilded star-fashion by a glint
from hell' (ll. 544–5); Guido, the 'main monster', has two 'goblin
creatures' for brothers (ll. 549–51), and these two 'had rolled the
starlike pest to Rome | And stationed it to suck up and absorb | The
sweetness of Pompilia' (ll. 554–6). Guido's palace is 'a fissure in the
honest earth' leading to 'nether fires' (ll. 559–61). The plot against
the Comparini is described as a 'foul rite' in which the 'satyr-family
. . . danced about the captives in a ring' (ll. 564–74); Pompilia, left
on her own, is the intended victim of an even more luridly imagined
sacrifice, combining occult worship and sexual violation: 'Fire laid
and cauldron set, the obscene ring traced, | The victim stripped and
prostrate' (ll. 581–2). As Guido and his four accomplices approach
the villa on the night of the murder, Browning sees them as a 'pack
of were-wolves' (l. 611) with 'blood-bright eyes, | And black lips
wrinkling o'er the flash of teeth' (ll. 616–17); Guido's 'master-stroke'
of using the name of Caponsacchi to gain entrance is compared
to Lucifer using the name of Gabriel to gain entrance into Eden
(ll. 622–3).[5]

Of the main characters in the poem, it is Caponsacchi who most
obviously takes up this rhetoricizing method; but he does so selectively. Although he idealizes Pompilia as 'The glory of life, the
beauty of the world, | The splendour of heaven' (vi. 118–19) he is
constantly alive and attentive to her humanity, or at the very least to
her womanliness. But he cannot really conceive of Guido as human
at all. Guido's hatefulness is self-evident to him, but he has no real
conception of why Guido is full of hate, or of what his hatred means.
The judges, he claims, should have seen plainly that Guido was evil:
it was written in his countenance, 'Large-lettered like hell's masterpiece of print' (vi. 1794). But when it comes to saying *what* was
'lettered', Caponsacchi can only offer 'some lust, letch of hate
against his wife' (l. 1796). Not even the Pope can do much better: his
analysis of Guido's behaviour, carefully grounded though it is on his
social origins and the circumstances of his life, is in the end as

---

[5] Milton's Satan doesn't in fact do this in *Paradise Lost*, but does disguise himself
as a 'stripling cherub' in order to get directions from Uriel as to how to get to Paradise
(iii. 630 ff.).

emotive as Caponsacchi's, or as the narrator's in book I, concluding with a vision of the entire Franceschini family as wild beasts 'Huddling together in the cave they call | Their palace' (x. 870–1), with Guido as wolf, his brother Paul as fox, his other brother Girolamo a 'hybrid' of both, and their mother 'The gaunt grey nightmare in the furthest smoke, | The hag that gave these three abortions birth' (ll. 910–11), a 'she-pard' too old and decrepit to do more than

> Lick the dry lips, unsheathe the blunted claw,
> Catch 'twixt her placid eyewinks at what chance
> Old bloody half-forgotten dream may flit,
> Born when herself was novice to the taste,
> The while she lets youth take its pleasure.

> (ll. 920–4)

Neither the Pope nor, of course, Caponsacchi, claims to 'sympathise just as much' with Guido as with Pompilia. The Pope is not responsible for Guido, but for judging him. (In some respects it is Tertium Quid, out of all the characters in the poem, who comes closest to Browning's own creative method.) It is to Guido himself that we must turn, and turn twice in the poem: for in his first monologue he exposes himself unwittingly and is the object of our ironic scrutiny, whereas in his second the tables are turned. In Guido's first monologue he is used by the form, but in the second he uses it. He moves from self-justification to self-revelation.

The 'truth' of Guido's life is hatred, but for the truth of his or any life to be made manifest it must come, as Browning had long ago argued in *Paracelsus*, from 'within ourselves', from the 'inmost centre in us all | Where truth abides in fulness' (i. 738–41). Hatred is Guido's 'imprison'd splendour' (l. 747), and it is fitting that his second monologue should take place in a prison, the counterpart of the 'baffling and perverting carnal mesh' (l. 744) of his physical body and social being, soon to be dissolved by death. Guido makes his escape at last, and we gain the fruit of him: he fulfils Browning's credo (if any single utterance deserves the name) in 'By the Fire-Side':

> How the world is made for each of us!
>   How all we perceive and know in it
> Tends to some moment's product thus,
>   When a soul declares itself—to wit,
>   By its fruit, the thing it does!

> Be Hate that fruit or Love that fruit,
> 　　It forwards the General Deed of Man,
> And each of the Many helps to recruit
> 　　The life of the race by a general plan,
> Each living his own, to boot.
>
> (ll. 241–50)

The earnestness of these lines, coming as they do after the impassioned lyric celebration of the lovers' union, is marked by their rhetorical clumsiness (the emphatic capitals, the banality and repetitiousness of the vocabulary and rhymes). And just as importantly, the lines mark a shift away from erotic union to the speaker's interpretation of it: he no longer narrates what has happened to himself and his wife, but reflects on the meaning of what has happened to *him*. He both enlarges the scale of the event by making it representative of the 'life of the race', and narrows it by reference to his own identity. A preoccupation with the self (associated in this poem, as often in Browning, with an autumnal landscape) inevitably follows from the idea that the 'General Deed of Man' is made up of countless individuals, 'Each living his own [life]'.[6]

The 'fruit' of Guido's life is Hate, the deed by which his 'soul declares itself' being both the murder of Pompilia and ('since speech is act', as Browning says)[7] the speech in Book XI by which he finally justifies it. Others in the poem see this, but see it always from the outside: like the Augustinian friar in Book XII, they look on Guido's crime as a spectacle, a 'strange human play | Privily acted', whose privacy is interrupted,

> And lets the world see the wild work inside,
> And how, in petrifaction of surprise,
> The actors stand,—raised arm and planted foot,—
> Mouth as it made, eye as it evidenced,
> Despairing shriek, triumphant hate,—transfixed,
> Both he who takes and she who yields the life.
>
> (xii. 548–53)

This 'petrifaction' of Guido and Pompilia in a tableau of Gothic horror contradicts the principle of reading which Browning enjoins on us in Book I: 'See it for yourselves, | This man's act, changeable

---

[6] For further discussion of 'By the Fire-Side', see Ch. 11.
[7] In *Red Cotton Night-Cap Country*, iv. 24.

because alive!' (i. 1364–5). The 'spectators of this scene' will get nothing from it except titillation of their senses or confirmation of their prejudices. The Pope, like the friar, takes Guido's truth to be revealed *by* a hideous accident, and *as* a symbol of hatefulness: like 'Alberic's huge skeleton unhearsed' in *Sordello* (vi. 788) it emerges in the light of day as a portent both of past and present horror:

> As when, in our Campagna, there is fired
> The nest-like work that lets a peasant house;
> And, as the thatch burns here, there, everywhere,
> Even to the ivy and wild vine, that bound
> And blessed the hut where men were happy once,
> There rises gradual, black amid the blaze,
> Some grim and unscathed nucleus of the nest,—
> Some old malicious tower, some obscene tomb
> They thought a temple in their ignorance,
> And clung about and thought to lean upon—
> There laughs it o'er their ravage,—where are they?
>
> (x. 619–29)

The 'old malicious tower' of course recalls 'Childe Roland to the Dark Tower Came' (and this is only one of a cluster of such images in Browning, which I discuss in the next chapter): this is how the Pope *perceives* Guido, how he interprets him, but it is not at all equivalent to Guido 'declaring himself' to be that thing.

From the other characters in the poem, then, including Browning in some of his narrative guises, we will get only 'readings' of Guido, almost all of them designed to fix him in some static form, to encapsulate him in an image, a gesture, an attitude. Guido's own story conducts us rather to a truth of identity which is mobile and polemic, and which comes, as we shall see, from the extreme stress of his ultimate ordeal.

Guido is 'made of many hates',[8] and these hatreds are his living medium, the ways in which he understands the world and himself. (In the summative way of *The Ring and the Book*, he is also an anthology of Browning's other haters: most are 'quoted' in him somewhere, and those he does not echo he prefigures.) Hatred is the source of Guido's creativity, of his aesthetic sense, of his sexual nature. Hatred gives him, like Sludge, a penetrative vision of social

---

[8] I adapt Domizia's phrase in *Luria*, ii. 4.

and moral hypocrisy, and, like the Duke in 'My Last Duchess', a despairing desire for what he destroys. It also gives him a grim humour: faced with Abate Panciatichi and Cardinal Acciaiuoli, his two appalled, squeamish interlocutors in his second monologue, Guido mocks their inadequacy to the task of bringing him to pious repentance. 'Name me a primitive religionist', he says, denying that he has ever been in any sense a Christian, and he cites a passage of Virgil in support:

> 'Tis in the Seventh Aeneid,—what, the Eighth?
> Right,—thanks, Abate,—though the Christian's dumb,
> The Latinist's vivacious in you yet!

> (xi. 1926–8)

Guido's social failure opens an especially rich vein of hatred. Browning shared with many Victorian writers, especially novelists, a bourgeois, Protestant, egalitarian dislike of the aristocracy: Guido has more than a touch, both physical and moral, of Rigaud/Blandois in *Little Dorrit*, for example. And yet a cry of authentic rage and pain comes out of Guido's ignoble depths; he is the poet of shabby nobility, of the shifts and miseries of the hard-up, unlucky, ill-favoured toff: the dingy follower of a Cardinal, who has 'waited thirty years' for advancement and seen 'many a denizen o' the dung | Hop, skip, jump o'er [his] shoulder' (v. 292–4), and who 'rarely missed a place at the table-foot | Except when some Ambassador, or such like, | Brought his own people' (v. 340–2). The juggernaut of the class war has rolled over him, and what it has left behind is not a pretty sight; Guido has an unsparing self-knowledge of his physical and moral repulsiveness, and a corresponding hatred for the person who made him feel it most. Perhaps there is no passage in either of his monologues so alive with the rancour of his own wounds as the long description in Book XI (ll. 961 ff.) of the roots of his hatred of Pompilia.

Are we to agree with Julia Wedgwood that Guido's energy of mind, his flashes of insight and wit, come from Browning's moral neutrality, his conviction that 'one may fetch fire from Heaven or Hell so that one's torch burns brightly', the demand of the 'artist mind' for 'intensity above every thing else'? I would rather put it in Chesterton's words: that what we see revealed in Guido are 'the grounds of the happiness of a thoroughly bad man' (Chesterton: 175).

'Be it life or death,' Thoreau wrote in *Walden*, 'we crave only reality.' Browning had this craving (sometimes, as with Thoreau

himself, in the form of nostalgia). His greatest personal hatreds were
not just for liars, but for liars whom he *saw through*.[9] In *The Ring
and the Book* Guido is represented by his enemies as an arch-liar:
manipulator, showman, forger. And he is *seen through*, principally
by the Pope: the basis of his condemnation is that he is found out,
detected, not just in the fact of the murder but in his entire identity.
The Pope—a Neapolitan, as Pompilia's lawyer notes, who 'relishes a
sea-side simile' (ix. 373)—compares him to the 'ambiguous fish' that
'Detaches flesh from shell and outside show, | And steals by moon-
light (I have seen the thing) | In and out, now to prey and now to
skulk' (xi. 485–8):

> And when Law takes him by surprise at last,
> Catches the foul thing on its carrion-prey,
> Behold, he points to shell left high and dry,
> Pleads, 'But the case out yonder is myself!'
> Nay, it is thou, Law prongs amid thy peers,
> Congenial vermin; that was none of thee,
> Thine outside,—give it to the soldier-crab!

(ll. 503–9)

To the Pope, such behaviour is especially ignoble because it represents
not the human failure to behave well, but a perverse belief 'in just
the vile of life' (l. 511). He sees a radical dissociation between the
outward signs of Guido's identity and his real inner faith. It is not
that Guido is a sinner who fails to live up to his own religious ideals
or social obligations; he is a sinner who cynically exploits these
ideals and obligations as a means of satisfying his appetites. Guido is
far from being irreligious: he has an *anti-religion*, a 'habitual creed':

> Honor and faith,—a lie and a disguise,
> Probably for all livers in this world,
> Certainly for himself! All say good words
> To who will hear, all do thereby bad deeds
> To who must undergo; so thrive mankind!

(ll. 515–19)

This analysis of Guido's mentality, which the Pope arrives at by
induction, is confirmed by Guido himself in both his monologues,

[9] The most notable examples are the medium D. D. Home (for whom see Ch. 3)
and Elizabeth Barrett Browning's false friend, Sophia Eckley—for whom see Porter:
57–68.

though in different modes. In his first, courtroom, speech, he cannot help exposing himself; in his second, death-cell, speech, he makes a terrible virtue of necessity.

We can see this difference microscopically but vividly realized in the way a single image is transformed between the two monologues. In the first, Guido tries to play on his judges' sympathy, but can't help his bent for cruelty coming out: he tells of his longing to go home to the country after his failed career at Rome, and chooses an 'innocent' rural pastime to illustrate the point: 'I am tired: Arezzo's air is good to breathe; | Vittiano,—one limes flocks of thrushes there' (v. 363–4). The image is proleptic: the snaring of birds antici-pates the deception (both sexual and financial) which Guido will practise on Pompilia and the Comparini; later, he will find his accomplices for the murder at Vittiano, his country estate. But in the second monologue the image reappears in a quite different context, as Guido contemplates with dread being *seen through* by the eye of God:

> When you cut earth away from under me,
> I shall be left alone with, pushed beneath
> Some such an apparitional dread orb;
> I fancy it go filling up the void
> Above my mote-self it devours, or what
> Immensity please wreak on nothingness.
> Just so I felt once, couching through the dark,
> Hard by Vittiano; young I was, and gay,
> And wanting to trap fieldfares:[10] first a spark
> Tipped a bent, as a mere dew-globule might
> Any stiff grass-stalk on the meadow,—this
> Grew fiercer, flamed out full, and proved the sun.
> What do I want with proverbs, precepts here?
> Away with man! What shall I say to God?

> (xi. 921–34)

Here is Guido's sense of the world as a Darwinian struggle, elevated to the cosmic scale, in which he is both predator and victim; here is his cruelty, and the pleasure he takes in it, attributed to God's exercise of power; here, too, is his egotism, his sense of isolation both in the negative sense of being 'left alone' and in the positive

---

[10] The fieldfare is a species of thrush (*Turdus pilaris*); the connection with the earlier passage is exact.

sense of being singled out. For the lines have Wordsworthian associations: Guido's boyhood is like that of the poet in *The Prelude*, whose
'joy' was to trap woodcocks, 'Scudding away from snare to snare',
alone beneath the moon and stars and, like Guido, admonished by
Nature in ways that mingle guilt with exaltation.[11] As the sun rises
on the boy it finds him out, detects him as the eye of God is
traditionally said to detect the sinner, and also annihilates him,
drinks him up like the drop of dew *to which it was itself compared*.
Immensity wreaks itself on nothingness: but this process, sublime
and ecstatic, is also *reciprocal*. It confirms Chesterton's profound
insight that even the most ignoble of Browning's characters, 'while
admitting a failure in all things relative, claims an awful alliance
with the Absolute' (Chesterton: 202).

In the light of these lines the Pope's indignation against Guido
begins to look, if not suspect, then incomplete or inadequate. It is an
inadequacy which the Pope himself unwarily exposes in his judgement
on the Comparini, those 'Sadly mixed natures':

> Never again elude the choice of tints!
> White shall not neutralize the black, nor good
> Compensate bad in man, absolve him so:
> Life's business being just the terrible choice.

> (x. 1234–7)

In the heat of the moment, the Pope seems to have forgotten that the
Comparini, being dead, are not going to get another chance either to
make this choice of tints or to elude it; but in any case the judgement
implies that their murderer, Guido, has conducted his life's business
more successfully than they. He, at least, has made the 'terrible
choice'. But the Pope never admits that Guido, too, has a hunger for
reality. The 'grounds of the happiness of a thoroughly bad man' are
the same as those of everyone else: hatred of lies, love of truth. Like
Braccio in *Luria*, Guido believes in 'one thing plain and positive; |
Man seeks his own good at the whole world's cost' (i. 132–3). He
disbelieves in the Pope's sincerity as much as Braccio disbelieves in
Luria's; everything the Pope stands for is a lie, which he must break
through; in his death-cell he bears an unexpected, a scandalous

---

[11] See *The Prelude*, i. 309 ff. I quote from the 1850 text, the one which Browning
would have known; in the 1805 version Wordsworth calls himself a 'fell destroyer', a
phrase he cut from the later text.

resemblance to another prisoner of the Church, the betrayed, tortured, and maddened speaker of 'The Confessional':

> It is a lie—their Priests, their Pope,
> Their Saints, their . . . all they fear or hope
> Are lies, and lies—there! thro' my door
> And ceiling, there! and walls and floor,
> There, lies, they lie, shall still be hurled,
> Till spite of them I reach the world!
>
> (ll. 1–6)

This, after all, is Guido's opinion, too; experience has taught him, like the speaker of 'The Confessional', that Christianity is a dead letter:

> 'Tis dead of age now, ludicrously dead;
> Honour its ashes, if you be discreet,
> In epitaph only! For, concede its death,
> Allow extinction, you may boast unchecked
> What feats the thing did in a crazy land
> At a fabulous epoch . . .
>
> (xi. 561–6)

With Browning's license Guido might be quoting Swift's *Argument against abolishing Christianity* (written in 1708, a mere decade after Guido's execution), which takes it for granted that 'The system of the Gospel, after the fate of other systems, is generally antiquated and exploded' and protests:

I hope no reader imagines me so weak to stand up in the defence of real Christianity, such as used in primitive times (if we may believe the authors of those ages) to have an influence upon men's belief and actions. To offer at the restoring of that would indeed be a wild project; it would be to dig up foundations; to destroy at one blow all the wit, and half the learning of the kingdom; to break the entire frame and constitution of things . . .[12]

This is precisely the tenor of Guido's sardonic fantasy, as, with 'a monster-laugh, | A madman's laugh' (xi. 581–2) he imagines the consequences of restoring 'real Christianity':

---

[12] The full title of the pamphlet is *An argument to prove that the abolishing of Christianity in England, may as things now stand, be attended with some inconveniences, and perhaps not produce those many good effects proposed thereby.*

Come, thus I wave a wand and bring to pass
In a moment, in the twinkle of an eye,
What but that—feigning everywhere grows fact,
Professors turn possessors, realize
The faith they play with as a fancy now,
And bid it operate, have full effect
On every circumstance of life, to-day . . .

Here's Rome believes in Christianity!
What an explosion, how the fragments fly
Of what was surface, mask and make-believe!

(ll. 587–93, 623–5)

The devil, of course, is quoting scripture here: 'we shall all be changed, in a moment, in the twinkling of an eye, at the last trump: for the trumpet shall sound, and the dead shall be raised incorruptible, and we shall be changed' (1 Corinthians 15: 51–2). The 'realizing' of Christianity would be the resurrection of a dead and corrupt faith into 'incorruptible' life, a transcendent event which, Guido's powerful irony implies, is as likely as the resurrection of the dead itself. In a series of satiric sketches (ll. 626–94) he imagines what life would be like if people behaved as their faith dictated, and concludes by contrasting the unreal 'Christian' with his actual counterpart:

Contort your brows! You know I speak the truth:
Gold is called gold, and dross called dross, i' the Book:
Gold you let lie and dross pick up and prize!

(ll. 695–7)

It is Christianity itself, Guido argues, which constitutes the 'surface, mask and make-believe' of life. What he can't bear about his fate is that it represents the victory of a lie. Like the Jews in 'Holy-Cross Day', he objects to being asked to pay lip-service to the noble ideals of his tormentors, 'Whose life laughs through and spits at their creed, | Who maintain thee in word, and defy thee in deed!' (ll. 85–6; 'thee' = Christ). So Guido to the Abate and the Cardinal:

You two come here, entreat I tell you lies,
And end, the edifying way. I end,
Telling the truth! Your self-styled shepherd thieves!
A thief—and how thieves hate the wolves we know:
Damage to theft, damage to thrift, all's one!
The red hand is sworn foe of the black jaw!
That's only natural, that's right enough:

> But why the wolf should compliment the thief
> With the shepherd's title, bark out life in thanks,
> And, spiteless, lick the prong that spits him,—eh,
> Cardinal? My Abate, scarcely thus!

(xi. 432–42)

It's a Marxist, or even pre-Marxist satire: property is theft (Proudhon's *mot* dates from 1840), and Guido's wordplay brings 'theft' and 'thrift' into uncomfortable proximity. Those who own and shear the sheep can claim no moral superiority over those who prey on them by other means. This is what Guido *knows*; and he knows it most intensely, and expresses it most eloquently, in the only condition in which the 'imprison'd splendour' of truth can 'dart forth', that of approaching death. As Paracelsus says,

> not alone when life flows still do truth
> And power emerge, but also when strange chance
> Affects its current; in unused conjuncture,
> Where sickness breaks the body—hunger, watching,
> Excess, or languor—oftenest death's approach—
> Peril, deep joy, or woe.

(i. 776–81)

This 'philosophy of extremity', as John Woolford calls it (Woolford 1977) applies on the grand scale in Paracelsus's own case, with his deathbed testament of faith in Part V, and in that of Sordello, similarly enlightened at the point of death in Book VI.[13] At the end of his second monologue, Guido makes a supreme effort to come to terms with the death facing him. Like Sludge, he is carried by sheer pressure of circumstance beyond the limits of his nature into a region of speculation where he is both free of himself and more truly, more intensely himself than he has ever been, or than he will be at the moment of his inevitable retraction. As Chesterton says of Sludge, 'when the last of his loathsome secrets has been told . . . then he rises up into a perfect bankrupt sublimity' (Chesterton: 195). Chesterton also convincingly defends the psychological realism and artistic necessity of Sludge's relapse into despicability at the end of the poem (pp. 197–8); by analogy, I would argue that Guido's sudden change of

---

[13] For a detailed discussion of Sordello's final vision, see pp. 186–9. The collapse of binary categories which is the core of Sordello's 'closing-truth' would, by analogy, question the basis for judging Guido as evil in an absolute sense; but more importantly it emphasizes the primacy of the 'soul's essence', the 'nucleus' of identity (a word which, as we shall see, Guido himself uses).

tone at the very end of his monologue, his panic-stricken plea for life at any cost, does not invalidate his profession of faith. I disagree with perhaps the majority of critics who see Guido's final appeal to Pompilia as a recognition of her goodness or even a sign of his last-minute conversion and salvation (along the lines of the 'late-repentant' in Dante's *Purgatorio*, among whom was classed Sordello).[14] Guido rather resembles the protagonist of *Pauline*, who envisages succumbing to temptation, yet insists: 'Still this is all my own, this moment's pride, | No less I make an end in perfect joy' (ll. 993-4).

What is the nature of this 'perfect joy'? It has two principal features: the acceptance of death, and a grossly physical assertion of hatred as the core of Guido's identity. By 'acceptance' I mean both a metaphysical understanding and an emotional exhilaration, the 'appropriate drunkenness of the death-hour' as Guido calls it (xi. 2326), which gives him a tremendous shot of rhetorical power. 'I begin to taste my strength', he says (l. 2328); this 'strength' is that of the free self, able at last to 'declare itself' with visionary eloquence:

> I see you all reel to the rock, you waves—
> Some forthright, some describe a sinuous track,
> Some crested, brilliantly with heads above,
> Some in a strangled swirl sunk who knows how,
> But all bound whither the main-current sets,
> Rockward, an end in foam for all of you!
> What if I am o'ertaken, pushed to the front
> By all you crowding smoother souls behind,
> And reach, a minute sooner than was meant,
> The boundary, whereon I break to mist?
> Go to! the smoothest safest of you all,
> Most perfect and compact wave in my train,
> Spite of the blue tranquillity above,
> Spite of the breadth before of lapsing peace
> Where broods the halcyon and the fish leaps free,
> Will presently begin to feel the prick
> At lazy heart, the push at torpid brain,
> Will rock vertiginously in turn, and reel,
> And, emulative, rush to death like me . . .
>
> (ll. 2346-64)

---

[14] The Pope sees Guido's only chance of salvation in these terms: 'So may the truth be flashed out by one blow, | And Guido see, one instant, and be saved' (x. 2126-7). But he does not predict that this will happen, and I do not see Guido's last despairing cry as evidence that it has.

The desire for death which Guido expresses here is at once lyrical and fierce, summoning the images of the tranquil sky, the brooding halcyon, and the leaping fish, only to reject them as unavailing emblems of creativity and freedom: 'tranquillity', 'breadth', and 'lapsing peace' become instead a medium of the 'lazy heart' and 'torpid brain'. In the end Guido sees himself not being carried helplessly and irresistibly towards his fate (being *bound* to the rock means being compelled to move towards it), but as rushing to embrace it. The very *rock* itself metamorphoses from noun to verb ('*rock* vertiginously') as the waves, by a fantastic twist of figuration, become what they behold.

If life is motion, then it is motion towards death; death gives life its *urgency*:

> 'tis death that makes life live,
> Gives it whatever the significance.
> For see, on your own ground and argument,
> Suppose life had no death to fear, how find
> A possibility of nobleness
> In man, prevented daring any more?
> What's love, what's faith without a worst to dread?
> Lack-lustre jewelry; but faith and love
> With death behind them bidding do or die—
> Put such a foil at back, the sparkle's born!
> From out myself how the strange colours come!
>
> (ll. 2374–84)

What Guido says of 'faith and love' applies, in his own case, to hatred and unbelief, the 'strange colours' of his identity. The 'possibility of nobleness' is also the possibility of degradation. Guido has had to 'dare' his crime as much as Pompilia her faithful endurance, or Caponsacchi his self-sacrificing love, or the Pope his courageous judgement.[15] What Guido is implicitly asking is that the value of his

---

[15] Browning uses one of his favourite phrases, from the last line of Christopher Smart's *Song to David* ('And now the matchless deed's achieved, Determined, dared, and done!') to describe Guido's action: he 'determined, dared and did | This deed just as he purposed point by point' (i. 801–2). It should be noted that of the four principal characters in the poem, three (Pompilia, the Pope, and Guido) are either literally on their deathbeds or close to death through extreme old age; Caponsacchi, the fourth, sees himself as figuratively dying: 'My part | Is done; i' the doing it, I pass | Out of this world. I want no more with earth. | Let me, in heaven's name, use the very snuff | O' the taper in one last spark shall show truth | For a moment, show Pompilia who was true!' (vi. 167–72).

life be acknowledged as much as that of theirs. It is an existential, not a moral affirmation: it posits a core of identity which must be taken for what it is, in its own terms. Even if there is a future life, Guido says, in which he is to be 'Unmanned, remade', still there must remain 'something changeless at the heart of me | To know me by, some nucleus that's myself' (ll. 2391–3). But in this life, at any rate, that 'nucleus' is present to him as an inviolable integrity of hatred:

> All that was, is; and must for ever be.
> Nor is it in me to unhate my hates,—
> I use up my last strength to strike once more
> Old Pietro in the wine-house-gossip-face,
> To trample underfoot the whine and wile
> Of that Violante,—and I grow one gorge
> To loathingly reject Pompilia's pale
> Poison my hasty hunger took for food.
>
> (ll. 2397–404)

The three images here are carefully chosen to represent in compressed form Guido's 'life', in the sense both of his history and his primary impulses and appetites. The thematic order starts with Guido's aristocratic disdain for Pietro, moves through his misogynistic hatred of Violante (women are both weak and crafty, both worms and snakes), and ends with his hatred of Pompilia as his natural enemy, a 'poison' hostile to everything he is or stands for. (At the same time, this rejection of Pompilia is Guido's last expression of desire for her, even if it is only the desire, like that of the stone lion in the church of San Lorenzo, to devour her 'prostrate figure'.) The three gestures— striking, trampling, vomiting—correspond to the deadly sins that rule Guido, the sins of anger, pride, and greed. The last, associated with Pompilia, is the most serious: it suggests (or rather, in the light of what Guido has already said in his monologue, confirms) that Guido has no sense of other people except as 'food'. And the three images are ordered in time, too: the first is a memory of the actual moment of murder, the second merges that moment with memories of Violante's habitual behaviour, and the third (again, the most disturbing) moves away from the murder to the sexual death that preceded it.

This, then, is Guido's 'truth'. Before she had read Guido's second monologue, Julia Wedgwood pleaded with Browning to spare his readers: 'But, oh, be merciful to us in Guido's last display!

Shame and pain and humiliation need the irradiation of hope to be endurable as objects of contemplation; you have no right to associate them in our minds with hopeless, sordid wickedness' (Curle: 163). Browning replied with less than his usual patience: 'Guido "hope?"—do you bid me turn him into that sort of thing? No, indeed!' (p. 167).

Dark Tower, Siren Isle, Ruined Chapel: Landscapes of Love and Hate

> There is no difficulty in finding a representative of Eros; but we must be grateful that we can find a representative of the elusive death instinct in the instinct of destruction, to which hate points the way.
>
> (Freud)[1]

> I did turn as he pointed . . .
>
> ('Childe Roland to the Dark Tower Came', l. 16)

I did turn as he pointed: 'Childe Roland to the Dark Tower Came' begins with hate pointing the way, and with Roland acquiescing in the gesture. A turning-point in the poem, like the 'turning moment of a dream' that Luria dreads:

> And always comes, I say, the turning point
> When something changes in the friendly eyes
> That love and look on you . . so slight, so slight . .
> And yet it tells you they are dead and gone,
> Or changed and enemies for all their words,
> And all is mockery and a maddening show!
>
> (iii. 106–10)

Luria represents the change as happening to him; but suppose it is happening *in* him? His self-pity is dramatically sterile, because it corresponds to an intended effect of pure pathos; the 'mockery' and 'maddening show' of Roland's nightmarish journey are alive because he generates them himself. Roland loves what he hates, desires what disgusts him, thrusts his spear 'to seek | For hollows' (ll. 123–4) as though emptiness were his object (his 'point'); he is Browning's

---

[1] 'The Ego and the Id' (1923) in Freud 1984: 383.

intensest figure of a divided nature. The other 'Nature', the landscape he describes, traps him in a sardonic and pitiless embrace. The poem darkly inverts Wordsworth's depiction of Nature as foster-mother, Muse, and benign teacher. (Browning had not forgiven Wordsworth, and a specific reminder of 'The Lost Leader' turns up in ll. 97–102 of 'Childe Roland' in the figure of Giles, the 'poor traitor, spit upon and cursed' by his own followers.)[2] Roland sees Nature with his mind's eye: he is thoroughly Wordsworthian in that, if not in hating what he sees (hating himself, in other words). Yet the language of the poem is itself divided between what might be called the moral and the aesthetic aspects of his self-hatred. 'What I seem to myself, do you ask of me? | No hero, I confess.' These words, from 'A Light Woman' (next but one to 'Childe Roland' in *Men and Women*), might describe Roland's overt self-image, but could not account for the exhilaration of his speech.[3] Browning later allowed this sense of mastery open play in the song 'Thamuris marching' in *Aristophanes' Apology*, where Thamuris marches 'gay | And glad . . . robed and crowned' (ll. 5189–90). But it is present in Roland's imagery (a compound of physical brutality and literary allusiveness which Browning was never to equal), in his syntactical grasp, and especially in the metrical pulse of his stanzas. Hatred is Roland's trumpet, and he blows it.

The fascination with dark and dreadful landscapes is not new, either in literature or art. (Browning's poem undoubtedly draws on visual iconography as well as on literature, as DeVane long ago demonstrated.)[4] 'Childe Roland' has a complex genealogy, many of whose branches (literary, social-historical, psychological) have been exhaustively traced. They range from landscapes of biblical desolation to the nightmare of Victorian industrial and urban development, from Dante to Dickens, from Bunyan to Byron, from Spenser to Sade. Alongside the numerous demonstrations of the poem's affinity with *King Lear* or *Pilgrim's Progress* we might set the equally numerous (and sometimes simultaneous) claims for the poem as *Browning's* masterpiece, the poem that quintessentially sums him up. But what is striking about the work which has been done on the

---

[2] Roland's pity for Giles contrasts with the vengeful attitude of the speaker of 'Italy in England' towards the 'perjured traitor', Charles, his boyhood friend.

[3] Harold Bloom notices an analogous effect in Browning's 'exuberance in declaring a highly personalized evangelical belief in Christ . . . in which fervor of declaration far surpasses in importance the supposed spiritual content of the declaration' ('Introduction: Reading Browning', Bloom and Munich: 3).

[4] See DeVane: 230–1.

poem is the lack of attention that has been paid to Browning's own
corpus. The major sources of 'Childe Roland' are other poems by
Browning, though to speak of 'sources' in this context may be
misleading. I prefer to think of 'Childe Roland' as one of a group of
Browning poems that act and react on each other: a family, engaged
in a family romance. I am going to focus on two other members of
this family, 'England in Italy' and 'By the Fire-Side', the first published ten years before 'Childe Roland', in *Dramatic Romances and
Lyrics*, the second alongside it in the first volume of *Men and
Women*.

In Chapter 6 I pointed out that the first appearance of the Dark
Tower in Browning's work is to be found in *Sordello*, in the
description of the 'one tower that remains' of the tyrant Alberic's
castle. By an irony of time, the symbol of hatred and cruelty has
become embedded in the fertile landscape of valley Rù. This combination recurs in 'England in Italy', in the passage where the speaker
imagines a journey to one of the isles of the siren off the coast of Sorrento:

> Oh, to sail round and round them, close over
>   The rocks, tho' unseen,
> That ruffle the grey glassy water
>   To glorious green,—
> Then scramble from splinter to splinter,
>   Reach land and explore
> On the largest, the strange square black turret
>   With never a door—
> Just a loop that admits the quick lizards;
>   —To stand there and hear
> The birds' quiet singing that tells us
>   What life is, so clear;
> The secret they sang to Ulysses,
>   When ages ago
> He heard and he knew this life's secret
>   I hear and I know!
>
> (ll. 213–28)

Among Browning's many strong misreadings of classical texts this
must rank as one of the boldest. We should begin by recalling who
the Sirens were and what they sang to Ulysses (Odysseus) in Book
XII of the *Odyssey*. Circe tells Odysseus: 'There is no home-coming
for the man who draws near them unawares and hears the Sirens'

voices; no welcome from his wife, no little children brightening at
their father's return. For with the music of their song the Sirens cast
their spell upon him, as they sit there in a meadow piled high with
the mouldering skeletons of men, whose withered skin still hangs
upon their bones.' As to the song itself, it is not (*pace* Sir Thomas
Browne in *Urn Burial*) a 'puzzling question', since Odysseus quotes it
verbatim: ' "Draw near," they sang, "illustrious Odysseus, flower of
Achaean chivalry, and bring your ship to rest so that you may hear
our voices. No seaman ever sailed his black ship past this spot
without listening to the sweet tones that flow from our lips, and
none that listened has not been delighted and gone on a wiser man.
For we know all that the Argives and Trojans suffered on the broad
plain of Troy by the will of the gods, and we have foreknowledge of
all that is going to happen on this fruitful earth."' Wisdom, then—
or 'this life's secret', in Browning's words—is what the sirens offer.
They were creatures with the bodies of birds and the heads of
women, and they inhabit a landscape in Homer remarkably reminis-
cent of Alberic the torturer in his Dark Tower.[5]

Neither Odysseus nor Browning's speaker hears the sirens' song
'unawares', of course. Odysseus listens safely strapped to the mast of
his ship. Browning's speaker unstraps himself and scrambles ashore.[6]
The unseen rocks will return with a vengeance in 'Childe Roland', at
the same crisis of revelation:

> What in the midst lay but the Tower itself?
>   The round squat turret, blind as the fool's heart,
>   Built of brown stone, without a counterpart
> In the whole world. The tempest's mocking elf
> Points to the shipman thus the unseen shelf
>   He strikes on, only when the timbers start.
>
> (ll. 181–6)

The poem closes, as it opened, with a gesture of pointing; but here
the 'mocking elf' is, in one aspect, Roland himself, just as he is also
the 'shipman', an Odysseus figure; an 'elf' is usually a supernatural

[5] In Homer the sirens are twins; Alberic, too, has his brother Ecelin: 'Kings of the
gag and flesh-hook, screw and whip, | They plagued the world' (vi. 768–9).
[6] The connection is reinforced by the unusual epithet 'grey' for the water, which is
Homeric. It was even stronger, apparently, in the original manuscript, where the word
'glassy' did not appear; Elizabeth Barrett quoted 'the grey sea-water', to which she
objected because the rhythm was not smooth enough. See Woolford and Karlin: ii.
353, and next note.

being, and sometimes a devil, but in Spenser's *Faerie Queene* he is a knight. In 'England in Italy' the 'strange square black turret' is, like the 'one tower left' of Alberic's castle, a remnant of a larger structure, also built by a tyrannical ruler.[7] The sirens have metamorphosed from death-dealing bird-monsters to birds, their flowery meadows no longer littered with bones (we are reminded of Alberic's 'huge skeleton' intruding on the pastoral harmony of Valley Rù). Their 'quiet singing' may rebuke the rhapsodic strains of Romantic poetry (Shelley's skylark, Keats's nightingale) but preserves the Romantic identification of birdsong with divine revelation: so even as birds the sirens turn out to be Homeric oracles of past and future knowledge.

Homer's sirens *promise* to sing to Odysseus of his own fate: the suffering he has undergone, and what lies in store for him on the 'fruitful earth'. It is a cunning appeal, because the emotions that dominate Odysseus are grief for the past and longing to reach his homeland, Ithaca. Nevertheless the sirens do not reveal his fate (nor would they have done so had he paid them a visit, except in the sense that his fate would then have been to be devoured by them). Their song—rather like 'Childe Roland'—is a reflexive utterance: it usurps the performance it precedes, and stops before that performance begins. Browning's sirens, on the other hand, do reveal 'this life's secret' to Odysseus, and to the poet; but *he* isn't telling. In a series of pronouns the speaker glides from 'tells *us*' to 'He heard' to '*I* know', from Romantic humanism to Romantic egotism. Odysseus, far from being a generalized or representative figure of mankind, is a mythic mask of the poet's dominating self, a staging post on the swift journey from communal to private vision. At which point the main business of the poem comes to as abrupt a halt as in the final line of 'Childe Roland'.

To understand this coupling of the egotistical sublime with the gesture of withholding (a turning inward, an inward pointing) we need to widen our focus, to draw back from our close scrutiny of the passage about the siren isle and the black turret and look at it in the context of the whole poem.

'England in Italy' is 'Childe Roland's' antithetical precursor. It is a

---

[7] The structure is in fact a cistern belonging to a tower built on 'il Gallo Lungo', the largest of the siren-isles, by King Robert I of Naples in 1330. In the manuscript of the poem the line originally read 'The square black tower on the largest'; the revision was prompted by Elizabeth Barrett, who objected to the abruptness of the rhythm, though she did not suggest the revised wording.

poem based on a landscape of love, of the beauty and fertility of Italy. The iconographical and ideological terrain of 'Childe Roland' is predominantly northern: Flemish and German painting, Protestant theology and literature. 'England in Italy' is—at first glance, anyway—a 'beaker full of the warm South', a celebration of Mediterranean luxuriance and sensuous life. Elizabeth Barrett, the poem's first reader, praised 'the rushing & hurrying life of the descriptions' and stated: 'For giving the *sense of Italy*, it is worth a whole library of travel-books.' This comment, which has its own undeniable truth, obscures an alternative reading of the poem which would place its descriptive energies in a very different light.

In both 'Childe Roland' and 'England in Italy' a daemonic energy informs the descriptions, though in one poem the mode is orgiastic and in the other grotesque or perverse. But when you look closely, the dividing line between pain and pleasure begins to blur, and some of the images in 'England in Italy' tremble on the verge of finding themselves in 'Childe Roland's' domain: the grape-harvest, for example:

> In the vat half-way up in our house-side
>   Like blood the juice spins
> While your brother all bare-legged is dancing
>   Till breathless he grins
> Dead-beaten, in effort on effort
>   To keep the grapes under
> For still when he seems all but master
>   In pours the fresh plunder
>
> (ll. 73–80)

A slight twist, and this might become the image of a damned soul; the grin on the face of the 'breathless' and 'dead-beaten' boy is certainly not funny, and we are not too far from the 'skull-like laugh' of the cripple by the roadside in 'Childe Roland'. As the speaker climbs mount Calvano (with its phonetic closeness to 'Calvary') he describes a landscape which, again, would require only a small shift of context to become nightmarish and Roland-like:

> As up still we trudged
> Though the wild path grew wilder each instant,
>   And place was e'en grudged
> 'Mid the rock-chasms, and piles of loose stones
>   Like the loose broken teeth
> Of some monster, which climbed there to die

> From the ocean beneath—
> Place was grudged to the silver-grey fume-weed
>   That clung to the path,
> And dark rosemary, ever a-dying,
>   Which, 'spite the wind's wrath,
> So loves the salt rock's face to seaward . . .
>
> (ll. 150–61)

What keeps the poem this side of pleasure is a recognition, as in 'Caliban upon Setebos', that violence and beauty in Nature are inseparably linked, that the world not only includes 'love' and 'wrath' as antithetical qualities but draws its vitality from the relation between them. The scene, where even the 'piles of loose stones' are imagined as evolutionary fragments, uncannily foreshadows Darwin (fourteen years before *Origin of Species*), even though the impersonal struggle for existence is represented in the language of emotion: grudging, clinging, wrath, love. In 'Childe Roland' the landscape is seen as wholly grudging, 'ever a-dying' in grim earnest, and Roland's horror at the struggle for existence is without a compensating admiration for the tenacity of living organisms:

> If there pushed any ragged thistle-stalk
>   Above its mates, the heads were chopped—the bents
>   Were jealous else.
>
> (ll. 67–9)

The metaphor here is political: it is a reactionary's sour view of egalitarianism. The deadness or negativity of this struggle may be compared with that of the 'bold hardy sprig of rock-flower' which pushes up through adverse soil in 'England in Italy': itself engaged in a struggle to survive, it becomes the focus of another struggle: 'For the prize were great butterflies fighting, | Some five for one cup' (ll. 31–2). The contest is vital: Darwinian struggle has an erotic drive (since death, as Darwin insisted, is a necessary part of the cycle of propagation); the Darwinian universe, seen in its true light, is not in the slightest bit malignant. But in 'Childe Roland' the action of 'wrath', which in 'England in Italy' is the very condition of 'love', is directed *towards* death, *points* to death as its ultimate object. It is as though the Darwinian universe had gone into reverse, as though a process of 'devolution' were under way, reminiscent of Tennyson's horrific image, in 'The Vision of Sin', of 'men and horses pierced with worms, | And slowly quickening into lower forms' (ll. 209–10).[8] What causes this is the felt presence, in the world of nature, of a *principle* of malignancy; immediately after the lines about the jealous bents, Roland continues:

> What made those holes and rents
> In the dock's harsh swarth leaves—bruised as to baulk
> All hope of greenness? 'tis a brute must walk
> Pashing their life out, with a brute's intents.
>
> (ll. 69–72)

Perhaps the most disturbing thing about such images is the very imaginative energy which informs them. Roland is erotically drawn to death, worships the power whose cruelty appals him, finds hatred, in the end, a more animating idea than love; but his *mode* of perception brings him closer to that of the speaker of 'England in Italy' than is comfortable for either of them.

It is not just that the protagonists of the two poems share certain features, but that the poems themselves are formally alike, sometimes in surprising ways. 'Childe Roland' is celebrated for its concentration and intensity of purpose, whereas 'England in Italy' has a quite false reputation as a travelogue, amiable and diffuse. On the contrary, not only does it have a highly ordered narrative structure, but one which connects it to 'Childe Roland', that of the quest or journey. In 'England in Italy' this quest, which will end up at the 'square black turret' on the siren isle, will also turn out, as in 'Childe Roland', to be an ambivalent affair.

The speaker's invocation of Ulysses as seeking 'this life's secret' from the sirens ignores a fundamental difference of purpose between himself and his mythic precursor. Quests are lonely affairs, as Paracelsus points out;[9] Odysseus, too, arrives home alone. But the purpose of Odysseus's journey is not a visionary revelation (which he sails past); it is the 'welcome from his wife'. Circe's threat makes as cunning an appeal to Odysseus as the sirens' song: she threatens him with the loss of his homecoming. But Browning's 'Odysseus' has no

---

[8] The whole poem, as has often been remarked, is an important precursor of 'Childe Roland': compare, for example, the lines which immediately follow the ones I have quoted, 'By shards and scurf of salt, and scum of dross, | Old plash of rains, and refuse patched with moss', with ll. 151–3 of Browning's poem: 'Now blotches rankling, coloured gay and grim, | Now patches where some leanness of the soil's | Broke into moss or substances like boils'.

[9] See the passage quoted on p. 99.

such motive: he wants to get to Circe, not escape from her. The last
lines of 'England in Italy' are a flash of impatience and indignation at
England's stagnant political system:

> Fortù, in my England at home,
>   Men meet gravely to-day
> And debate, if abolishing Corn-laws
>   Be righteous and wise . . .

> (ll. 287–90)

The speaker has come to Italy to get away from all this; he is greedy
for experience which he can appropriate, and for a politics which
will match that daemonic and lawless impulse. In another *Men and
Women* poem, 'De Gustibus—', Browning makes the connection
between southern climate, radical politics, and sexual licence even
more explicit:

> A girl bare-footed brings and tumbles
> Down on the pavement, green-flesh melons,
> And says there's news to-day—the king
> Was shot at, touched in his liver-wing,
> Goes with his Bourbon arm in a sling.
> —She hopes they have not caught the felons.
> Italy, my Italy!

> (ll. 33–9)

The girl's bare feet have very different connotations from those of
the woman in 'Italy in England'. The speaker of that poem (the
companion-piece to 'England in Italy') is not an Englishman but an
austere Italian exile, reminiscing about the time when he was a
fugitive hiding from the Austrians; he finds a lofty Marian symbol in
the poverty of the peasant-woman who befriends him: 'Planting each
naked foot so firm, | To crush the snake and spare the worm' (ll. 61–
2). Among its other excellences 'De Gustibus—' offers a witty
sending-up of 'Italy in England', a dignified work in which the
speaker works hard to sublimate his sexual attraction to his rescuer
into a patriotic idealization of Italian womanhood. The speaker in
'De Gustibus—', not being an Italian, is under no such constraints:
his girl is barefoot because she is savage, an erotic link between the
two items she brings, the 'green-flesh melons' (an emblem of her own
sexuality: young, gamey, raw) and the 'news' of the attempted
assassination. Her 'tumbling' the melons down is itself both a violent

or revolutionary gesture and a sexual one.[10] It is the 'liver-wing' that is 'touched' because the liver is traditionally the seat of sexual desire. A wildness or lawlessness prevails in Italy, or rather (and this is the crucial *turn*) in the *appetite* for Italy, for its interpenetrating sensations of food, sex, and violence. The girl's lawless hatred for the 'legitimate' ruler is like a lightning-rod for the speaker's arousal, which bursts out in his ejaculation 'Italy, *my* Italy!' These are what the speaker *loves* and *owns*.

Browning's love of Italy had the special generosity that springs from a deeply gratified self-interest. He wrote to Elizabeth Barrett in 1845 (in a passage closely connected with the composition of 'England in Italy') of an 'old belief—that Italy is stuff for the use of the North, and no more ... strange that those great wide black eyes should stare nothing out of the earth that lies before them!' (Kintner: 50).[11] In a letter to Isa Blagden of 1866, when he was writing *The Ring and the Book*, he wrote with unaffected candour: 'my liking for Italy was always a selfish one,—I felt alone with my own soul there' (McAleer 1951: 239). This is wholly the condition of the speakers in 'De Gustibus—' and 'England in Italy'. In the latter poem the speaker's separation is enacted through the narrative itself. For he, too, has his barefoot girl, Fortù, whom he addresses at the start of the poem.[12] He is lodging in a farmhouse on the Sorrento peninsula. Fortù, a daughter of the family, is frightened of an approaching storm, and the speaker tries to comfort her:

> I was sure, if I tried,
> I could make you laugh spite of Scirocco:
> Now, open your eyes—
> Let me keep you amused till he vanish

[10] The combination of 'girl', 'tumbles' and an injured king—*Ophelia*: 'Quoth she "Before you tumbled me, | You promis'd me to wed"'; *Claudius*: 'O, yet defend me, friends; I am but hurt'—suggests the suitably ghostly presence of *Hamlet* in this passage of a poem which begins 'Your ghost will walk ...'

[11] For an account of Browning's correspondence with Elizabeth Barrett in the period of the poem's composition, see Woolford and Karlin: ii. 342–3.

[12] Fortù is of indeterminate age: in the first line the speaker calls her 'my loved one', but l. 3 ('On my knees put up both little feet') suggests a child; in any case she could not be his mistress, because he is a lodger at her mother's farm, in the midst of a devout Catholic community. All the children (including the young ones) are at work, but Fortù is being comforted by the speaker because she is afraid of the storm; he cajoles her with titbits and she falls asleep on his shoulder, which all sounds child-like; on the other hand she is old enough to manage a pert response to him at the end of the poem ('Such trifles', l. 286). I believe that Fortù *is* a child, but that Browning wished to suggest, without specifying, an erotic element in the speaker's feelings about her.

> In black from the skies,
> With telling my memories over
> As you tell your beads;
> All the Plain saw me gather, I garland
> —Flowers prove they, or weeds.

(ll. 4–12)

At the start of the poem, then, it looks as if what the speaker is proposing is a 'weak' commemoration—not the rapture of Words-worthian memory, 'that inward eye | Which is the bliss of solitude' ('I wandered lonely as a cloud', ll. 21–2). He will tell his memories as Fortù tells her beads—that is, *while* she does so, and *in the same manner*—the rosary, a favourite Protestant target of Catholic mumbo-jumbo, signifies the speaker's own conventional tourist-piety. A 'garland' is a throw-away item. But this opening is deceptive. For the speaker, a stranger in a strange land, does find himself alone in the end. He is twice abandoned in the poem, and once (as we have already seen) leaves his companion behind. The first abandonment is Fortù's, who falls asleep at l. 128 and wakes up *after* the vision of the siren-isle in ll. 222–8. The speaker exhorts her: 'Now, open your eyes', but she doesn't. Elizabeth Barrett half-humorously objected that the speaker's vivid descriptions were 'very little adapted to send anybody to sleep', missing the point that Fortù's sleep is symbolic of *unawareness*: 'strange that those great wide black eyes should stare nothing out of the earth that lies before them!'[13] The dramatic monologue form secretes a Wordsworthian lyric of self-realization. This lyric is tied to the progress of the storm which Fortù evades but which the speaker embraces. The storm that cows her senses awakens and sharpens his.

When the storm reaches its height ('Scirocco is loose!', l. 116) the speaker shifts from his 'rushing, hurrying' account of the life of the farm into an account of a climb he made up mount Calvano, one of the highest points in the Piano di Sorrento which commands a sweeping view across the plain itself and the Gulf of Sorrento, including of course the siren-isles. He is still addressing Fortù, but she is safely asleep; nor does he need to refer further to the storm, since his narrative contains and expresses it. Now comes the second abandonment:

---

[13] It should be stressed that the English share this state in 'Home-Thoughts, from Abroad': 'who wakes in England / Sees, some morning, unaware . . .' (ll. 3–4).

> Last eve I rode over the mountains—
>   Your brother, my guide,
> Soon left me to feast on the myrtles
>   That offered, each side,
> Their fruit-balls, black, glossy and luscious,
>   Or strip from the sorbs
> A treasure, so rosy and wondrous,
>   Of hairy gold orbs.
> But my mule picked his sure, sober path out,
>   Just stopping to neigh
> When he recognised down in the valley
>   His mates on their way
> With the faggots, and barrels of water;
>   And soon we emerged
> From the plain . . .
>
> (ll. 133–47)

The boy, of course, is a false guide; but the speaker, now openly a Bunyanesque pilgrim, won't be tempted to stray from the 'sure, sober' path (which, of course, gets narrower and stonier as it climbs) by the 'luscious' fruits of the wayside.

Besides the Christian of *Pilgrim's Progress*, the speaker is also a Moses, bent on revelation. Not that he leaves his inferiors behind as comprehensively as the students in 'A Grammarian's Funeral', for whom the climb up the mountain means a rejection of the 'common crofts, the vulgar thorpes ... Sleeping safe on the bosom of the plain' (ll. 3–5). A remnant of Romantic political feeling survives in the mule's acknowledgement of his burdened fellows down below: the 'faggots, and barrels of water' which they are carrying link them to the Gibeonites, the 'hewers of wood and drawers of water' of Joshua 9: 23, who in *Sordello* (iii. 799) denote the common people. Nevertheless, a disturbing moment of choice awaits him at the top of the mountain. At first he experiences a unified, or undifferentiated rapture:

> He climbed to the top of Calvano,
>   And God's own profound
> Was above me, and round me the mountains,
>   And under, the sea,
> And with me, my heart to bear witness
>   What was and shall be!
>
> (ll. 171–6)

Like Shelley's dreamer in *The Triumph of Life* ('the deep | Was at my feet, and Heaven above my head', ll. 27–8), the speaker situates himself at an intersection of immensities; his play with prepositions of space ('above', 'round', 'under', 'with') identifies his perceiving and reflexive eye as the centre of things, so that even 'God's own profound' forms only one dimension. How can the speaker go further? By decomposing the vision, by showing the Romantic unity of sky, earth, and sea to be itself an illusion from which the speaker must decisively turn:

> Oh heaven and the terrible crystal!
>> No rampart excludes
> The eye from the life to be lived
>> In the blue solitudes!
> Oh, those mountains, their infinite movement!
>> Still moving with you—
> For ever some new head or breast of them
>> Thrusts into view
> To observe the intruder—you see it
>> If quickly you turn
> And, before they escape you, surprise them—
>> They grudge you should learn
> How the soft plains they look on, lean over
>> And love, they pretend,
> —Cower beneath them—the flat sea-pine crouches,
>> The wild fruit-trees bend,
> E'en the myrtle-leaves curl, shrink and shut—
>> All is silent and grave—
> 'Tis a sensual and timorous beauty—
>> How fair, but a slave!
> So I turned to the sea,—and there slumbered
>> As greenly as ever
> Those isles of the syren . . .

(ll. 177–99)

Heaven's open invitation is sealed off in the first four lines; it's clear that we are to hear no more about it. It is the 'eye', not the 'I', which 'No rampart excludes', and the speaker wants more than this speculative apocalypse. Not a life *to be lived* but *this life's secret*.

What about the mountains? They turn out to be in a sinister relation of sexual and political power to the plains beneath them (a very Shelleyan idea, this). Notice how the myrtles plundered by the boy-guide (with the kind of unthinking male energy that Wordsworth describes in 'Nutting') are re-figured as shrinking female presences, caught up in a repellent sado-masochistic fantasy. It is the quickness of the speaker's awareness, his *turn* that surprises their unpleasant secret and saves him from what happens in 'Childe Roland', where it is the mountains which ambush and entrap the pilgrim:

> For looking up, aware I somehow grew,
>   'Spite of the dusk, the plain had given place
>   All round to mountains—with such name to grace
> Mere ugly heights and heaps now stol'n in view.
> How thus they had surprised me,—solve it, you!
>   How to get from them was no plainer case.
>
> (ll. 163–8)

The tentativeness of 'aware I somehow grew', the plaintiveness of the appeal to the reader in l. 167, above all the punning shift from 'plain had given place' to 'no plainer case'—all emphasize the bafflement and slowness of response which Roland displays all through the poem until the 'trap shuts' in l. 174 and his mind (and the whole poem) puts on a tremendous burst of speed. The speaker of 'England in Italy' is literally and imaginatively emancipated from this condition. One good turn deserves another: 'So I turned to the sea'. And with this the visionary journey to the siren-isles is launched. Unlike Roland approaching, out of a landscape of terror and menace, a moment of profoundly unwelcome self-recognition, the speaker approaches the siren-isles (abode of mythic monsters, let us recall) with sublime self-confidence. Walter Savage Landor saw why, when he closed his poem 'To Robert Browning' (written after he received his complimentary copy of *Dramatic Romances and Lyrics*) with an image drawn from the poem:

>   warmer climes
> Give brighter plumage, stronger wing: the breeze
> Of Alpine heights thou playest with, borne on
> Beyond Sorrento and Amalfi, where
> The Siren waits thee, singing song for song.

The speaker is himself a siren; Fortù, less daring than Ulysses, sails through his invocation asleep. The 'black turret | With never a door' is the site not of an apocalyptic confrontation but of an assumption of power. 'Burningly it came on me all at once, | This was the place!'

cries Roland. And Thamuris, too, is fatally fired up: 'Therefore the morn-ray that enriched his face, | If it gave lambent chill, took flame again | From flush of pride: he saw, he knew the place' (*Aristophanes' Apology*, 5245–7). But the speaker of 'England in Italy' is not overmatched. He knows where he is going.

It is tempting to leave the matter there—with a benign dark tower to set against the malign one in 'Childe Roland'—but Browning has not made things that simple. The speaker's vision of the siren-isles is one of creative power, but this power is not only, as I remarked earlier, kept to himself ('I hear and I know'—but I'm not telling *you*), it is also *conditional*. It has often been said of 'Childe Roland' that it has a paradoxical narrative structure, since the retrospective telling of the story in the first person assumes an aftermath, a survival of the speaker which the story itself seems to disallow. Robert Langbaum, comparing the poem to Eliot's 'Love Song of J. Alfred Prufrock', acutely resolves this paradox: 'the disparity of tense between the utterance and the situation enhances the disequilibrium between them; it shows the utterance as not directed toward the situation, as not concerned with altering it, but as ultimately self-directed because concerned with extracting from the situation a pattern for self-understanding' (Langbaum: 198). The poem takes place in a psychological present dramatized as a historical past.[14] In contrast, the narrative structure of 'England in Italy' is scrupulously faithful to 'real time'; though it plays tricks with its narrative tenses at a crucial juncture, it does so *within* the framework of the speaker's monologue. As we have seen, the progress of the speaker's memories follows that of the storm, whose climactic moment may be thought to coincide with the speaker's exclamation 'I hear and I know!' But more important is the fact that the speaker's memory of standing on the top of Calvano prompts him to propose the journey to the siren-isles to the (sleeping) Fortù, so that the *present tense* of the utterance is in fact illusory. What the speaker actually felt on the summit is elided in favour of what it occurs to him to say to Fortù when he tells her about it; and this elision is followed by a sequence which culminates in an 'impossible' affirmation merging past, present, and future: 'O when shall we sail there . . . Oh, to sail round and round them . . . To stand there and hear . . . I hear and I know!'

---

[14] Technically this represents the inversion of a device undoubtedly familiar to Browning from Latin literature, the 'vivid present'.

The consequence of this narrative sleight-of-hand is that there *is* an aftermath in 'England in Italy', since the speaker's visionary trip to the siren-isles is private, sealed from his listener (Fortù, who misses the whole thing) and from us (since we are not told what the speaker hears and knows). The storm ends, the sun comes out, and the speaker resumes his 'amusing' vein of observation and anti-Catholic satire:

> All is over! wake up and come out now,
>   And down let us go,
> And see the fine things set in order
>   At church for the show
> Of the Sacrament, set forth this evening;
>   To-morrow's the Feast
> Of the Rosary's virgin, by no means
>   Of virgins the least—
> As we'll hear in the off-hand discourse
>   Which (all nature, no art)
> The Dominican brother these three weeks
>   Was getting by heart.
>
>   (ll. 245–56)

It is not too hard to locate the irony here—that Fortù has missed the speaker's 'fine things set in order', that a 'sacrament' has taken place to which she has been denied access, that the 'Rosary's virgin' looks back to the speaker's rosary of memories ('telling' his story turns out to have been a rite with some purpose after all), finally that the 'performance' of the Dominican brother (the Dominicans were chiefly responsible for spreading the use of the rosary as a devotional exercise, hence the hit at them) is to be set against the speaker's own 'off-hand discourse'. Whether the speaker's feelings coincide with Browning's or not (there is evidence that they do),[15] they evidently form the other side of the coin of being 'alone with one's own soul' in Italy, of which the speaker's account of his journey up mount Calvano was the lyrical face. It is not too harsh, I think, to see the

---

[15] For example, his contemptuous allusion to superstitious Italian piety in a letter to Elizabeth Barrett during the period of the poem's composition: 'would not I engage to bring the whole of the Piano (of Sorrento) in likeness to a red velvet dressing gown properly spangled over, before the priest that held it out on a pole had even begun his story of how Noah's son Shem, the founder of Sorrento, threw it off to swim thither, as the world knows he did? Oh, it makes one's soul angry, so enough of it' (Kintner: 55).

speaker's retreat into a shell of alienation and irony as hateful here, or too far-fetched to point out that the final image of Italy in the poem (which began with the speaker calling Fortù his 'loved one') is that of a 'scorpion with wide angry nippers' (l. 285).

It would be too much to say that the speaker ends by hating Fortù or even despising her, but it does seem that the revelation of 'this life's secret' carries the price of her exclusion, and that the 'love' which he expresses for Italy is—in this poem, at any rate—not entirely generous or disinterested. In 'Childe Roland' this exclusion of the female is taken to drastic lengths: Roland, ostensibly a knight-errant, has no lady either physically accompanying him (like Spenser's Red Cross Knight at the beginning of *The Faerie Queene*) or in his mind; the one moment of human tenderness in the poem is the speaker's memory of a fellow-knight: 'Cuthbert's reddening face | Beneath its garniture of curly gold', an image blighted by 'one night's disgrace' (ll. 91–2, 95). Nor is he palely loitering after meeting La Belle Dame Sans Merci or any of her sisters. What 'Childe Roland' does have is a horrific displacement of the erotic across the physical features of the landscape, so that Roland continually encounters images of bestiality, impurity, mutilation, and disease. Sometimes the sexual association of these images is made obvious, as in the twist given to a favourite Victorian moral tale when the speaker comes across a 'sudden little river . . . as unexpected as a serpent' (ll. 91–2):

> Drenched willows flung them headlong in a fit
> Of mute despair, a suicidal throng:
> The river which had done them all the wrong,
>   Whate'er that was, rolled by, deterred no whit.
>
> (ll. 97–100)

Suicide by drowning (in the *Serpent*ine, for example, where Harriet Shelley drowned herself) may be seen as a rite of purification, but the 'fallen' or abandoned maidens here are flinging themselves into the very element of 'wrong'. In the perpetual suspension of their 'headlong' fall they are still ravished brides, not of 'quietness' but of 'mute despair'.

Do such images articulate fear and hatred of sexuality and of the body (specifically the female body), and may the Dark Tower itself, described as a 'round squat turret', be in one of its menacing aspects an image of distorted and threatening female sexuality? (The turret on the siren-isle, I might add, is square.) I would say rather that the sexuality which Roland sees scattered and disfigured over the landscape of the poem is his own, and that this sexuality identifies itself with both male and female types. To go back to the suicidal willows: their 'mute despair' repeats Roland's own attitude when, 'quiet as despair' (l. 43), he turns out of the highway and plunges into his own undoing. Impotence and exhaustion mark the 'blind horse . . . Thrust out past service from the devil's stud' (ll. 76–8), which the speaker hates so passionately that his self-identification with it is almost too forcibly suggested.

In both 'Childe Roland' and 'England in Italy' an erotic preoccupation with the self, solitary and exposed, manifests itself in the imagery of love and hate which constitutes the landscape. Neither of these poems is about relationship, and indeed they might both be thought to achieve their aims by the sacrifice of relationship. I turn now to a poem with, apparently, the opposite design. If any of Browning's poems is founded on relationship, it is 'By the Fire-Side'. Nevertheless, here, too, I shall argue that it is the self to which, in the end, the poem turns.

'By the Fire-Side' has perhaps the most intricate narrative structure of any Browning poem of comparable length, and I must spend a little time puzzling it out, because it makes a significant difference to my argument about the relation between this poem and, in particular, 'Childe Roland'. It begins with the speaker anticipating what he will do 'when the long dark Autumn evenings come', that is in old age, 'life's November' (ll. 2, 5). He imagines himself day-dreaming over a book by the fire-side, returning in memory to his youth in Italy. (The process is remarkably like a dissolve in a film which signals a flash-back.) His memory is of a 'ruined chapel' in an 'Alpine gorge' (ll. 31–2) which he visited with his wife. He describes the surrounding landscape in detail, concluding at l. 100. So far both the time-frame of the poem and its syntax are perfectly clear; then both become suddenly and maddeningly opaque. The speaker bursts out:

> My perfect wife, my Leonor,
>> Oh, heart my own, oh, eyes, mine too,
> Whom else could I dare look backward for,
>> With whom beside should I dare pursue
> The path grey heads abhor?

For it leads to a crag's sheer edge with them;
   Youth, flowery all the way, there stops—
Not they; age threatens and they contemn,
   Till they reach the gulf wherein youth drops,
One inch from our life's safe hem!

With me, youth led—I will speak now,
   No longer watch you as you sit
Reading by fire-light, that great brow
   And the spirit-small hand propping it
Mutely—my heart knows how—

When, if I think but deep enough,
   You are wont to answer, prompt as rhyme;
And you, too, find without a rebuff
   The response your soul seeks many a time
Piercing its fine flesh-stuff—

My own, confirm me! If I tread
   This path back, is it not in pride
To think how little I dreamed it led
   To an age so blest that by its side
Youth seems the waste instead!

               (ll. 101–25)

Most readers would, I think, start by assuming that 'My perfect wife, my Leonor!' is an interjection which brings the speaker back to the 'dramatic present' or 'real time' in which the monologue is taking place. This follows from the assumption (also the natural and obvious one) that the whole poem *is* a dramatic monologue, addressed from the beginning to the speaker's wife.[16] But if this is the case, what does the speaker mean by saying 'I will speak now' in l. 111, as though he hadn't been speaking to her up to then? A further, and even more vexing question arises because of the past tense of 'led' in the same line. This seems to indicate, contrary to the impression given in the first part of the poem, that the speaker *is* in old age, an indication apparently confirmed by the reference to 'an age so blest' in l. 124. At this point the time-frame of the poem seems to have collapsed on itself, or rather two time-frames have merged, that with which the poem begins and that which it imagines in the future, so that the speaker inhabits, and speaks from, a double

---

[16] The very last words of the poem, which repeat the opening, support this reading: 'the whole is well worth thinking o'er | When the autumn comes: which I mean to do | One day, *as I said before*' (ll. 263–5, my italics).

identity. Only at the end of the poem, with the words 'which I mean to do | One day', are the two time-frames disengaged.

But in my view the reader is not meant to think of the whole poem as spoken aloud. On the contrary: the first part of the poem is an internal monologue, and what the speaker imagines himself remembering and reflecting on in the future *includes* the exclamation 'My perfect wife, my Leonor!'. The past tense of 'led' is therefore explained by its being part of this imagined future utterance. It is at this word 'led', indeed, that the speaker breaks off and returns to the dramatic present with the words 'I will speak now'—which is when he starts speaking aloud. He *stops* speaking at l. 255, with the words 'One born to love you, sweet!'. The last two stanzas of the poem resume and conclude the internal monologue.[17]

If my understanding of this structure is right, then it means that the speaker undertakes his journey of memory *twice*: once on his own, in silence (ll. 1–110), and once in the company of his wife. The difference between these two journeys is of crucial importance, since it suggests a swerve away from the pattern of expectation set up by 'England in Italy' and 'Childe Roland', that of a quest in the mode of the 'egotistical sublime'. That this swerve is not wholly accomplished is part of the interest of the poem: it shows how hard Browning found it to write of erotic mutuality without its becoming another reflection of his, or his speakers', subjectivity.

When the poem begins the speaker anticipates an old age of sterility, closure, and loss, the sense of which is sharpened by the playful imaginative energy of the young:

> How well I know what I mean to do
> When the long dark Autumn evenings come,
> And where, my soul, is thy pleasant hue?
> With the music of all thy voices, dumb
> In life's November too!

---

[17] I owe this suggestion to Mr John Woolford, who points out that immediately after l. 255 the speaker continues, 'And to watch you sink by the fire-side now | Back again' (ll. 256–7), implying that her attitude of attention to him has ceased, i.e. that he has stopped speaking; he now sees her 'Musing by fire-light' (l. 258) over what he has told her. There is one difficulty remaining, which concerns the fact that the speaker addresses his wife in ll. 121–2 ('If I tread | This path back') as though she already knew what 'this path' referred to; but I think this is solved by the lines immediately preceding, which claim a telepathic understanding between the couple: 'When, if I think but deep enough, | You are wont to answer, prompt as rhyme' (ll. 116–17). She has followed his unspoken train of thought up to the point at which he begins to speak aloud.

I shall be found by the fire, suppose,
  O'er a great wise book as beseemeth age,
While the shutters flap as the cross-wind blows,
  And I turn the page, and I turn the page,
Not verse now, only prose!

Till the young ones whisper, finger on lip,
  'There he is at it, deep in Greek—
Now or never, then, out we slip
  To cut from the hazels by the creek
A mainmast for our ship.'

(ll. 1–15)

His wife is strikingly absent from this picture (it is poignant to remember that Elizabeth Barrett Browning was indeed absent from Browning's own old age, when the description of reading a 'great wise book', Aristotle's *Ethics*, figures in one of his last poems, 'Development'). She is 'there' in the dramatic setting of the poem, sitting across from him, but the speaker only confirms this at l. 112. In the beautiful lines which describe the way that reading leads to day-dreaming, the speaker passes alone through the 'branch-work' of his thoughts and only then is joined by his wife: 'I pass out where it ends . . . we slope to Italy at last' (ll. 20, 24). This passage is figured as an escape from the 'young ones' who believe they are escaping *him*: the opportunity they seize (like Fortù's brother who abandons the speaker of 'England in Italy' to gather fruits by the wayside) in fact frees him to pursue his more adventurous inward journey.

The journey leads to a sexualized landscape, the 'woman-country' of Italy (l. 28), and, at once, to a gesture of pointing:

Look at the ruined chapel again
  Half way up in the Alpine gorge.
Is that a tower, I point you plain,
  Or is it a mill or an iron forge
Breaks solitude in vain?

(ll. 31–5)

The indeterminacy of the object (tower? mill? iron forge?) is juxtaposed with the certainty of the gesture itself ('I point you plain'): what matters is not the name of the structure but that there is *something* there, something to be pointed at, a mark of interrogation, the trace of a meaning. At the same time this something 'Breaks solitude in vain', its meaning is unexpressed or thwarted. As in 'Childe

Roland', *pointing* is followed by *turning*: 'A turn, and we stand in
the heart of things; | The woods are round us, heaped and dim'
(ll. 37–8). The speaker and his wife find themselves 'in the heart
of things', but do not yet recognize the 'powers at play' in the
woods (l. 237).

As they climb towards the chapel, the speaker describes a landscape
where Eros riots in rich and strange displacements; but here, too, as
in 'England in Italy', the speaker's perceptions have an edge of
violence, excess, or decay: 'small ferns fit | Their teeth to the
polished block' of the boulder-stones that line the path (ll. 49–50),
autumn 'crimson[s] the creeper's leaf across | Like a splash of blood'
(ll. 56–7), the 'sudden coral nipple' of the 'rose-flesh mushrooms' has
'bulged' at dawn (ll. 62–3), the stream by the chapel 'is stopped in a
stagnant pond | Danced over by the midge' (ll. 69–70), the chapel
and the bridge that leads to it are 'Blackish-grey and mostly wet'
(l. 72) and 'here again, how the lichens fret | And the roots of the ivy
strike!' (ll. 74–5). The chapel itself is a 'Poor little place' serving
people from 'scattered homes' who eke out their living as charcoal-
burners, hemp-dressers, or fowlers (ll. 76–85). The 'bit of fresco'
over the porch may represent 'John [the Baptist] in the Desert', but
the speaker can't really tell: it 'has borne the weather's brunt' (ll. 86–
90). To these images of impoverishment and depletion are added,
finally, a Wordsworthian image of intense *withholding*, of numinous
silence:

> And all day long a bird sings there,
>   And a stray sheep drinks at the pond at times:
> The place is silent and aware;
>   It has had its scenes, its joys and crimes,
> But that is its own affair.
>
>   (ll. 96–100)

This, as I have argued, is the culminating point of the *first* journey of
memory: it leads to this 'silent and aware' place, a 'spot of time'
which evidently has a secret but will not give it up. And this secret
turns out to be the speaker's own: the moment of recognition and
union which the speaker and his wife experienced by the chapel is
itself one of the 'joys and crimes' associated with the place.[18] But in

---

[18] The reference to a bird singing recalls 'England in Italy', where 'the birds' quiet
singing' reveals 'this life's secret' to Ulysses, and to the speaker; but the crucial
difference is that in 'By the Fire-Side' the secret is told to us, as well.

order to gain access to this experience, in order not to 'break solitude in vain', the speaker must repeat the journey, must draw his wife into the tender and erotic play of memory:

> Come back with me to the first of all,
>   Let us lean and love it over again—
> Let us now forget and then recall,
>   Break the rosary in a pearly rain,
>   And gather what we let fall!

> (ll. 146–50)

This image of the rosary recalls 'England in Italy', whose speaker compares telling his memories to Fortù telling her beads. But whereas he and Fortù are at odds in that poem, in 'By the Fire-Side' the relationship between husband and wife is so strong that they can play with loss, sure of recuperating what they 'let fall'.[19]

In this intimate communion the speaker resumes his narrative, and this time the silence is charged with the possibility (in narrative terms the *inevitability*) of revelation:

>   the silence grows
> To that degree, you half believe
>   It must get rid of what it knows,
>   Its bosom does so heave.

> Hither we walked, then, side by side,
>   Arm in arm and cheek to cheek,
> And still I questioned or replied,
>   While my heart, convulsed to really speak,
>   Lay choking in its pride.

> (ll. 157–65)

The physical closeness of the lovers is not a sign of their union: 'One near one is too far' (l. 230). It is not enough to be *near*: what the speaker desires (what his heart wants 'to really speak') is complete union, where 'each is sucked | Into each' (ll. 128–9); the making of 'one soul' (l. 131) whose oneness will reach even beyond the apocalypse, 'When earth breaks up and Heaven expands' (l. 133). It is the moment at which this union occurred which the speaker can now at last narrate, mimicking in his account how close they came to missing it:

---

[19] In fact it is the breaking of the rosary which precipitates the 'pearly rain' which the lovers gather up like manna in the wilderness.

We stoop and look in through the grate,
  See the little porch and the rustic door,
Read duly the dead builder's date,
  Then cross the bridge we crossed before,
Take the path again—but wait!

Oh moment, one and infinite!
  The water slips o'er stock and stone;
The west is tender, hardly bright.
  How grey at once is the evening grown—
One star, the chrysolite!

(ll. 176–185)

All the indications are there, but the lovers nearly fail to take their chance: they can see inside the locked church but not enter it, they 'Read duly the dead builder's date' instead of their own urgent present, they cross back over the bridge and are on the point of retreating from the very site of revelation. The 'moment, one and infinite' takes place at twilight, on the threshold of night, and is symbolized by the 'One star'.[20] But the lovers do take the chance: their awareness of the 'moment' leads to the breaking of the 'bar . . . between life and life'; they are 'mixed at last | In spite of the mortal screen' (ll. 233–5).

This attainment of perfect mutuality corresponds to Childe Roland's solitary defiance; the 'moment, one and infinite' answers the 'one moment' which, for Roland, 'knelled the woe of years'. And yet, if there is something triumphant about Roland's despair, something which suggests the *achievement* of his loss, then there is something equally disturbing about the speaker's insistence, in 'By the Fire-Side', on an ecstatic *secondariness*. For it turns out that perfect love is mutual, but not equal; there is a hierarchy of souls, in which the speaker's authority, his power to perceive and express, is blissfully subordinated to his wife's, a subordination which is to extend, as I said earlier, into the afterlife:

---

[20] The star is almost certainly called a 'chrysolite' because of the echo of *Othello*, v. ii. 146–9: 'Nay, had she been true, | If heaven would make me such another world | Of one entire and perfect chrysolite, | I'd not have sold her for it.' Othello's exclamation, coming after his murder of Desdemona, provides Browning with an inverse source for his image, Shakespeare's tragedy of broken trust contributing to his lyric of 'entire and perfect' love. Such inverse allusions are very common in Browning.

Oh, I must feel your brain prompt mine,
   Your heart anticipate my heart,
You must be just before, in fine,
   See and make me see, for your part,
New depths of the Divine!

(ll. 131–5)

She for God only, he for God in her; another way of putting it is that Browning imagines himself as Eglamor in *Sordello*, who, in the 'golden courts' of heaven, lags perpetually (but blissfully) behind the 'upward flight' of the greater artist whom he worships.[21] Yet there is something troubling about this identification of the speaker with the secondary and the dependent, since it runs counter to the absolute authority implied by the very form of the dramatic monologue, a form which, like that of all autobiographical fiction, does not easily tolerate the intrusion of other voices.

It is tempting, of course, to read the poem as a reflection of Browning's attitude to his own wife, especially given the supporting evidence from his letters both to her and about her. 'I *know*—that you are immeasurably my superior', he wrote to her in April 1846; 'while you talk most eloquently and affectingly to me, I *know* and could prove you are as much my Poet as my Mistress' (Kintner: 638). After her death he wrote to Isa Blagden: 'the simple truth is that *she* was the poet and I the clever person by comparison' (McAleer 1951: 365). Even so plausible a biographical reading, however, cannot account for the fact that in the poem the speaker's wife is twice described as *mute* (ll. 115, 257), that the power to speak (and to remember) is vested by the speaker solely in himself, that the poem begins and ends with what *he* means to do, that what happens in the scene by the little chapel is the sealing of *his* destiny ('One born to love you, sweet!') and, by implication (since the poem is the text of this love), the renewing of *his* poetic creativity. Powerfully though he evokes the landscape of sexual bliss, he is no less driven by the exaltations and anxieties of his own will than Childe Roland, crossing the waste land of hatred to his sublime undoing.

[21] See vi. 793–814, and the note on this passage in Woolford and Karlin: ii. 765. For another reading of the speaker's secondariness, see Leslie Brisman's essay 'Back to the First of All: "By the Fire-side" and Browning's Romantic Origins' in Bloom and Munich: 39–58.

Bibliography

All quotations from Browning are to the first editions of the poems. For poems written up to 1846 I have used the Longman edition (Woolford and Karlin); thereafter references are to the original volumes. The only alterations concern the standard use of single quotation marks and the elimination of repeat marks before each line in passages of direct speech. Quotations from Browning's courtship correspondence with Elizabeth Barrett (Kintner) have been checked against the holograph manuscripts and occasionally corrected. In both letters and poems Browning sometimes employs a two-point ellipsis (. .) where modern punctuation would use a dash. Editorial omissions in quoted passages are indicated by the usual three-point ellipsis (. . .). Quotations from the Bible are to the Authorized Version of 1611 (in modernized form); quotations from Shakespeare are to the Alexander edition (London and Glasgow: Collins 1951).

ALLINGHAM, H., and RADFORD, D. (eds.), *William Allingham's Diary* (1907; Fontwell: Centaur Press, 1967).

ARMSTRONG, I. (ed.), *Robert Browning*, Writers and their Background (London: G. Bell, 1974).

BLOOM, H., and MUNICH, A. (eds.), *Robert Browning*, Twentieth Century Views (Englewood Cliffs, NJ: Prentice-Hall, 1979).

BROWNING, V., *My Browning Family Album* (London: Springwood Books, 1979).

BURTON, J., *Heyday of a Wizard: Daniel Home the Medium* (London: George C. Harrap, 1948).

CHESTERTON, G. K., *Robert Browning*, English Men of Letters (London: Macmillan, 1904).

COLERIDGE, SAMUEL TAYLOR, *Collected Works*, vol. xiii: 'On Logic' (London: Routledge, 1981).

COLLINGWOOD, W. G., *The Life and Work of John Ruskin*, 2 vols. (London: Methuen, 1893).

CURLE, R. (ed.), *Robert Browning and Julia Wedgwood* (London: John Murray and Jonathan Cape, 1937).

DARWIN, CHARLES, *The Expression of the Emotions in Man and Animals*, Popular Edition, ed. F. Darwin (London: John Murray, 1904).

DAHL, C., and BREWER, J. L., 'Browning's "Saul" and the Fourfold Vision: a Neoplatonic-Hermetic Approach', *Browning Institute Studies*, iii (1975), 101–18.

DeLaura, D. J., 'Ruskin and The Brownings: Twenty-Five Unpublished Letters', *Bulletin of the John Rylands Library*, liv (1972), 314–56.

De Quincey, Thomas, *Recollections of the Lakes and the Lake Poets*, Penguin English Library (Harmondsworth: Penguin Books 1970).

DeVane, W. C., *A Browning Handbook*, 2nd edn. (New York: Appleton-Century-Crofts, 1955).

—— and Knickerbocker, K. L. (eds.), *New Letters of Robert Browning* (London: John Murray, 1951).

Firth, C. H., and Furnivall, F. J. (eds.), *Robert Browning's Prose Life of Strafford* (London: Kegan Paul, 1892).

Freud, Sigmund, *Case Histories II*, Pelican Freud Library, vol. 9 (Harmondsworth: Penguin Books, 1979).

—— *On Metapsychology: The Theory of Psychoanalysis*, Pelican Freud Library, vol. 11 (Harmondsworth: Penguin Books, 1984).

Gill, S., *William Wordsworth: A Life* (Oxford: Clarendon Press, 1990).

Goldfarb, R. M., 'Hiram H. Horsefall and Company: the Audience for Mr. Sludge, the Medium', *Research Studies* (Washington State University), xli (1973), 192–200.

Griffin, W. H., and Minchin, H. C., *The Life of Robert Browning,* 3rd edn. (London: Methuen, 1938).

Grosart, A. (ed.), *The Complete Prose Works of William Wordsworth*, 2 vols. (London: Macmillan, 1876).

Hawthorne, Julian, *Shapes that Pass: Memories of Old Days* (London: John Murray, 1928).

Hazlitt, William, *The Complete Works*, ed. P. P. Howe (London: J. M. Dent, 1931).

Heydon, P. N. and Kelley, P. (eds.), *Elizabeth Barrett Browning's Letters to Mrs. David Ogilvy 1849–1861* (New York: Quadrangle/The New York Times Book Co. and The Browning Institute, 1973).

Home, D. D., *Incidents in My Life* (London: Longman, Green, 1863).

—— *Incidents in My Life, Second Series* (London: Tinsley Brothers, 1872).

Hood, T. L. (ed.), *Letters of Robert Browning* (London: John Murray, 1933).

Horsman, E. A. (ed.), *The Diary of Alfred Domett* (Oxford: Oxford University Press, 1953).

Huxley, L. (ed.), *Elizabeth Barrett Browning: Letters to Her Sister, 1846–1859* (London: John Murray, 1929).

Irvine, W., and Honan, P., *The Book, the Ring, and the Poet* (London: The Bodley Head, 1974).

Irwin, T., *Classical Thought*, History of Western Philosophy, i (Oxford: Oxford University Press, 1989).

Jenkins, E., *The Shadow and the Light: A Defence of Daniel Dunglas Home, the Medium* (London: Hamish Hamilton, 1982).

KARLIN, D., 'Browning's Paired Poems', *Essays in Criticism*, xxxi (July 1981), 210–27.

—— 'Browning, Elizabeth Barrett, and "Mesmerism" ', *Victorian Poetry*, 27, nos. 3–4 (Autumn–Winter 1989), 65–77.

KELLEY, P., and HUDSON, R. (eds.), *The Brownings' Correspondence* (Winfield, Kan., 1984–   ).

KELLY, R., 'Daniel Home, Mr. Sludge, and a Forgotten Browning Letter', *Studies in Browning and His Circle*, i, no. 2 (Fall 1973), 44–9.

KENYON, F. G. (ed.), *The Letters of Elizabeth Barrett Browning*, 2 vols. (London: Smith, Elder, 1898).

—— (ed.), *Robert Browning and Alfred Domett* (London: Smith, Elder, 1906).

KINTNER, E. (ed.), *The Letters of Robert Browning and Elizabeth Barrett Barrett 1845–1846*, 2 vols. (Cambridge, Mass.: Harvard University Press, 1969).

LANGBAUM, R., *The Poetry of Experience* (1957; Chicago: University of Chicago Press, 1985).

LANDIS, P. (ed.), *Letters of the Brownings to George Barrett* (Urbana: University of Illinois Press, 1958).

MCALEER, E. C. (ed.), *Dearest Isa: Robert Browning's Letters to Isabella Blagden* (Austin: University of Texas Press, 1951).

—— (ed.), *Learned Lady: Letters from Robert Browning to Mrs. Thomas Fitzgerald* (Cambridge, Mass.: Harvard University Press, 1966).

MARTIN, R. B., *Tennyson: The Unquiet Heart* (London: Oxford University Press and Faber, 1980).

MATTHEWS, G., and EVEREST, K., *The Poems of Shelley*, Annotated English Poets, vol. i (Harlow: Longman, 1991).

MAYNARD, J., *Browning's Youth* (Cambridge, Mass.: Harvard University Press, 1977).

MELCHIORI, B., *Browning's Poetry of Reticence* (Edinburgh: Oliver and Boyd, 1968).

MEREDITH, M. (ed.), *More Than Friend: The Letters of Robert Browning to Katharine de Kay Bronson* (Waco, Tex., and Winfield, Kan.: Armstrong Browning Library and Wedgestone Press, 1985).

MILLER, B., *Robert Browning: A Portrait* (London: John Murray, 1952).

—— 'The Séance at Ealing: A Study in Memory and Imagination', *Cornhill Magazine*, clxix, no. 1013 (Autumn 1957), 317–24.

MILLS, J., *Womanwords* (Harlow: Longman, 1989).

ORR, A. S., *Life and Letters of Robert Browning* (London: Smith, Elder, 1891).

PETERSON, W. S. (ed.), *Browning's Trumpeter: The Correspondence of Robert Browning and Frederick J. Furnivall* (Washington, DC: Decatur House Press, 1979).

PETTIGREW, J., and COLLINS, T. J. (eds.), *Robert Browning: The Poems*, 2 vols. (New Haven, Conn.: Yale University Press, 1981).

PHELPS, W. L., 'Robert Browning on Spiritualism', *Yale Review*, xxiii (Sept. 1933), 125–38.

PORTER, K. H., *Through a Glass Darkly: Spiritualism in the Browning Circle* (Lawrence: University of Kansas Press, 1958).

PROUST, MARCEL, *Remembrance of Things Past* [*A la recherche du temps perdu*], trans. C. K. Scott-Moncrieff and T. Kilmartin, 3 vols. (Harmondsworth: Penguin Books, 1983).

RICKS, C. (ed.), *The Poems of Tennyson*, Annotated English Poets, 2nd edn., 3 vols. (Harlow: Longman, 1987).

ROBERTS, A., 'Euripidaristophanizing: Browning's *Aristophanes' Apology*', *Browning Society Notes*, vol. 20, no. 2 (1990–1), 32–45.

ROYLE, N., *Literature and Telepathy: Essays on the Reading Mind* (Oxford: Blackwell, 1990).

RYALS, C. DE L., *Browning's Later Poetry* (Ithaca, NY: Cornell University Press, 1975).

SHATTOCK, J., and WOLFF, M. (eds.), *The Victorian Periodical Press: Samplings and Soundings* (Leicester University Press and University of Toronto Press, 1982).

SHAW, W. D., *The Dialectical Temper* (Ithaca, NY: Cornell University Press, 1968).

SURTEES, V., 'Browning's Last Duchess', *London Review of Books*, vol. 8, no. 17 (9 Oct. 1986).

TENNYSON, HALLAM, *Tennyson: A Memoir* (London: Macmillan, 1899).

WARD, M., *Robert Browning and his World*, vol. ii (London: Cassell, 1969).

WOOLFORD, J., 'Browning's Philosophy of Extremity', *Browning Society Notes*, vol. 7, no. 2 (July 1977), 41–53.

—— *Browning the Revisionary* (London: Macmillan, 1988).

—— and KARLIN, D., *The Poems of Browning*, Annotated English Poets, vols. i and ii (Harlow: Longman, 1991).

Index